MONOPOLIES
IN
AMERICA

BOOKS BY CHARLES R. GEISST

Wall Street: A History

100 Years of Wall Street

*Exchange Rate Chaos: Twenty-five Years of
Finance and Consumer Democracy*

Investment Banking in the Financial System

*Entrepot Capitalism: Foreign Investment and
the American Dream in the Twentieth Century*

*Visionary Capitalism: Financial Markets and
the American Dream in the Twentieth Century*

The Political Thought of John Milton

A Guide to Financial Institutions

A Guide to the Financial Markets

*Raising International Capital: International Bond
Markets and the European Institutions*

Financial Futures Markets
(cowritten with Brendan Brown)

MONOPOLIES IN AMERICA

Empire Builders and Their Enemies

from Jay Gould to Bill Gates

CHARLES R. GEISST

OXFORD

UNIVERSITY PRESS

2000

OXFORD
UNIVERSITY PRESS

Oxford   New York
Athens   Auckland   Bangkok   Bogotá   Buenos Aires
Calcutta   Cape Town   Chennai   Dar es Salaam   Delhi
Florence   Hong Kong   Istanbul   Karachi   Kuala Lumpur
Madrid   Melbourne   Mexico City   Mumbai   Nairobi   Paris
São Paulo   Singapore   Taipei   Tokyo   Toronto   Warsaw

and associated companies in
Berlin   Ibadan

Copyright © 2000 by Charles R. Geisst

Published by Oxford University Press, Inc.
198 Madison Avenue, New York, New York 10016

Oxford is a registered trademark of Oxford University Press, Inc.

Library of Congress Cataloging-in-Publication Data
Geisst, Charles R.
Monopolies in America : Empire builders and their enemies
from Jay Gould to Bill Gates / Charles R. Geisst.
p. cm.   Includes bibliographical references and index.
ISBN 0-19-512301-8
1. Monopolies—United States—History.
2. Big business—United States—History.   I. Title.
HD2757.2.G45   2000   338.8'2'0973—dc21   99-14340

1 3 5 7 9 8 6 4 2

Printed in the United States of America
on acid-free paper

For Meg,
a chip off the old writer's block

CONTENTS

PREFACE

THE HISTORY OF MONOPOLIES in America is relatively short but manages to encompass most of the important developments in industry, Wall Street, and political thinking over the last 130 years. Within that entire time, no one single history has ever been written touching upon the constant tug-of-war that developed between Washington and corporate America. Since the days of the nineteenth-century industrialists, bigness in industry and the role of government in curbing it have added many colorful personalities and strong ideologues to the overarching debate about the nature of the American experiment and the attempts at controlling free market capitalism. Many of the original questions are still raised today and have a strange aura of déjà vu surrounding them. In the immediate post–Civil War years, concern over the spread of the railways and their attempts to consolidate were widespread. John D. Rockefeller's dominance of the oil market and Carnegie's tight grip over the steel industry all have been replayed in one form or other within the last decade. In many cases the corporate names involved in these battles have remained the same, as have the monopoly issues themselves. Jay Gould and Commodore Vanderbilt would easily recognize the issues confronting antitrust law today: in many ways they helped create them.

I would like to thank my agent, Tom Wallace, and editor at Oxford University Press, Peter Ginna, for their unflinching support while I tackled this topic. I am especially grateful to Tom Stanton and Ron Chernow, whose knowledge of the institutions and personalities of the monopolists proved invaluable. By sharing their expertise, they helped me keep the narrative on track.

MONOPOLIES
IN
AMERICA

INTRODUCTION

MILLIONS OF PEOPLE have played the popular board game Monopoly. Millions of others have played the real-life version in the business world. The rules are simple: Accumulate as much property as possible and win. The principles have not changed since Monopoly was first marketed in 1935—an unfortunate roll of the dice and the aspiring game monopolist can spend some time in jail. The rules and stakes for monopolists in real life have not changed substantially, either. Unlike in the board game, however, those accused of monopoly rarely ever spend time in jail.

While everyone plays the board game by moving pieces around the track and landing on various properties, here the game departs from reality because in the business world there are various time-proven ways of attaining a dominant position. What methods are considered acceptable and unacceptable are the subjects of intense and constant debate. They all revolve around a basic question: What is fairness in business? What remedies are sought against companies that allegedly break the rules of fair play? Do the rules of fair play actually apply in hotly competitive businesses? Unfortunately, in the American experience these questions are not adequately answered in all cases. Like the society they reflect, they rely both upon very general principles, somewhat timeless in nature, and on court decisions that have been very transient.

Throughout the first seventy-five years of big business in America, "monopoly" was a convenient charge to level at large industrial organizations. Opponents of big business, whether they were American aristocrats, socialists, investigatory journalists, or the competition, leveled the charge time and again at the rapidly expanding industries that quickly transformed American life after the Civil War. In many cases the accusations were true, but in others they were vastly exaggerated. This was to be expected, since society was industrializing quickly, and charges of monopoly often were a sign that the pace of change was almost too fast. Antimonopolists have never been Luddites, however. They have never advocated stopping the technologies and the capital used to support them, insisting only that they be used equitably. The American ideal of making money while reaching a large market has never admitted naysayers to its ranks. Antitrust laws seek to restrain the powerful from badgering the weak economically. Not since the days of the nineteenth-century critics has anyone suggested that they be used to return to a more idyllic past, to a simpler society.

The history of monopoly formation in the United States is the history of economic and industrial power, ideology, and consumerism all rolled into one. What is most astonishing about its growth and development is the fact that the history is only about a century and a quarter old, spanning the time from Jay Gould and the railroad era to contemporary computer software engineers. Within that relatively short period, monopoly became public economic enemy number one and then receded into relative obscurity. The paradox it presents is simple. Businesses grow larger and larger to produce more goods. Economies of scale set in, so that producing more costs less and more profit is realized. Once that desirable stage is reached, it is time to call the lawyers, because charges of monopoly are not far behind. But beginning in the late 1970s, antitrust forces have been much less enthusiastic in pursuing alleged monopolists. Activity that would have been frowned on before World War II is now seen as economically healthy and as posing no threat to the political or economic order.

How regulators view alleged monopolies reflects the dominant political and economic ideologies of a period. Antitrust actions quickly became the battleground between different philosophies of democratic government and the state. Liberals in the Hamiltonian mold have used it as a tool against big business, seen as a predatory power capable of subjugating the population to its unelected will. They view a strong federal government as a potent counterbalance to the power of big business, which may often act undemocratically in its quest for profits and increased market share. Conservatives, on the other hand, tend to view it much more benignly, seeing big business as the provider of jobs and economic well-being. They draw their philosophy from Thomas Jefferson, who favored the power of the states over a strong federal government. Commerce was essentially a state matter, and actions by the state against business were incursions into often forbidden territory. Over the years the Jeffersonian position has been used to defend business against interference from Washington. Inconsistencies have appeared constantly as the political landscape changed. What was considered a monopoly in 1911, when Standard Oil and American Tobacco were broken up, was not applied again in 1919, when the Supreme Court refused to dismantle U.S. Steel. These were among the first of numerous court decisions that seemed to depend upon the ideological bent of the Supreme Court at the time. Separating antitrust or antimonopoly thought from the larger context of political and economic ideology is impossible. And that thought has extended to smaller companies as well. The history of antitrust action contains many notable cases where large companies were not involved but monopoly was still suspected. Small companies conspiring to fix prices or conquer a market often have received more attention than larger companies, which can be very expensive to prosecute. Both the IBM and AT&T antitrust cases in the 1970s and 1980s took over ten years to prosecute. Smaller cases reach court more quickly and provide antitrusters with quicker results.

Conventional wisdom has it that there have been four great merger periods in American history—in the 1880s and 1890s, in the 1920s and early 1930s, in the 1960s, and most recently in the 1980s and 1990s. The 1920s provided the original subjects of Monopoly. The game was purchased by Parker Brothers from Charles Darrow of Pennsylvania, who based it upon the most obvious monopolies of his day—utility companies and land developers. A closer reading of the history of the last century shows that this identification of merger periods is not quite accurate, however. The *entire* period of American capitalism since the Industrial Revolution has been an unrelenting trend toward consolidation. When the companies involved in those mergers become large enough, monopoly eventually rears its head. The phenomenon has been continuous since the modern corporation appeared in the latter part of the nineteenth century. The very apparent lack of serious antitrust activity by the Justice Department over the last two decades of the twentieth century attests to merger as more than simply a trend. It has become a corporate way of life, slowed down only by uneasy stock markets or poor economic conditions.

The constant force creating bigger and bigger businesses is a natural consequence of free enterprise capitalism. The relentless quest for better products, expanding markets, economies of scale, and enhanced profits make constant growth a logical outcome of corporate enterprise. Critics of capitalism and monopolies in the last century looked at them through Marx's lens. Monopoly was the final stage of capitalism. Once it had been achieved, commercial life had reached its pinnacle—it had nowhere else to go. The final goal toward which it was being driven had been achieved. But the critics of monopoly never got any farther than describing the process. No one offered any suggestions as to where society might venture next. That suggests that antimonopoly thought in the nineteenth century was mostly rhetoric, aimed at fattening the wallets of the muckrakers who made a living by criticizing business in general.

Adding to their intriguing past, monopolies often have come into being under dominant personalities. Monopolists have tended to be strong individuals who forged industrial empires with genius, a good bit of luck, and frequently ruthless disregard of the competition. Wall Street has aided them in their quest for expansion, playing an integral part in their history. The public's reaction to them has been mixed. Some see them as godsends, providing employment and economic well-being. Others see them as symptomatic of business gone amok, the great enemy lurking within. But no one disputes that the economy could not have grown to its present strengths without them. One inescapable fact emerges from the history of monopolies: Sometimes the public has been willing to tolerate a monopoly operating in the market, but it is much less inclined to be tolerant when the company is run by a "monopolist."

Since the railroads began consolidating after the Civil War, there has been a distinct difference between monopolies and monopolists. Monopolies were considered endemic to capitalism from the very beginning. Socialists were not alone in viewing them in that light. The principal inventor of the railroad locomotive, George Stephenson, said as much before the Civil War. He was able to predict the need for a monopoly to consolidate the new era of rail transportation because the costs of starting a railroad were so high that competition would have proved ruinous and inefficient. He was foretelling the rise of men such as Cornelius "Commodore" Vanderbilt and Jay Gould well before the new industry was even born. The men who created them, the much-reviled monopolists of the nineteenth century, became larger than the organizations they created. Most of them were men of little privilege and scant formal education who clawed their way to the top of the economic ladder by hard work and sheer ingenuity. The head of the Antitrust Division of the Justice Department in the late 1930s, Thurman Arnold, said that they "built on their mistakes, their action was opportunistic, they experimented with human material and with little regard for social justice. Yet they raised the level of productive capacity beyond the dreams of their fathers." But their lifestyles and personal philosophies earned them the enmity of the newspapers. Once the political cartoonists and satirists of the post–Civil War era realized that they made good press, their reputations and images were under constant scrutiny and ridicule. Muckraking was born with the monopoly movement. The power of the press helped create public animosity toward big business and tycoons. And it also made them folk heroes.

Alleged monopolists also had to defend their wealth. Sometimes that has been a difficult proposition. When William Vanderbilt inherited his father's wealth in the nineteenth century, politicians, including British prime minister Gladstone, openly questioned whether $100 million was too much for one person to hold. The amount superficially pales in comparison to the fortune of Microsoft's Bill Gates, some seven hundred times that of Vanderbilt. But in conservatively adjusted terms, Vanderbilt's fortune today would be roughly equal to Gates' estimated billions. Vanderbilt also had the advantage of having much of it in cash. One of the key signs of monopoly over the years has been the wealth of the alleged monopolist. If it is extraordinary, the implication is that there must be fire when one smells that much smoke.

Defining a monopoly has always been a tricky business. Before the Industrial Revolution, a strong antimonopolist tradition had been inherited from English common law. That tradition equated monopoly power with that of the state. The British crown granted letters patent to merchants, giving them the exclusive right to provide certain goods or services. Those patents in principle were similar to patents granted by governments today: They allow an innovation a bit of breathing space to develop before the idea loses its legal protection. It is tolerated as a monopoly for a determined period of time. From the beginning, monopoly power has been closely intertwined with both the state and business. Separating the two has often been difficult. Traditionally, business has been suspicious of the centralized powers of the state, fearing interruption with the process of making money. Conversely, advocates of strong, decisive central government often suspect business of gravitating toward monopoly if not restricted for the sake of competition and fair pricing.

Attempting to be more precise has often been a problem, as can be quickly seen when reading the major antitrust cases of the last hundred years. *Monopoly control* means that one company dominates its industry, being able to set prices, control production, and often raise barriers to competitors wishing to enter the field. Occasionally, if that business is extremely capital-intensive and strategically vital, it may be protected by government itself. In that case it is referred to as a *natural monopoly*. If there are several firms in the same industry controlling things, they are classified as an *oligopoly* (though that term is less popular today than in the past). The degree to which the members of an oligopoly collude to influence prices is central. Tightly knit ones, where members of the group enter into specific agreements to control price or production, is referred to as a *collusive oligopoly*. This term often replaces the formerly popular term *cartel*. Over the last twenty-five years, *shared monopoly* has been a more popular way to describe oligopolies that have a virtual stranglehold on their respective industries.

Remedies against monopolies can be classified in several ways. Before the Civil War, the only viable way to attack an alleged monopoly was through the commerce clause of the Constitution. The same was true of the post–Civil War period, when the railroads were attacked for causing hardship to the farmers. That culminated in the creation of the Interstate Commerce Commission (ICC) in 1888. While that agency began to come to grips with the railroads, industry was quickly consolidating in its great trust phase, which lasted until World War I. The Sherman Act was passed in 1890 to counter the growth of trusts and their effect upon competition and prices, but its language was very broad. Not all litigation attempted under it was successful, and the Clayton Act was passed in 1914 in an effort to tighten the noose on trusts. This second law tried to come to grips with vertical mergers as well as horizontal ones, the type most easily identified during the period of the formation of the great trusts between 1880 and 1910. A *horizontal merger* was one between two firms in the same industry—the case of a large fish swallowing a smaller one in an attempt to expand the market for its goods and services while posing a danger to the competition. A *vertical merger* was one between two companies in related but dissimilar businesses. The DuPont company bought a sizeable stake in General Motors during the 1920s, when it realized that the auto maker would make an ideal customer for its plastics. Eventually it was forced to sell it because the arrangement had the effect of barring others from competing for business with GM because of the vertical arrangement.

Monopoly power evolved quickly over the years. It can be defined as the ability of a company to drive competitors out of business by using its dominant market position. One of the most common ways of accomplishing this is by undercutting competitors' prices, driving them out of the market, and then raising prices again. This is technically known as *predatory pricing*. The practice was common in the nineteenth century and was practiced notably by Cornelius Vanderbilt in the shipping business. He became so feared by his competitors that they actually paid him not to compete with them. Conversely, it can also be defined as a dominant company that refuses to lower prices in the wake of lower costs, costing the consumer too much money. That is known as *price leadership* and usually means that a dominant company sets prices for its industry. Competing firms refuse to undercut the market leader for fear of retaliation. Or it could also mean a company using its dominant position to keep others out of its industry. This was the favorite technique of John D. Rockefeller in establishing

Standard Oil as the largest company on earth. It could provide obstacles to others, capitalizing on its role as market leader to ensure that new ideas or technologies are not introduced by the competition. These techniques are known as *barriers to entry*. One favorite trick of monopolists is to put the squeeze on a competitor by cutting its financial lifelines, forcing it out of business. The fate of Samuel Insull, the notorious Chicago utilities baron of the 1920s, at the hands of an eastern banking syndicate was evidence of this power.

Charges of monopoly made in the past have employed all of these arguments in one form or another. Naturally, political will is necessary to bring charges or make them stick, and prevailing political ideologies play a major role in determining the course of antitrust matters. For the first seventy-five years of the industrial age, prosecuting monopolies was difficult, but at least the enemy was identifiable. After the Korean War, the environment, and the monopolist, changed. The *conglomerate* appeared, an organization that grew larger by merging companies with no apparent relationship to each other. Antitrusters were alarmed because none of the existing antimonopoly laws seemed to apply. There was no clear evidence that these organizations stifled competition, nor did they appear to practice predatory pricing or even price leadership.

The actual number of antitrust laws at the federal level is quite small. Most companies are sued for violating either the Sherman Antitrust Act or the Clayton Act. But there are other notable pieces of legislation, passed decades ago and not superficially antitrust laws at all, that have been even more effective in breaking up monopolies. The Glass-Steagall Act, the Bank Holding Company Act, and the Public Utility Holding Company Act appear to have been more consequential in breaking up the money trust and the utility monopolies than any of the pure antitrust laws. And there have also been some less-than-effective attempts at antitrust legislation. The Robinson-Patman Act of 1937, complex and contentious because of its avowed purpose of protecting the small businessman against the larger at all costs, may be the one piece of antitrust legislation that was actually Luddite in nature. It has been criticized by both liberals and conservatives as too vague and potentially disruptive to economic growth in the name of distant nineteenth-century ideals.

In the post–World War II period the ideas of the New Deal remained alive through members of the Supreme Court and Congress whose careers spanned the 1930s through the 1970s. As a result, many ideas first used in the 1930s were resurrected later. In 1935 Congress prohibited the large utility companies, and especially those controlled by J. P. Morgan, from expanding by using the *death sentence* provision: A utility could not own more than one operating system. That part of the law effectively blocked the giant utility holding companies from crossing state lines and lasted until the 1990s. The same idea was also used in a bill to block banks from crossing state lines in the 1960s, another prohibition that lasted until the 1990s. Ideas of the New Deal Democrats lived on for years in these and other laws that were antitrust legislation hiding in sheep's clothing.

The critics of antitrust law have much to complain about, and its advocates have much to celebrate. Monopolies have been identified and sometimes stopped, while others escaped its grip. But one inescapable fact remains: When a business organization becomes so large that it attracts the attention of regulators, its power will be challenged. Students of democratic societies recognize that when large organizations wield concentrations of economic power, political power is not far behind. The unnamed fear behind this realization is of a drift toward European-style fascism, where the power of large organizations supplants the role of the individual in society. That unacceptable outcome is the force that propels antimonopoly thinking, as imperfect as it may be. However, as the world grows smaller through globalization and as businesses cross national boundaries with relative ease, that fear is receding. Taking its place is another, greater fear of the consequences of curbing business as the population grows and demand for goods and services grows with it at the same time as resources dwindle. Antimonopoly theory and practice are at a crossroads in this delicate economic balancing act.

The relatively brief history of monopolies in the United States has been enormously affected by the fall of Soviet Communism. After the dismemberment of the Soviet Union, there has been a tacit acknowledgment that capitalism caused its downfall. The inexorable demands for capital in an increasingly competitive world put too much pressure on Communism, with its emphasis upon noncompetitive state guidance of industry. The system failed because it could not find the capital necessary for development, research, and production. Dying with it was the idea that big is necessarily evil. American business was quick to adopt the idea and adapt it for its own purposes. Now bigness in business has taken on a new importance as the savior of jobs, the provider of economic well-being, and a source of wealth for shareholders in companies that merge. Whether this attitude will prevail in the long run depends ultimately upon whether antitrust ideas can adapt themselves to the rapidly changing environment.

I

THE "MONOPOLIST MENACE"
(1860–1890)

What we call Monopoly is Business at the end of its journey.
The concentration of wealth, the wiping out of the middle
classes, are other names for it.

— HENRY DEMAREST LLOYD

MONOPOLIES HAVE A LONG and colorful history in the United States. They have usually been associated with industry, especially in the post–Civil War period. But their history is much older, originating in Elizabethan England. By the time the American colonies became independent, the terms *monopoly* and *antimonopolist* were already well established. Yet nothing was written about monopolies in the Constitution, and no mention was made of them in the writings of the founding fathers. However, several states felt strongly enough about them to prohibit them in their constitutions in the months following independence. Less than a century later, they were the most discussed topic in the country.

The great public relations problem for the industrialists of the post–Civil War era was that the monopolies they created were considered the very embodiment of conspiratorial business methods, at odds with the best American libertarian tradition. But were these not the enterprises that helped make the United States dominant during the Industrial Revolution? Without what would be called monopoly consolidation, the great railroads would not have stretched from coast to coast. Without the rail-roads, farmers would not have been able to get their products to market to feed the growing population. And without the other monopolies the rail-roads helped create, oil and steel production would not have reached record levels, because distribution would have been difficult. Was this snowball effect good or bad for the country? Industrialists naturally said it was beneficial, while many critics, still rooted in the mercantilist era, were not quite as sure.

More than a few businessmen could be excused for asking openly what they had done wrong in assembling great industrial enterprises only to find that they were considered enemies of the public. In some extreme cases they were even considered enemies of democracy. Even more ironic was the fact that they were derided by the same critics who extolled the virtues of American industrial prowess. What they encountered was an economic and ideological battle that was deeply rooted in the past and showed an apprehensiveness about the future. The most strident critics of monopolies came from the literary establishment, who often distorted facts and history in order to make a point and sell books and magazines. They were not able to create the antimonopoly tradition by themselves; the idea that accumulating economic power was intrinsically bad was a characteristic inherited from the English common-law tradition.

The admiration for money, on one hand, and the fear of bigness, on the other, were problems that were never adequately sorted out in the nine-teenth century. When combined with the religious and ideological fervor of the time, they could be perplexing; at other times they were humorous. One of the best-known examples of preaching what would later become known as the "gospel of wealth" was Russell Conwell, a popular Baptist minister whose famous "Acres of Diamonds" speech was one of the most famous and often-delivered orations of the nineteenth century. Claiming that it was every Christian's duty to "get rich" because making money "honestly is to preach the gospel," Conwell was an unabashed admirer of American capitalism. Delivered several thousand times over his career, his speech was said to have earned him over $5 million in fees. In the opposite vein were the remarks of Congregationalist minister Washington Glad-den, the father of the Social Gospel movement. Gladden held that "what men call natural law [survival of the fittest] by which they mean the law of greed and strife is unnatural . . . the law of brotherhood is the only natural law." These diametrically opposed points of view would clash time and again in the debate over monopolies and vividly illustrated the American ambivalence surrounding wealth and power.

There were more serious social parallels. The America observed by Alexis de Tocqueville in the early 1830s was a country that was ruled locally by the town meeting and in which the economy and social life were mostly agrarian. Every man was equal to every other, and a sense of fairness prevailed. But there was also the America bulging at the seams, the America of manifest destiny, teeming with immigrants and "go west, young man" ideology. In expansionist America, railroads and industry grew quickly along with petroleum refining, steel production, and new forms of communication. This was the country where economies of scale ruled supreme and where small-town America was viewed only as part of a larger market. Industrialists expanding rapidly were viewed with distrust by those at the local level. They were equated with dizzying progress and material well-being but also with rapacious profits and autocratic political intentions.

In the twenty years preceding the Civil War, American business altered its regional character and began to show potential for nationwide expansion. The railroads developed quickly into a revolution that would soon link the continent. After the war, business increased even more rapidly. As it did, ingenuity spawned new industries and with them new industrial forms. One, the trust, was the predecessor of what we now know as the holding company. The trust was essentially a shell company that held the stock of others "in trust," and it set off howls of protest from both the states and the federal government. Congress responded by passing the Sherman Act in 1890, shortly after trusts (then understood as monopolies) began organizing. What was the basis of the protests? What was so repugnant about this new form of industrial combination?

"Monopolies are odious, contrary to the spirit of free government . . . and ought not to be suffered," declared the Maryland State Constitution in 1776. Several other state constitutions expressed similar sentiments. They were referring not to industrial monopolies as known today but to monopolies granted by the British crown that dated back two hundred years to the reign of Elizabeth I. Although the crown granted various monopoly patents to supporters, they were disliked by the public generally. A member of Parliament under Elizabeth I stated unequivocally that "I cannot . . . conceive with my heart the great grievances that the town and country which I serve suffereth by some of these monopolies; it bringeth the general profit into a private hand, and the end of all is beggary and bondage of the subject." In fact, the uproar at granting patents became so shrill that Elizabeth herself responded to the fuss by stating that some of the monopolies "would presently be repealed, some suspended, and none put in execution, but such as should first have a trial according to the law for the good of the people."[1] In societies that were just beginning to shrug off vestiges of the Middle Ages, concern was growing for the artisan class, which would have been seriously hurt if monopolies were granted to some members of the society. What would these existing businessmen do if they were suddenly barred from earning a living because the crown decided arbitrarily to grant someone exclusive privilege to produce a good or render a service? Normally the crown did so because it could derive revenues from the sale of the monopoly to that person or trading company. English jurist William Blackstone defined the problem succinctly: "The subject in general is restrained from that liberty of manufacturing or trading which he had before." Three hundred years later, opponents of monopolies in the United States would take the queen's remark literally and use the courts in fighting the great industrial combinations that had grown rapidly since the Civil War.

Resentment of monopolies became deeply ingrained in English political thought. As time passed they became consonant with mistrust of the powers of the monarchy. The English republican and democratic theories of the seventeenth century found their way into the American Constitution and the Federalist Papers. John Adams was an avid reader of political thought and blanched at the very thought of anything but a democratically elected assembly for America. The work of John Locke provided both a framework for the framers of the Constitution and a necessary antidote to more frightening theories, such as those of Thomas Hobbes. Locke's most popular idea was that property was one of man's basic rights because it was an extension of the individual. Hobbes's *Leviathan*, published in 1651, described the emerging modern state as one in which absolute power naturally appeared as a force to be reckoned with. Bigness versus smallness was not a purely American preoccupation but was inherited directly from the British.

Antimonopoly sentiments were also strong in the new republic. The Whiskey Rebellion of 1794, when Washington County in western Pennsylvania rebelled over a federal excise tax on whiskey production, prompted George Washington himself to leave the daily rigors of the presidency temporarily in order to subdue the rebellion. The demands made by the rebels were remarkably similar to the arguments the American colonists themselves made against the British and had a distinctly antimonopolist ring. Whiskey was both consumed and used as a quasi currency on the western frontier at the time. The rebels claimed the government tried to use the tax to assert central control over citizens, seriously confusing legitimate power with tyranny. This was not materially different from the argument made by the Elizabethans against the crown. Similar complaints against monopolies were also heard on the American frontier at the time of the Louisiana Purchase. The American settlers in St. Louis and points west found themselves at a disadvantage compared to the French and Spanish fur trappers who already inhabited the area and who had been granted exclusive rights to develop the area by their respective crowns. They possessed an exclusivity that the newly arrived Americans found difficult to match. The Americans would come to dislike monopolies in whatever form they detected them.

Once the corporation became a widely used form of business organization, antimonopolists had a new enemy that replaced the state. The modern business corporation that emerged after the Civil War possessed many of the same trappings of power as a government but without any of the constitutional checks. Fixing prices, ignoring the plight of the workingman, and acting purely in the name of profit characterized all the great industrialists of the age. Their wealth and ingenuity were offset by their capricious use of power and tendencies to behave as autocrats without regard for their constituencies. After the Civil War a movement arose to counter their alleged abuses of economic power.

The fear of monopolies was not necessarily the same as fear of monopolists themselves. The two could and were easily separated before the Civil War. Monopoly was originally coincidental with the power of the state, the new industrial state that was emerging. After the Civil War the topic became much more complicated when the monopolists came to prominence. These entrepreneurs were successful without the intervention of the crown or state, and there were few political ways to curtail their industrial power. What happened instead was that muckraking journalists began to expose monopolists and their dreaded creations, and public accountability began to take on a new dimension not seen before in American affairs.

Those who forged great industrial empires were easy targets of the antimonopolists because they made tangible products with clear lines of supply. But other monopolists were more elusive. Those who created empires built upon finance were much more difficult to accuse, let alone actually prove to have engaged in anticompetitive practices. Compounding the problems were those who dabbled in both. Cornelius Vanderbilt, his son William, and Jay Gould are examples of those who created wide-ranging empires using shadowy stock market techniques to finance themselves. While their clear goal was making money, it was often difficult to tell which technique they preferred: Were the railroads their main obsession or merely a smoke screen for stock market raids? What was clear is that the three came to be known as monopolists. Large, octopuslike organizations now had recognizable leaders that cartoonists and other journalists could rant about. The public outcry was always greatest when these large organizations seemed to be making exorbitant amounts of money for their proprietors.

Almost from the beginning of the great monopoly debate, financing industrial expansion became a serious problem for the antimonopolists. Finance developed to the point where even those ostensibly opposed to it could not help but be drawn into its web. The stock market had become the personal preserve of many of the early industrialists and some swashbuckling traders who made personal fortunes at the expense of others. The term "robber baron" was later applied to those industrialists who made great fortunes while apparently ignoring the plight of the workingman and scoffing at the public will. The allure of accumulating great wealth in a short time even drew some of the fiercest critics of the age into embarrassing positions. Some critics of the robber barons and their empires, such as Charles Francis Adams Jr., were known to take the occasional plunge in the market, often with less than successful results. The fact that they were unable to beat the barons at their own game made their protests shriller.

The great industrialists, almost to a man, possessed as much knowledge of finance as of their respective industries. Without it, they would not have made their marks. Andrew Carnegie, John D. Rockefeller, and Jay Gould were all able financiers. Those most closely associated with the stock market, notably Gould, used an intricate knowledge of the market to raise cash by sometimes dubious, but perfectly legal, means. One technique perfected by Gould was known as locking up cash. Knowing when the supply of funds in the money market would be tight, especially during seasonal adjustments of the money supply, Gould would borrow large sums of greenbacks, using securities as collateral. That would exacerbate an already tight situation and force interest rates higher, knocking down the stock market. This created a paradise for short sellers, who were waiting for a downturn so that they could buy at lower prices to cover their positions. Pushed to the extreme, this often caused market slowdowns and panics. It also made speculators avid devotees of greenbacks when others were fussing about the new currency's lack of gold backing. Equally important was that such tricks allowed the young market manipulators to raise money, something that most lacked early in their careers. Stock market raiding was actually a way of raising capital to be used in further ventures.

A more serious issue was the nature of the monopolies being assembled. The first industry in the post–Civil War era to undergo consolidation was the railroads. Almost from the beginning, the nature of the railroads was seen as something quite different from other industries. George Stephenson, the principal inventor of the steam-powered locomotive, declared early on that railways would have to unite, or consolidate, to avoid duplicating the heavy, capital-intensive costs that would prove ruinous if two railroad companies sought to compete for the same market. Costs to the consumers would have to rise as a result. But if they could consolidate with other companies serving adjacent areas, then the costs would eventually come down and long-distance travel and shipping would be made cheaper. (This was one of the first warnings about what would a century later be called capital barriers—a situation in which setup costs are so high that whoever establishes one successfully ultimately controls the fate of the industry and is able to bar others from entry). Because the costs of running a railroad were fixed, the only way to recoup those costs and make a profit was to carry as many passengers or as much freight as possible. Large systems would be able to run more efficiently than smaller ones, and so the natural tendency for railroads was to consolidate in order to contain costs. Lurking in the shadows were the aspiring monopolists who would seize the opportunity to consolidate and rig prices at the same time, costing the public heavily. The great debate had begun. Ironically, however, capitalism invited consolidation, and consolidation invited monopoly. The circle had been closed long before industrial expansion had been completely set in motion.

Later in the nineteenth century writers and commentators would begin to distinguish different types of monopolies, realizing that the term was too general for the expanding economy. Railroads, John D. Rockefeller's petroleum monopoly, and Carnegie's domination of the steel industry became known as *industrial monopolies,* or *industrial trusts.* A trust was a company organized to hold the stock of others, the predecessor of the holding company. But a larger question still loomed: Were monopolies and trusts the same thing? John Moody, one of the fathers of investment analysis, added some clarity to a confusing situation. "Monopoly is not a combination itself; the monopoly element, if there be any, is something distinct from the mere organization or Trust," he wrote in 1904. He concluded on a note that would prove useful in the years ahead. "When men form corporate organizations . . . they do not form monopolies. They take advantage of monopoly in one way or other but they do not create it."[2] Success had to be achieved before monopoly could be claimed. The distinction was useful, even though it did not cover all possible circumstances. For example, since many of these businesses were capital-intensive, competition from other quarters was sometimes unrealistic. In that case, these industries were referred to as *natural monopolies.* These organizations were difficult to control, as shown by the railroads. They were vital to the Industrial Revolution, and foolish regulations over them could have disastrous economic consequences. Another type of monopoly, the *government-granted monopoly,* became an issue in the twentieth century.

SUNSHINE AND WATERING

Charles Francis Adams Jr., the first of the self-styled critics of the railroads, became well known on account of his essays on the century's archetypal bad boy, Jay Gould. Adams recognized the financial problems monopolies posed in his essay *The Railroad System,* published in 1871. The consolidation of the railroads into large systems had both organizational and financial elements. The financial aspects were accomplished mostly through stock watering, a tool perfected by Daniel Drew and Jay Gould, his protégé. Stock watering was a common technique whereby additional stock was added in a company despite the fact that this diluted its asset value substantially. Watering actually weakened a company's financial statements and eroded what shareholder value existed. But investors regularly ignored the practice when buying stocks they thought had excellent prospects. Often they relied upon inaccurate press reports about companies, reports which were often planted by those with vested interests in the companies' fortunes. The stock market was a dangerous place for investors in the nineteenth century and took its toll on more than one fortune, but investors always came back for more, providing financing for railroads with dubious management. Naturally, railroads became the focus of the first antimonopoly attacks. The cast of characters running some of the better-known rail lines made the attacks easy.

Critics of monopolies, like their antitrust counterparts later, often came from the aristocratic, propertied class, which viewed modern industrialists with some distaste. Later the role of critic would transfer itself to intellectuals. While the modern corporation was emerging during the Civil War period, not everyone considered it a blessing. Distaste for trade and commerce still abounded in both the United States and Europe. "Did you ever expect a corporation to have a conscience, when it has no soul to be damned, and no body to be kicked?" asked Edward Thurlow, a British member of Parliament, at the end of the eighteenth century. "Business?" quipped Alexandre Dumas, son of the novelist, in 1857. "It's quite simple: it's other people's money." Fifty years later Louis Brandeis would borrow that phrase in the title of a book that was to become the gospel of the antitrust movement. Men who engaged in commerce were not thought to be in the same intellectual class as those engaged in a traditional serious profession. Making money was essentially a dirty business. Those who were of superior intellect had to provide a check on those with grandiose ambitions. Much of the thinking about early monopolies and antitrust issues was dominated by these concepts of noblesse oblige.

Hailing from the country's best-known political family, Charles Francis Adams Jr. was the great-grandson of John Adams, grandson of John Quincy Adams, and son of Charles Francis Adams, a diplomat. His brothers Henry and Brooks also became historians and writers of note. Educated at Harvard, like most of his family, Adams was drawn to the law but found it unsatisfying. After serving in the Civil War at Gettysburg, Antietam, and Richmond with the Union Army, he returned to civilian life determined to make his name in the public realm. Unlike his father or grandfather, he embarked on a career not as a politician or diplomat but as an essayist. His target became the railroads and the railroad barons. His timing proved impeccable. Jay Gould provided both Charles and his brother Henry with all the fuel they would need to enhance their reputations as guardians of the public good.

The Adamses displayed a long-standing distaste of the rough-and-tumble in American politics, preferring a life of letters and commentary. A major affront in the family history occurred early when Harvard University decided to give Andrew Jackson an honorary degree after Jackson defeated John Quincy Adams in the presidential election of 1828. Brooks Adams later recalled his grandfather's description of the newly elected president as a "barbarian who could not write a sentence of grammar and hardly could spell his own name." Honor forbade them from engaging in the commercial frays of the period and political plunder, for which Jackson and later Ulysses S. Grant were well known.

In 1869 Charles and Henry wrote *A Chapter of Erie*, outlining the shenanigans of Jay Gould and "Jubilee" Jim Fisk in running the Erie Railroad from their opulent New York City headquarters. A year later, in *The New York Gold Conspiracy*, Henry Adams recalled the attempt by Gould to corner the New York gold market, purportedly with the unwitting assistance of President Grant. Both works became classics of the day and two of the first examples of muckraking literature. The Erie book launched Charles' career as a critic of the railroad industry, while the gold essay propelled Henry into the front ranks of what would later become known as muckraking journalists. In Charles' case, the essay was somewhat self-serving since he desperately wanted to make his mark in the public realm as a critic of railroad management. There were other railroad barons who easily could have been the target of his pen, such as Cornelius Vanderbilt, but

Gould's latest adventures were headline news and invited the inevitable barbed criticisms.

All of the virtues and benefits associated with the railroads were under a shadow as long as Gould and Fisk ran one of the East Coast's best-known lines. The railroads became one of the first attempts at monopoly concentration in the post–Civil War period. Jay Gould would always claim that by amalgamating the railroads, he was providing considerable employment, especially in the western states. Charles Adams' criticism of Erie was aimed at the excesses of its management and the quality of its senior personnel. The New York Central, Cornelius Vanderbilt's railroad, came in for the same criticism from Adams, who often compared it to the Pennsylvania Railroad, considered to be the best-run system in the country at the time. While the New York Central was described as an empire run by Vanderbilt, the Pennsylvania was seen as a republic, run in conjunction with the politicians of the state. But the people and politicians in Pennsylvania still came under Adams' criticism as being "not marked by intelligence; they are, in fact, dull, uninteresting, very slow and very persevering."[3] It was just this sort of plodding dullness that made corporations work relatively efficiently. His assessment of the unimaginative Pennsylvania Railroad would prove ironic, however. The president of the line at the time of the Civil War, Thomas Scott, had a young assistant who was bound to move on to better things. Andrew Carnegie proved to be better at forging a career in the steel industry and left the Pennsylvania shortly after the war to set up the Keystone Bridge Company.

Adams described how Vanderbilt and Gould used autocratic methods to run their companies like personal fiefdoms, and he established them in the public mind as magnates without conscience. *The Economist* used similar language when it described the antics of Fisk and Gould at the Erie headquarters: "They are absolute dictators—neither rendering accounts, permitting discussion, nor regarding any interest but their own. They openly maintain an Opera House, with Ballet and Orchestra, out of the revenues of the railroad."[4] Monopoly power was endemic to capitalism as it was developing in the United States, but being a monopolist was its tawdry side. And historically, monopoly was synonymous with tyranny. That link would provide an emotional platform with which to fight monopoly over the next fifty years.

The ideological underpinnings against monopolies were reinforced by the Anglo-American common-law tradition. Although there were no specific federal or state statutes prohibiting monopolies, there was a body of common law that could be invoked to prohibit it in some forms. As early as 1859 a case in Louisiana showed that combinations to restrain trade could be struck down by state courts if the courts were convinced that prices were unnecessarily propped up and trade in goods restricted by the agreement.[5]

Cornelius Vanderbilt engaged in just the sort of practices that common law proscribed. He often would undercut a competitor in order to woo its customers, ruining the other business. Once the customer was doing business with him, Vanderbilt would raise prices again to previous levels. His business practices were so feared by his competitors that they actively paid him not to compete with them; in hearings before the House of Representatives in 1860, two steamship lines admitted that they paid him over $500,000 per year not to compete. The president of one company testified that "the arrangement was based upon there being no competition and the sum was regulated by that fact." But despite the strong tradition of law against such agreements, especially when they had an impact upon public monies (the steamship companies carried mail), Vanderbilt was never prosecuted by the House, many of whose members were assumed to be in his back pocket.[6]

Writing about monopolies and relying upon common law were not going to curtail their power. The states took the lead by establishing commissions to control corporate behavior, some before the Civil War, and within ten years of the establishment of the first railroads, some states passed laws attempting to curtail their power by limiting their potential profits. Nineteenth-century critics and commentators were preoccupied with the power of companies as measured by their assets. Too high a return suggested a combination of wealth and power that many considered highly dangerous. Comparing corporate assets to those of individuals was a favorite tool of antimonopolists who wanted to show the absolute size of the new corporate leviathans. The state utility commissions that developed to control the railroads found these comparisons useful in their attempts to limit the corporations. From the very beginning of the battle, economics and ideology would be mixed in an acrimonious argument about who knew what was best for the country.

Early attempts at railroad regulation were sketchy at best, but after the Civil War, railroad rates became a pressing issue, especially for farmers. In 1867 Oliver Hudson Kelley, a former clerk with the Bureau of Agriculture, founded the Granger movement in Minnesota. The movement was opposed to what it saw as excessive railroad freight charges, which it considered detrimental to the economic development of rural areas. The Grangers immediately found a receptive audience, and within seven years over twenty thousand local Granges were established, with nearly a million members. The Grangers' political demands were decidedly antimonopoly. They pressed for antimonopoly legislation and a national income tax in addition to railroad reform.

The Grangers began organizing about the same time that Charles Francis Adams pushed for a Massachusetts commission on railroads to be established. The state legislature obliged by creating the Massachusetts Board of Railroad Commissioners in 1869, and Adams became one of its three original members. The body quickly became known as the "sunshine commission" because its avowed purpose was to cast sunshine onto the railroad problem in the state. But the legislation that created it gave the commission—a "model, weak agency"—no power to enforce its recommendations.[7]

As the railroads grew larger, new issues arose constantly requiring attention—more than any individual agency could possibly handle. Rail road rates were a problem. Some states had already mandated a maximum level of profit be set on railroads so that they would not enrich themselves at the consumers' expense. Safety issues were a serious problem. Some of the railroads had appalling records of accidents and passenger fatalities. Many lines, including the New York Central, published a list of accidents occurring on their rails in their annual reports, but it was not out of a sense of public duty; the reports were required by state law. Later, George Westinghouse developed the air brake in response to the problem.

Abuse of investors was another problem. Stock watering was enriching many railroad barons. Some were able to merge two companies and create a new company whose capital substantially exceeded the sum of the old companies' capital, creating a new sort of Wall Street alchemy not seen before. The railroads seemed to be profiting at the expense of the investing public.

CAVALRY CHARGE

Cornelius Vanderbilt's New York Central and Jay Gould and Jim Fisk's Erie were perhaps the best-known corporations in the country, thanks in no small part to the activities of the men who headed them. Newspapers of the day continually ran stories about the industrialists, many of whom were members of the "Millionaires and Monopolists Club" that frequently dined at Delmonico's in New York, flagrantly showing off their wealth. The ostentatious displays only invited more criticism. Noted cartoonist Thomas Nast regularly set his sights on the management of Erie, especially on its links with the notorious Tweed ring of Tammany Hall fame. All the publicity that Jay Gould received from the time that *Chapters of Erie* was written made him a legendary figure in financial circles, and he attained the distinction of being perhaps the most vilified figure on Wall Street. Rival traders whom he had beaten in the markets regularly accosted him, the best-known incident occurring at Fraunces Tavern in the Wall Street area when a fellow diner pummeled him on account of a shady business deal. Being the butt of criticism and the occasional attack only made him more resolute, however, and by the time he died in 1892 he had amassed one of the country's largest fortunes.

The New York legislature helped the railroads' cause immeasurably. In one of the more comical twists in railroad history, the New York railroad commission, established in 1855, was bought off by the railroads and recommended its own abolition, which was granted two years later. Some well-meaning laws were evaded by the railroads; one law passed by the New York legislature in 1850 allowed the state to determine what was to be done with any excess profits earned by the railroads. Railroad managements had been hostile to any suggestions that their profits were "excessive" and devised ingenious schemes to mask their profitability. They falsified their accounts to make it appear that they had invested large sums of capital in physical improvements that were never actually performed. They also bought off legislators so that they could continue busi-

Jay Gould Swinging Between His Varied Interests, by Keppler. *Puck*, n.d.

ness as usual while the state legislatures looked the other way. One such group of legislators in the New York Assembly became known as the Black Horse Cavalry. This bipartisan group of representatives would push through legislation favoring big corporations at a proper price, usually $5,000 to $10,000 a vote.[8] Jay Gould withdrew $500,000 from the coffers of the Erie to bribe them so that he could fight impending litigation over his control at the railroad. As *The Economist* sarcastically noted, such goings-on were natural for New York in general, where "burglary, theft, and even murder, are incessant."

Upon the death of Cornelius Vanderbilt, who often traveled to Albany accompanied by William "Boss" Tweed of Tammany Hall to influence legislators, his estate went to his son William, who proved a worthy successor. For the first forty years of his life Billy was sequestered on a family farm on Staten Island because the Commodore considered him a bit slow. But after assuming the Vanderbilt empire, he proved equal to the task of running the businesses. Known for his blunt remarks, much like his father, he spared no verbiage when angered. His most enduring remark was "The public be damned," a reaction to hearing what a reporter told him of the public's perception of his wealth and power. When discussing those in the state legislature who would make his life difficult in order to up the ante,

Jay Gould in the Robbers Den, artist unknown.

he was even more clear. "When I want to buy up any politician," he quipped in 1882, "I always find the anti-monopolists the most purchasable—they don't come so high."

The young Theodore Roosevelt was a member of the legislature in the 1880s, during the heyday of the Black Horse Cavalry, but unlike many of his colleagues there, Roosevelt, from one of the country's best-known families, was a relentless reformer who opposed the "cavalry's" tactics. He became involved in investigating a New York State Supreme Court judge, T. R. Westbrook, suspected of aiding Jay Gould in his acquisition of the Manhattan Elevated Railway Company. After discovering a note written by Westbrook to Gould clearly stating that "I am willing to go the very verge of judicial discretion to protect your vast interests," Roosevelt initiated an investigation of the judge by the state legislature.[9] This was one of the early reforming actions taken by the young Roosevelt. He was also successful in persuading the legislature to reduce the fare on the elevated railroad from 10 cents to 5 cents. The reduction was popular with the public but certainly less so with Gould. The rationale for the rate decrease was clear. In 1881 the elevated tramway served over 75 million customers, earning $5.3 million in the process. Even the rate cut did not seriously hamper Gould's ability to make money, and the company doubled its number of passengers and its earnings over the next ten years.[10] But Roosevelt established a reputation as a reformer that would carry through to his presidency and pose serious problems for big business.

Laws passed to protect the public from monopolies often inadvertently led to stock watering. Vanderbilt, Drew, and Gould were masters of the technique. Drew was the first and most notorious, being called the "speculative director" of Erie by Adams because of his penchant for speculating with his own company's stock. In one particularly well-publicized escapade, Vanderbilt doubled his personal fortune by issuing new stock in the New York Central. A state law restricted his New York Central from issuing new stock in order to acquire the Hudson River Railroad, so Vanderbilt bought off enough members of the New York legislature to allow the railroads to consolidate. He then quickly issued $44 million worth of new stock in the combined company that was valued at a premium of 80 percent. With only a printing press to aid him, he almost single-handedly doubled the value of the company on paper. Investors seemed delighted, and the stock rose dramatically. The affair led Adams to conclude later that "according to the books of the company, over $50,000 of absolute water had been poured out for each mile of road between New York and Buffalo."[11] Even Adams had to acknowledge that the New York Central/Hudson amalgamation was one of Vanderbilt's "great masterpieces." Most commentators of the period calculated that Vanderbilt's personal share from the watering was $6 million—in cash, not in watered stock.

At the same time, the speculative fever of the post–Civil War years gripped even those who appeared least likely to be interested. Charles Francis Adams Jr. was a frequent speculator in the stock market, known for investing heavily at times in the shares of the railroads. He was a margin trader who had to borrow money more than once to satisfy his broker for loans on stocks that did not perform well. It is not clear whether he speculated in the stock of railroads that ultimately he would later have commercial dealings with. Many investors of the day held positions in Erie, one of the most popular stocks of the time. Adams, for his part, made very little money in his speculations.

Jay Gould learned the new art of controlling information well; he often used journalists to plant news about stocks he intended to manipulate. He eventually bought the *New York World* so that he could manipulate financial information and control the flow of information on companies in which he had a vested interest.

The muckraking lent a shrill tone to the antimonopoly debate, but it was not without its adulatory side. Vanderbilt, Drew, and Gould were all men of limited or no education who nevertheless had managed to accumulate sizeable fortunes. Vanderbilt, perhaps the best example of a self-made man of his era, was once told of an English peer's remark that it was a pity he had no formal education. The Commodore replied, "You tell Lord Palmerston from me that if I had learned education I would not have time to learn anything else."[12] And their wealth made them legends on Wall Street, despite the fact that they helped ruin more than one unsuspecting trader. The public admired them as long as they did not create financial panic by their actions—a charge that was easily leveled at Gould on several occasions. The real resistance came from the Granger movement, which argued that the railroads' price-rigging activities were keeping farmers from earning a decent living. Its arguments were difficult to dispute but equally difficult to act upon, for legal precedents were not well established. Ironically, one of the precedents that would help serve the Granger cause in the post–Civil War years came about as the result of a lawsuit instituted by one of Vanderbilt's early employers.

In his twenties and early thirties Vanderbilt worked for a steamship company, owned by Thomas Gibbons, that provided service between New York and Philadelphia via New Brunswick, New Jersey. The ship would travel from New York to New Brunswick, and then passengers would complete the rest of the journey by coach to Trenton and then steamship again down the Delaware River to Philadelphia. The service proved very popular with passengers because it was faster than any other in existence.

But it also ran afoul of New York's monopoly given to Robert Fulton and Robert Livingston for steamship transportation in its own waters. New Jersey proved more competitive and approved of the service, threatening to retaliate against New York if it confiscated any of the ships making the run. Vanderbilt, operating as a captain for Gibbons, was instrumental in ensuring that the operation would continue, by continuously avoiding New York officials who attempted to stop the service. Finally, Gibbons sued in the New York courts to obtain relief against his pursuers. He was represented by Daniel Webster. He lost the case and carried the battle to the federal courts, claiming that the opposition's actions were in violation of the commerce clause in the U.S. Constitution. There he met with success. The case, *Gibbons v. Ogden*, became one of the landmark decisions of the court under Chief Justice John Marshall. New York courts had written that Congress had no power to control internal commerce, which was what they claimed the New York–New Jersey dispute involved. But the Supreme Court disagreed. In 1824 Marshall wrote that the power of the commerce clause was "complete in itself, may be exercised to its utmost extent, and acknowledges no limitations, other than are prescribed in the Constitution."[13] The Fulton monopoly was broken, interstate transportation was given an immediate boost. The decision contributed to the success of the area in establishing itself as the center of American commerce and transportation. It also contributed indirectly to Vanderbilt's already formidable reputation as one of the leaders in American shipping.

Even before the Civil War, railroads were challenging shipping as the most efficient means of transportation but were not setting profitability records by any means. Most railroad building was occurring in New England and the Middle Atlantic states. The western frontier and the South did not experience great growth until after the war. Only when the consolidations began did the returns on the rails begin to increase. And stock watering was certainly part of it. In one of the early financial analyses of the railroads in 1884, it was stated that the investment in the railroad companies did not exceed the amount of debt outstanding, meaning that they were excessively capitalized, or watered, by 50 percent; this figure agreed with Adams' assessment of five years before.[14] General productivity and profitability rose after the war and stayed high until the end of the century, due mainly to the railroads' westward expansion and their continued consolidations. Over twenty-nine thousand miles of track were laid between 1870 and 1875, exceeding the length of all of the existing track laid since 1830. But the twenty years after the war also witnessed a constant struggle between the states and the railroads that was mostly the Grangers' doing. Freight rates were excessively high when simple economics would have suggested otherwise.

The federal government did not yet have the means to curtail the interstate activities of the railroads, so the job was left to the states. In one situation that led to the most noteworthy of what are referred to as the "Granger cases," Illinois passed some very restrictive laws on those industries within its borders that it considered were operating in the public interest, notably the railroad and agricultural storage businesses. A man named Munn was charged and convicted with operating a grain warehouse without a license. He then sued to challenge the authority of the state. The Illinois Supreme Court upheld his conviction, and he appealed again. When *Munn v. Illinois* eventually found its way to the U.S. Supreme Court, the entire matter of interstate commerce and due process came to the surface. The Court ruled in 1877 that such businesses were "clothed with a public interest" and were rightfully subject to Illinois' supervision.[15] Munn's earlier conviction was upheld, and the Granger movement won a significant victory in its fight over the railroads and their agents who helped control interstate commerce.

The Granger victory was important for the antimonopolist movement because as the rails spread rapidly into the South and the West, opening many of these areas to nationwide commerce for the first time, farmers there would be at the mercy of the railroads unless meaningful regulations could be enacted. What the Court suggested in *Munn* was that the states could control railroad freight rates in the absence of congressional action on the larger issue of the regulation of interstate commerce. Clearly, a waiting game was in effect; Illinois' jurisdiction was fairly clear in *Munn*, but as the railroads became larger the issue became more clouded. As railroads grew and crossed state lines, using the states simply for passage, it became difficult for individual states to control them. The *Munn* decision was not the end but only the beginning of a long history of judicial rulings concerning interstate commerce. The real question was when Congress would finally decide to act and take up the issue of regulation.

STATES' PREROGATIVES

Railroads were not the only monopoly issues during the Reconstruction era. As the country became more industrialized, the extraction and pro-cessing of natural resources also became the object of antimonopolists' scrutiny. Because of the capital-intensive nature of such industries, they were more properly known as industries in which natural monopolies were quickly developing. Natural monopolies—electric power generation and water supplies would also fall into this category in the future—would soon be recognized for their peculiar characteristics and would all even-tually fall under government protection of one sort or other. Antimonop-oly thinking quickly covered the ground from state-granted monopolies to interstate commerce within the short course of fifty years. However, *Munn* is remembered as an example of a commerce case rather than an antitrust case since it sought not to regulate a monopoly or break it up but only to set fair rates. *Antitrust,* the term now used to encompass litigation against violations of monopoly laws, was not yet appropriate in the period before 1890, since trusts had not yet been organized and the Sherman Act had not yet been passed. By necessity, early antimonopoly action had to take place under the guise of commerce. Only after the Sherman Act passed in 1890 did the federal government have the tools to fight antitrust cases. The battleground before that was littered with cases and statutes that fell under several different categories, although their intent was very clear.

Another strong case was made for railroad regulation after the failure of Jay Cooke & Co. and the Northern Pacific Railroad in 1873. Jay Cooke, the Civil War financier who had personally organized the sale of Treasury bonds during the conflict, had taken possession of most of the stock of the Northern Pacific. The railroad was in a severely depleted condition, and Cooke, something of a novice in railroad finance, acquired it. After the market panic of 1869, caused by Gould's gold-cornering operation, investors became increasingly wary of speculative adventures in the long period of depression that followed. Depositors at Cooke's bank eventually learned of his ownership of the Northern Pacific and began to withdraw funds from the bank. As a result, Cooke went into bankruptcy when he could not meet their liquidity demands. His failure caused the panic of

1873, another in the long history of financial downturns precipitated by the robber barons and financiers.

The tug-of-war between the states and the corporations put pressure on the federal government. A federal solution to the problem of interstate commerce was needed because the tide had shifted against the states' attempts to limit businesses within their borders. Adams recognized the problem and the inadequacy of the states' attempts to control the railroads as early as 1871. "It is scarcely an exaggeration to say that our legislatures are now universally becoming a species of irregular boards of railroad direction," he noted in examining the links between government and the railroads.[16] Shortly after the states' temporary victory in the Supreme Court, another famous court case helped to unravel some of the success the states had won in *Munn*. In *Wabash Railway Co. v. Illinois*, 1886, the Court ruled that the states could not regulate railways simply passing through the state. It considered applications of the *Munn* decision to commerce a "deleterious influence upon the freedom of commerce among the states." More important, it also suggested that regulation "should be done by the Congress of the United States under the commerce clause of the Constitution."[17] This was a clear acknowledgment that federal law, not just a patchwork of state laws and court rulings, would be necessary to control the railroads. The message was received loud and clear by Congress, which reacted quickly to create the first federal regulatory agency.

The Interstate Commerce Act was passed in February 1887 after a long, torturous debate. No congressman wanted to be seen impeding progress of the rails, but no one wanted to be seen ignoring the will of the public, either, especially since robber baron cartooning had become something of a national industry. The act created the Interstate Commerce Commission, the first congressionally sanctioned agency designed to oversee interstate commerce. It embodied the Granger principle that railroads were subject to public regulation. Railroad pooling (price fixing) and giving rebates to customers were expressly forbidden. At first it appeared to be a victory for the movement that had built up over the previous twenty years. The railroads appeared to be shackled and the public will acknowledged.

The railroads were sorely lacking capital and unified direction at the time, and not all railroad people opposed the idea of a federal commission.

An executive of the Pennsylvania Railroad stated in 1884 that "a large majority of the railroads in the United States would be delighted if a railroad commission or any other power could make rates upon their traffic which would ensure them six per cent dividends, and I have no doubt, with such a guarantee, they would be very glad to come under the direct supervision and operation of the National Government."[18] Andrew Carnegie, a heavy user of the railroads, concurred: "The Interstate Commerce Commission is to become one of our greatest safeguards." But the hopes soon evaporated. It became apparent within a few short years that the ICC's powers would not be taken seriously. Its significance for the first twenty years of its life lay in the fact that it was even created in the first place. However, in the aftermath of the bill being passed, the barons of finance and of the railroads grouped their considerable talents and assets together at the behest of J. P. Morgan to deal with the new "crisis." He called the railroad barons to his New York residence on January 8, 1889, to discuss the momentous changes that could be wrought by the new ICC.

Railroads presented an opportunity for Morgan. His reputation as one of the country's premier bankers was already well established. An earlier deal in which he helped William Vanderbilt sell a sizeable portion of New York Central stock to foreign investors added to his reputation as a canny financier of American business. The railroads' constant infighting presented a window of opportunity for someone who possessed what they did not: access to large amounts of capital and the diplomatic skills to match, a necessity when dealing with the states and the federal government. Morgan recognized the capital problems surrounding the railroad industry and realized that whoever ultimately controlled the capital flows effectively controlled the railroads.

Answering his call were Jay Gould, representing the Missouri Pacific; George Roberts of the Pennsylvania; Frank Bond of the Chicago, Milwaukee & St. Paul; and A. B. Stickney of the Chicago, St. Paul & Kansas City. Also present was Charles Francis Adams Jr., who for the past five years had been at the head of the Union Pacific. After serving on the Massachusetts sunshine commission until 1879, he then served a five-year stint on the Eastern Trunk Line Association's board of arbitration before taking the top job at the railroad. He characterized the first five years of his stewardship as successful before it began to go badly wrong. At the time of the meeting, he was still riding the relatively high crest of a wave. The ostensible purpose of the meeting was to see that the provisions of the new commerce act were enforced and that stable rates were achieved across the country. But as the antimonopolists feared, a major consolidation phase among the railroads was about to be attempted, with a financier at its helm rather than a railroad man.

OPPORTUNITY KNOCKS

The plight of the railroads immediately after the passing of the Interstate Commerce Act gave J. P. Morgan an opportunity to unite the railroads under his unofficial aegis. The railroad chieftains argued among themselves constantly and would always be opposed to each other's actions unless they were united under one banner. Answering Morgan's call signaled the dawn of a new era in the development of American industry. Previously, private investment bankers had raised capital for growing industries, but now they were inviting themselves into the deals as well. The result was that industrialists now shared corporate boards with their main bankers. The financiers brought some sorely needed financial discipline to the table.

Competition was the topic of the Morgan meeting. If it could be reduced among the railroads, then greater prosperity would be shared by all. A sore point among the railroad barons was the building of parallel rail lines by outside parties. In order to reduce competition, the barons usually bought out the upstart companies, sometimes at exorbitant prices. Opportunists realized that if they built what appeared to be a competing line alongside an established one, the larger railroad would have to acknowledge it and eventually buy it out. A group of entrepreneurs in 1878 built the Nickel Plate Railroad in order to "compete" with William Vanderbilt on the Chicago route. Vanderbilt eventually bought them out at great cost, doing something that he himself had previously forced others to do many times. In 1883, another competing company, called the West Shore Line, was formed on the other side of the Hudson River from his New York Central route. Again he bought out the owners at exorbitant rates, issuing more worthless stock to finance the acquisition. The result was more overcapitalizing of his own companies by stock watering, so the public eventually bore the costs of the "competition" among the rail lines. The fears of

George Stephenson about a natural consolidation in the industry based upon its enormous costs were shared by others and were now being exploited. Between the Nickel Plate and the West Shore, a thousand extra miles of unneeded track were added to the Vanderbilt system.[19]

Andrew Carnegie also engaged in the same practice himself in order to reduce the freight rates charged to his steel company. Discovering that the Pennsylvania Railroad charged different rates to different customers, he purchased several hundred miles of a line so that he could ship his steel products himself to the Great Lakes ports rather than pay the railroad what he considered to be exorbitant costs. Within a short time, his old boss Thomas Scott, now president of the Pennsylvania, called him to his office to press him to abandon his plan. But Carnegie was adamant, resolving to fight the railroad monopoly tooth and nail. As he recalled, Scott put it to him simply: "If you will stop building that line from the lakes to your works, we will do what you ask." To this the steelmaker replied, "That cannot be. I have agreed to build that line . . . it has to be built."[20] He compromised with the railroad by allowing them to continue to do some of his business, and everyone walked away from the table happy. But not all railroad customers had Carnegie's economic clout when dealing with the varied rate structures.

William Vanderbilt and Gould had been at odds for years, and both were also in open conflict with the Pennsylvania Railroad, the force behind many of the machinations and the object of many others in turn. Morgan was a close ally of William Vanderbilt. Both Adams and Gould privately agreed that such an alliance of railroad men was necessary. The internecine competition among the railroads of the past was doing no good for rate structures and the public's opinion of the railroads. He and Gould discussed the possibility of a general organization designed to include all of the railroad presidents. Adams also pushed for including the new ICC commissioners.[21] But nothing came of the idea. Morgan then picked up the gauntlet and called his own meeting shortly thereafter.

The major issue among the railroad barons was the condition of the western rails. Cutthroat competition prevailed, and their business tactics were aggressive, to say the least. While the eastern lines were also in a state of intense competition, they were relatively quiet when compared to the goings-on in the West. Morgan proposed a reinstatement of pooling arrangements, conceived in a way that would not violate the Interstate Commerce Act. When the act made these pools illegal, it had also caused chaos among the railroad companies, since pools, although smacking of cartels, were a relatively efficient way of allocating resources. Morgan proposed a return to pools through a commission drawn from among the assembled. But not all of the railroad heads thought this was a good idea. Roberts, of the Pennsylvania Railroad, complained that bankers could not be trusted because they were making money on both sides of the railroad issue. They made underwriting fees by selling shares in the "competing" lines as well as by serving the larger rail systems. This was a serious complaint raised by the railroad executives against Wall Street. Recognizing the problem, Morgan stated his intention to avoid underwriting competing lines. The bankers were "prepared to say that they will not negotiate and will do everything in their power to prevent the negotiation of any securities for the construction of parallel lines or the extension of lines not approved by the executive Committee," he stated, leaving the impression that his committee actually stood in place of the ICC.[22] This was one of the first clear indications that the railroad presidents and their bankers considered themselves to be working alongside the newly minted federal commission. Ultimately, the Morgan-led commission failed, succumbing to the competitive natures and petty differences among the railroad men. Adams' recollection of railroad people was characteristically condescending: "In the course of my railroad experiences I made no friends . . . nor among those I met was there any man whose acquaintance I valued. They were a coarse, realistic, bargaining crowd."[23]

Whatever fear the railroad barons inspired was compounded by the development of the trust, a new form of industrial organization most often associated with John D. Rockefeller and the Standard Oil Company. Until the 1880s, most concern with monopolies centered around the ability of large companies to fix prices, charging the public what they wished. While the railroads argued that was hardly the case, the hard proof was in the actual prices the railroads charged their customers. The Granger movement constantly argued for lower rates to benefit farmers. The great irony was that it took another monopolist, John D. Rockefeller, to successfully negotiate lower rates for his own industrial organization. The lesson of raw power was about to be taught to the antimonopoly movement: Lower rates would be negotiated by someone whose power even the railroads envied, not by the farmers.

The home of Rockefeller's Standard Oil empire was Ohio. His refining companies operated from Cleveland, the first home of the oil industry. Rockefeller's rise in the oil industry was spectacular. He and his partner Henry Flagler originally entered the refining business in 1863. By 1870 the Standard Oil Company had been formed. Standard Oil quickly became the leviathan of its day, gobbling up smaller oil companies in the process. Rockefeller was the largest refiner in the country, and the railroads conceded the lower rates he demanded, recognizing the importance of this new industry. Within five short years Standard Oil, other oil refiners, and the railroads had helped form the first cartel, the South Improvement Company. One of its main aims was to negotiate lower haulage rates from the railroads that were anxious to carry the oil to market. In 1871 Rockefeller and Flagler met with railroad representatives in a New York hotel and hatched a scheme whereby Standard Oil and a handful of other refiners would receive rebates for shipping on the major railroads, notably the Pennsylvania (under Thomas Scott), the New York Central (under Cornelius Vanderbilt), and the Erie (under Gould and Fisk). If that were not enough of a competitive edge, the refiners were also to receive a rebate for every barrel of oil shipped by their competitors who were not members of the South Improvement Company. The railroads were only too happy to have the business, and the cartel substantially tightened its grasp on the oil market.

In 1882 the Standard Oil trust was officially organized. Unlike a cartel, which was an arrangement between companies not under common ownership, a trust combined all under one shell company that owned the stock of the others. The shares of fourteen oil companies were transferred to the trust and came under the control of nine trustees, including Rockefeller. The actual duties of the trustees were unclear, but the new company wielded an enormous amount of economic power, although the trust document itself remained out of public view, known only to those who were parties to it. The expansion of the new oil industry was greatly aided by the railroad barons. Without them, the oil industry would not have prospered so quickly. The rapid organization of the oil refiners proved to farmers that they too would have to organize if they wished to benefit from lower rates. But their organizational abilities were inferior to those of the new oil magnates. Their respective impacts went in opposite directions. The Granger movement led to state laws and favorable Supreme Court rulings against the railroads. The refiners negotiated the sort of rates the farmers envied and made a fortune in the process. The railroads were suspected of aiding and abetting the great industrial trusts, but the problem was complex and difficult to prove. Nevertheless, the ability of the railroads to lower shipping costs for favored customers only reinforced the argument made against them and resulted in the Interstate Commerce Act.

Using railroads to their advantage also helped the trusts grow at the expense of their competition. Rockefeller and other industrialists were accused of bullying smaller competitors and threatening to ruin them if they did not agree to merge. Strong-arm tactics were sometimes used against these smaller firms, but usually it was the threat of losing their businesses entirely that made many of them accede to the trusts' offers. One small oil distributor from Marietta, Ohio, had a long history of opposing Standard Oil in any manner he could. George Rice tried in vain for years to negotiate rates with the railroads that would enable him to lower his prices, but to no avail. Standard Oil stood in his way every time. Rockefeller did not undercut prices in order to force him out of business. Instead, the larger company used railroad rates to accomplish the same end less visibly. If Rice did not accept the competitive situation as he found it and tried to undercut Standard, he could expect the railroads, under Rockefeller's influence, to increase his freight charges to unreasonable levels. At the same time, the rebate would be activated, and Standard would receive money for every gallon that Rice shipped at the higher price. All of this kept the trust's profits high. During the post–Civil War period, the price of oil at the wholesale level had collapsed from over 40 cents per barrel to under 10 cents, and it remained at that level until the 1920s. But the savings were not being passed along to customers. In one case, Rice offered oil in Tennessee to a customer at 18 cents a gallon when Standard Oil's agents offered it at 21 cents. The buyer was afraid of offending the trust and declined his offer. Rice complained to the ICC, and an executive of the local railroad accused of discriminating against Rice was fired. Rice also made other complaints to the ICC, which found for Rice every time. Still, Rice complained, "The product has become cheaper but the Trust people have done all they could to prevent it."[24] Later, Standard Oil proposed to buy his company, but Rice protested that the offer was just a ploy. "Yes, I know their tactics," he asserted during an interview on a visit to New York. "They will trump up any kind of a charge to accomplish their ends and excite prejudice for their benefit. But I have this to say—I have never gone into any court with reference to the Standard Oil Company and its freight rates except when I found the company or the trust was grossly trespassing upon my rights." Rockefeller's view of Rice, on the other hand, was that he was a blackmailer, trying to sell out to Standard Oil at an exorbitant price. One of Rockefeller's lieutenants reported to his boss after meeting with Rice that he "admitted that it could be better to occupy friendly relations with us and assumed to be willing to make some arrangement, but extortion was written in every lineament of his countenance and burdened every syllable that fell from his lips."[25]

In the late 1880s, after the informal agreements between the oil companies and railroads had been put into place and after the trust was officially formed, the railroads and the oil companies came under investigation in several states. A New York Senate committee had a long laundry list of questions that it wanted answered, and it summoned John D. Rockefeller, among others, to answer them. Attesting to the oil companies' increasing power, William Vanderbilt testified that "if this thing keeps up, the oil people will own the railroads." However, the president of Standard Oil was less than forthcoming in his responses to the committee's questions. When asked if he was a member of the Southern Improvement Company before its demise, he replied simply, "I was not." Technically, he was correct because his interrogator made a mistake, using *Southern* instead of *South*. When he was asked whether some companies in the trust enjoyed favorable freight rates from the railroads, Rockefeller replied, "I do not recall anything of that kind." Finally, when asked if he was familiar with the ICC ruling regarding George Rice, he replied, "I read they made a decision, but I am really unable to say what that decision was."[26] Although Rockefeller provided no real light on the workings of the trust, the committee did ask to see, and was shown, the original document organizing the trust. It then published the document, making it accessible to interested parties. A small ray of sunshine entered previously dark corporate maneuverings, providing the public an opportunity to see for the first time what the Standard Oil trust was, and was not.

The New York investigation did have one positive effect for the opponents of Standard Oil. By making the Standard Oil trust agreement public, it ensured that it would be reprinted. Years later, in 1889, the attorney general of Ohio, David Watson, happened to pick up a copy of a book entitled *Trusts* by William Cook, a New York attorney. In it he found a copy of the Standard Oil trust agreement quietly produced seven years before. After reading it, he realized that it was illegal under Ohio law for a state-chartered company to transfer ownership outside the state. He consequently sued for the breakup of the Standard Oil Trust.[27] Watson reportedly was offered bribes and was subject to heavy outside pressure not to proceed with the case from, among others, Mark Hanna, the industrialist turned politician and deal maker. Hanna was later to back William McKinley for governor of Ohio and, after that, for president; Hanna himself was later elected to fill John Sherman's vacated Senate seat. But Watson remained steadfast. He had close contact with the Rice matter several years before and knew something of the corporate and legal tricks employed by Standard Oil. True to form, Standard Oil denied that it was actually part of the trust. The ploy did not work. The suit was successful, and the trust was ordered to disband by an Ohio court. However, it failed to do so immediately, with the result that the affair provided something of a public relations coup for Ohio but little else.

Standard Oil had other public relations problems as well. The tide of public opinion was building against it, and the executives of the company realized this. One wrote to Rockefeller in 1887, "We have met with a success unparalleled in commercial history, our name is known all over the world, and our public character is not one to be envied. . . . We are quoted as the representative of all that is evil, hard hearted, oppressive, cruel (we think unjustly) but men look askance at us, we are pointed at with contempt."[28] One of the sources referred to was a young journalist who had made the trusts a personal mission, Standard Oil's version of Charles Francis Adams Jr.: Henry Demarest Lloyd. In 1881 the *Atlantic Monthly* ran an article entitled "The Story of a Great Monopoly," written by the young financial editor of the *Chicago Tribune*. The criticism of the oil trust made Lloyd instantly famous and paved the way several years later for his best-known book, *Wealth Against Commonwealth*. In another article, in the *North American Review* in 1884, he continued his attack, displaying a solid knowledge of the history of monopoly concentrations. He wrote that "when Stephenson said of railroads that where combination was possible competition was impossible, he was unconsciously declaring the law of all industry." His work was roundly attacked from conservative quarters, but its influence was widespread in the English-speaking world; the father of English social Darwinism, Herbert Spencer, remarked during a visit to New York in 1882 that "I hear that a trader among you [Rockefeller] deliberately endeavored to crush out every one whose business competed with his own."[29] Thanks to Lloyd, the leviathan was now on public view.

Lloyd was born in 1847 and raised in New York City. He graduated from Columbia University and its law school and became active in the political movement to ferret out Boss Tweed and the corrupt Tammany Hall crowd after graduation. But he favored writing over an active political career and took a job at the *Tribune*, where he quickly became an editor. Within a short time he married the daughter of one of the paper's owners. Some years later he left the paper and took up freelance writing full-time, living off his own earnings plus his wife's substantial endowment. Not wanting for physical comforts or money, he devoted himself to attacks on big business and the trusts. His personal style and political views, which were far to the left of Adams and reminiscent of European socialism, so antagonized his father-in-law that Lloyd was purposely not made trustee of his children's bequest from their grandfather. Nevertheless, he continued to attack the evils of big business until his death in 1903. However, his writings were highly effective and paved the way for Ida Tarbell's even more influential book, *The History of the Standard Oil Company*, published twenty years later.

The antitrust contingent was not the only faction using magazines and books to press its case. In a well-known 1889 essay in the *North American Review*, Andrew Carnegie expressed his belief that the period of trust formation was ephemeral and soon due to dissipate. He stated unequivocally in "The Bugaboo of Trusts," "To those who quote the Standard Oil Company as an evidence that Trusts or combinations can be permanently successful, I say, wait and see. . . . As a student of political economy [I] apply to it the principles which I know *will* have their way, no matter how formidable the attempt to defeat their operations." Carnegie believed that the trust would disappear after Rockefeller and his closest associates died or retired from the company. That was part and parcel of his general ideas concerning competition and freedom in society. However, it appeared that society was less patient with the trust problem. The age of managerial capitalism had arrived; companies increasingly were being run by professional managers, not only by the founders or their heirs, and there was no reason to believe that the giant trusts would disappear with their founders.

SUNSET?

Standard Oil was not the only trust operating at the time the antitrust legislation was passed. The period prior to 1890 was indeed the age of big business. The tobacco trust known as the American Tobacco Company was formed early in the same year the Sherman Act was passed, the industry having undergone a consolidation several years before. In 1884 the sugar-producing industry underwent a consolidation when seventeen companies united to form the Sugar Refineries Company; in the previous years margins in the sugar business had fallen, but after the trust was formed they began to rise again. When New York took the company to court in 1890, the trust shifted its operation to New Jersey, a friendlier home to big business. The move was necessary from a corporate point of view in order to preserve the new American Sugar Refining Company's share—about 75 percent—of the refining capacity in the country.

A change was becoming noticeable in attitudes toward monopolies. The power of the state was no longer equated with monopolistic power, as it had been a hundred years before. Modern industrialization had proven that monopolies were not intrinsically bad and that society would tolerate them as long as they produced fair prices and an increasing standard of living. When they failed to do so, or were alleged to fail, the public turned quickly against them. Antitrust laws were passed in a handful of midwestern states, notably Kansas, Nebraska, and Michigan as well as Texas.[30] Most were prompted by the activities of the railroads. However, the patchwork of state legislation made it necessary for the federal government to act. Sentiment was building in Washington to curb the trusts, admittedly a difficult job. Newly elected president Benjamin Harrison made the trusts the subject of his first congressional address. Senator John Sherman of Ohio sponsored the legislation that bore his name, the Sherman Antitrust Act, sometimes referred to as the Magna Carta of the antitrust movement. In the debate preceding its passage, he declared that "the purpose of this bill is to enable the courts of the United States to apply the same remedies against combinations which injuriously affect the interests of the United States, that have been applied in the several states to protect local interests."[1] Cartoonists had a least depicting bloated senators on the payroll of the trusts. Others portrayed trusts as a problem to be rooted out along with anarchy, a problem that was assumed to be at the root of contemporary labor troubles.

Many in Congress believed that the Sherman bill was unconstitutional and would be struck down by the Supreme Court. Senator Vest argued that trusts were directly protected by high American tariff barriers, a commonly held belief at the time. Many motions were also made to send the bill to the Judiciary Committee, but Sherman prevailed and the bill was passed. In its brief eight sections, totaling only two pages, the bill outlawed combinations that restrained trade. It stated that "Every contract, combination in the form of trust or otherwise, or conspiracy, in restraint of trade or commerce among the several States, or with foreign nations, is hereby declared to be illegal." But the crime was only a misdemeanor, punishable by a maximum fine of $5,000. Much like the Interstate Commerce Act before it, the Sherman Act was more symbolic than effective, and not many businessmen took it seriously.

The vague language and the small fines appeared to make the Sherman Act impotent in the face of the modern corporation. But if it had been too specific, its intent would have been lost. The language was general enough to be used in the future without being subject to claims that the law was out of date. Sherman's biographer claimed another reason for the general language, one that goes to the heart of the American attitude toward monopolies: "It is to be noted that up to this time neither in the Congress nor in the country at large had the opinion gained any appreciable support that these aggregations of capital, familiarly known as trusts, were the result of a process of evolution. They were universally condemned as grasping monopolies, formed for the sole purpose of benefiting their projectors at the expense of the general public."[32] The framers of the law did not appreciate the longer tradition behind the trusts that had developed since independence. They felt a general law would solve the problem of trusts by protecting against their reach. The generally worded law would meet several important tests in the following decade and would become the cornerstone of the antitrust tradition. Unlike the Interstate Commerce Act, the Sherman Act did not create a commission, and so detractors could not claim that it left its execution to a small staff with little true experience in regulation, like the ICC. Clearly, the language and brevity of the Sherman Act made it clear that the Supreme Court or a lower court would have to deal with alleged constraints of trade. The long arm of the law would be the U.S. Department of Justice.

The long saga of Charles Francis Adams Jr. and Jay Gould came to an abrupt end about the same time the Sherman Act was passed. Since taking over the presidency of the Union Pacific, Adams had been in a constant state of turmoil with its creditors, bankers, and shareholders. The railroad's old problems had never been completely sorted out. It was saddled with a mountain of floating-rate debt that made it impossible to obtain new financing easily. Adams had been in discussion with Barings about arranging new financing when the venerable British bank collapsed under the weight of some ill-advised investments in South America. As a result, Adams was left with no recourse when Jay Gould quickly reappeared on the scene.

Gould became involved with the Union Pacific shortly after its founding during the Civil War. The construction company that built it, the Crédit Mobilier company, became involved in one of the nastiest scandals of the postwar era over charges of padded costs and bribing of congressmen. Much of its problem stemmed from its dual nature as a government-created company with private investors. Gould ran the company until the 1880s, when he divested himself of his interests and pursued other railroad opportunities in the Southwest. In 1890 the Union Pacific was in much the same position it had been when Gould previously ran it. Costs had soared and profits were falling. Adams had taken to publicly berating employees for the company's failures. About the same time, rumors began in the marketplace that were vintage Gould. Newspapers began to report less-than-favorable stories about the Union Pacific and its management. One particular paper, thought to be aiding Gould, reported that "a general feeling prevails in railroad circles that Union Pacific is managed by Harvard graduates who have big heads and small experience."[33] Remarks made by the Adams brothers about Gould twenty years before were about to come home to roost.

Gould assumed the finances of the company in order to put it back on its feet. The trade-off was Adams' resignation. In retrospect, Adams shrugged off the entire affair as the natural end of an unhappy experience. "In 1890, I was at last thrown forcibly out of the utterly false position from which, I am obliged to confess, I did not have the will power to extricate myself. Ejected by Jay Gould from the presidency of the Union Pacific, I at last, and instantly, fell back on my proper vocation."[34] True to form, Adams was more concerned with his latest project, a biography of fellow lawyer-turned-writer Richard Henry Dana *(Two Years Before the Mast)*, who died in 1880, than he was with the railroad. His removal signaled a brief victory for the monopolists over their critics. It also demonstrated that education and culture were not necessarily essential ingredients for running a large commercial enterprise. As one senator of the period characterized the likes of Dana and Adams, "those damned literary fellers" did not necessarily make good businessmen.

Social philosophy was more to their liking. When Gould sacked Adams, it was symbolic of the victory of the new order over the old guard in American politics. Within fifty years, the name Adams would be relegated to second place when discussing the country's oldest families. Certainly no one would remember them as pillars of industry. But the theoretical underpinnings of their attitude toward the new order lived on. Brooks Adams wrote the introduction for his brother Henry's *The Degradation of the Democratic Dogma*, published in 1919. In it, they pulled no punches discussing those who appeared on the other side of the aristocratic view of progress in a democracy. Henry had already compared Alexander the Great to Ulysses Grant, and concluded that "the progress of evolution from President Washington to President Grant, was alone evidence enough to upset Darwin."[35] Society's essential forces were dissipating in a barrage of self-indulgence; the aristocratic preference for ideals and rational discourse was being eroded and degraded by forces beyond man's control. While it all sounded very pessimistic and presaged similar thoughts by Oswald Spengler, it was an open admission that the likes of

Gould and Rockefeller had succeeded in forging a new society not thought of before the Civil War. Not mentioned but certainly understood was the fact that monopoly, that sinister force so disliked by the British and the colonial Americans, was responsible for this revolutionary trend in the quality of life. Yet the Adamses' criticisms were more than just aristocratic rhetoric. They provided the basis for what would become known as the Harvard school of antitrust economics. But first, antitrust thought itself had to be developed. The combination of economics and social criticism would become central to the ideas of the Progressives and New Dealers of the future.

The first hundred years of monopolies in the United States were characterized by a trend toward regulation at both the state and federal levels. However, the larger problem in the nineteenth century remained the definitions of *monopoly* and *trust*. As the economy and society expanded, trusts would appear across a wide spectrum of industries, spawning an all-out attack by the federal government. The attack was as ferocious as the growth of big business itself but lacked the consistency to be considered a serious threat to the designs of business expansion. The saga of monopolies had just begun. Both sides would be claiming victory in the years ahead.

2

"GOOD"
AND "BAD"
TRUSTS
(1890–1920)

*A holding company is a thing where you hand an accomplice
the goods while the policeman searches you.*

—WILL ROGERS

IN THE 1890S MONOPOLIES AND TRUSTS were popular topics of
conversation. Caricatures of monopolists and trust busters were often
found in the popular magazines and journals. John D. Rockefeller,
Andrew Carnegie, J. P. Morgan, and Jay Gould achieved the status of
household names. Unflattering caricatures of them by Thomas Nast, W.
A. Rogers, and Louis Dalrymple in the newspapers and magazines kept
them in the public spotlight. And their reputations extended far beyond
the shores of the United States. Europeans, and especially the British,
appeared fascinated by their nouveau riche cousins who had risen from
humble beginnings to lofty positions in society. These industrialists were
the very embodiment of what the United States symbolized—hard work,
opportunity, and, most important, a laissez-faire economy. But it would
not be long before the tide quickly started to change. By the last decade of
the nineteenth century even some of the hardened industrialists were
sounding the death knell of trusts. "To leave monopolists in control would
not be tolerated by the people, therefore there must be control and that

control, as far as one sees, must be in the hands of the general government," wrote Andrew Carnegie.

The years of reformist pressures placed upon Congress finally led to the breakthrough that opponents of big business hoped for. Populism was the first great grassroots political movement in the country, and it owed much to big business for its very existence. Without the railroads, the Granger movement would probably never have been formed. Even after the ICC was formed, the movement did not wither but picked up additional strength. Big business and agrarian interests constantly came into conflict after the turn of the century. Much of the tension would be seized upon by the Progressive movement, which formalized many of the Populists' early complaints about bigness. Lumping business into one category and blankly stating that it was inimical to American values vastly overstated the case. It did, however, make for good press, and Wall Street and business generally found themselves on the opposite side of the fence from the reformers. And the reformers themselves formed a wide spectrum. Fiery Populists such as William Jennings Bryan traced their intellectual origins back to Thomas Jefferson, whose vision of a relatively weak central government dovetailed nicely with Tocqueville's observations about an America where local democracy prevailed. Strong federalism was inimical to the interests of the rural farmer, who was out of touch with, and underrepresented in, the new industrialized era. More important for the development of monopolies and antitrust legislation was the folklore of the Populist movement. As Richard Hofstadter, a historian of the reform movement in the United States, noted, in the Populist mind history was a series of conspiracies by the Jews and Wall Street financiers against true American values. The battle against monopolies was a battle of the good (but simple) folk against the evil cabal of financiers and industrialists.

Industrialists and their bankers were driven by profit, while the Populists were driven by fear of industrialization and the unknown. While it was difficult to specifically define a Populist, the general aura of conspiracy led to some strange intellectual alliances. The anti-industrialist alliance included agrarian firebrands such as Bryan as well as disaffected aristocrats such as the Adamses. The Adamses were hardly Populists but their early writings about Jay Gould only proved what the Populists already knew: A strange man with a Jewish-sounding name had conspired to corner the gold supply of the country. The Populists saw Morgan's resolution of the 1894 financial crisis by selling bonds to British investors to shore up the gold reserve as nothing more than a blatant attempt to sell the country out to foreign interests; Henry Adams sounded the same sour note when he attributed the crisis in the markets to the "Jews of Lombard Street." Joseph Pulitzer, owner of the *New York World* (which he had purchased from Jay Gould), was even more hostile, calling the Morgan rescue group a group of "bloodsucking Jews and aliens."

The sentiments expressed on the East Coast paled in comparison with conspiracy theories that came from the heartland. A book entitled *Seven Financial Conspiracies Which Have Enslaved the American People*, by S. E. V. Emery, published in 1887, gained a wide audience in the Midwest and gave an account of how the country had become enslaved by the bankers' cabal. After the Civil War, Wall Street financiers conspired to manipulate the currency by developing an appetite for gold that silver or greenbacks could not satisfy. Theories like this produced some strange bedfellows. As Richard Hofstadter noted, the greenbackers and the silver advocates held a common notion that produced many further conspiracy theories, like Emery's. They maintained that the gold backers were trying to create a currency contraction by refusing to recognize silver. The resulting squeeze would make their assets more valuable, leaving the common man out in the cold. This was allegedly the long-range plan of what was dubbed the Anglo-American Gold Trust. The notion became one of the better-known conspiracy theories among Populists.

The years of muckraking journalism were beginning to take their toll on large industrial organizations, and the public was incensed by the revelations of novels such as *The Jungle*, by Upton Sinclair. Even more ammunition was provided by nonfiction exposés such as Ida Tarbell's *The History of the Standard Oil Company*, which provided a well-researched, revealing corporate history of the giant company. Not all muckraking was in the same genre. Frank Norris' book *The Octopus* appeared in 1901. It told a disheartening story of the clash between wheat farmers and the railroads in California. He concluded the novel with the sort of prose that left little doubt as to his message: "Men—motes in the sunshine—perished, were shot down in the very noon of life, hearts were broken, little children started in life lamentably handicapped; young girls were brought to a life of shame." Jack London commented that Upton Sinclair's *The Jungle* "depicts what our country really is, the home of oppression and injustice. . . . What *Uncle Tom's Cabin* did for the black slaves *The Jungle* has a large chance to do for the white slaves of today." Some of it bordered on extremism—at times, the extremism was as intense as the offenses themselves—but the reading public clamored for it. "The men with the muck-rake are often indispensable to the well-being of society," said Theodore Roosevelt in 1906, borrowing a phrase from English poet John Bunyan, "but only if they know when to stop raking the muck." The efforts put pressure upon the federal government to investigate the trusts and utilize the Sherman Act by filing suit against what it considered egregious violators.

The muckrakers themselves came from a variety of backgrounds. Some were socialists, while others were just journalists looking for a good scandal. Their efforts pushed big business into the limelight and kept it there for decades. Their impact upon public opinion was incalculable. The period between the passing of the Sherman Act and the beginning of World War I became a frenzied hunt for monopolists, real and imagined. The financial panics of 1893–94 and 1907 and the Spanish-American War provided diversions from what could have otherwise been called the age of pursuit. Suits were filed against a broad array of industries, so broad that it was suspected that trustbusters saw a problem everywhere they looked. Suits were brought against the oil, tobacco, telephone, cotton oil, sugar, shoemaking machinery, steel, heavy industrial equipment, whiskey, and railroad industries, to name but a few. As Theodore Roosevelt noted, the Puritan ethic still held sway when Americans thought of business. They appreciated hard work but disliked stifling the competition.

Both Roosevelt and William Howard Taft adeptly used trust-busting to their own political advantage. In the years immediately following the Sherman Act, lawsuits began slowly. Only eighteen cases were filed in federal courts prior to Theodore Roosevelt's first administration. But during the Roosevelt, Taft, and Wilson administrations, over 230 cases were brought before the courts, involving most of the major industries at the time. Not all were successful, but those that were set the tone for the decades to follow.

Not everyone was convinced that the Sherman Act was successful. The number of mergers occurring in 1899, over 1,200, suggested that business was consolidating at an a more rapid rate than ever before. Experiences with different types of business organization were mixed. The cartels, such as the South Improvement Company, were short-lived because it was very easy to show how they tried to restrain trade. Was it possible that the Sherman Act made loose combinations such as cartels easy targets while allowing trusts to slip through because of its general language? Trusts were certainly more formidable. Equally, did the act force companies to merge in order to remain competitive and avoid prosecution? The Supreme Court certainly did not help. The combination of the loose language of the act and the Supreme Court's interpretation of it probably did more to aid in the consolidation of industry than any other single factor in the late 1890s.

Two forces were compelling industry to consolidate during the latter quarter of the nineteenth century. One was the general price deflation of the period, pushing profit margins down along with prices. The other was the severe economic slowdown experienced after 1893. When these two were considered along with the protective tariffs passed by Congress to protect American trade, it was easy to see why businesses were combining. It was in their best interests to do so. In a sense, the federal government created an environment that was conducive to big business, and then tried to prosecute those that took full advantage of it. Precedents had already been established, leading some industries to believe that they were immune from the language of the Sherman Act. Rockefeller's successful avoidance of Ohio laws by forming the Standard Oil trust, the ability of agricultural industries to hide behind selective tariffs, and the railroads' pooling arrangements all suggested that perhaps the new law would not be effective.

Tariffs also helped the growth of trusts immeasurably. By taxing foreign imports, they helped the trusts reduce competition and avoid outside pricing influences. The chairman of the American Sugar Refining Company, Charles Havemeyer, testified that the "mother of all Trusts is the customs tariff law." Many shared his view. In 1890 Congress passed what was known as the McKinley tariff, named after William McKinley, a Republican congressman from Ohio and chairman of the House Ways and Means Committee. But protective tariffs proved politically dangerous. Associated with the trusts, they were considered protection for the likes of Rocke-

THE FAVORED GUEST.

Serving Up Favors for Monopolists, artist unknown. *Puck*, 1889.

feller, Carnegie, and the scores of agricultural trusts around the country. Popular reaction caused McKinley to lose his seat in 1890, and he returned to Ohio, where he successfully ran for governor. In 1896 he ran for president against William Jennings Bryan in a race dominated by the silver question. He was supported in both races by Mark Hanna, the political kingmaker from Ohio. Bryan was so strongly in favor of silver that at his nomination in 1896 he thundered to his opponents, "You shall not crucify mankind upon a cross of gold." Vested interests lined up on either side of the question. A newspaper war broke out between gold advocates on the East Coast and the silver faction on the West Coast. Joseph Pulitzer's *New York World* charged a conspiracy among the silver advocates that was nothing less than a silver trust. Among them was Pulitzer's publishing rival

Uncle Sam Fending Off the Trusts, by Rogers. *Puck*, 1893.

William Hearst, whose mining interests made him one of the West Coast's richest men. Hearst's own newspapers fired back retorts, but it was clear that the very word *trust* was enough to raise ire on both sides of the issue.[1]

McKinley prevailed in the election, although he still had his detractors. He was a frequent butt of Mark Twain's humor, as the essayist linked him and Hanna to the larger American imperialist movement of the late nineteenth century. Twain's fondness for Republicans was well documented. "No one has ever seen a Republican mass meeting that was devoid of the perception of the ludicrous," he once remarked. The political cartoonists of the day gleefully used McKinley's countenance at every opportunity to illustrate the evils of the relationship between the Republicans and big business. *The Economist* later noted that "Mr. McKinley, as everyone knows, was mainly elected by the Trusts. . . . During [his] Presidency the power and wealth of the Trusts have grown to such gigantic proportions that it is now said that they control about 90 percent of the industrial capital of the United States."[2] The assessment was not far from the mark. During McKinley's presidency, only three antitrust cases were filed, while the number of mergers between companies increased dramatically. One

Western Populists Pushing Their Favorite Trojan Horse,
by Rogers. *Harper's Weekly*, 1895.

year in particular, 1899, set a record for mergers that was not equaled again until the banner stock market year of 1929.

The growth of trusts in the 1890s was indirectly influenced by the Sherman Silver Purchase Act of 1890. This other Sherman bill effectively created a dual metal standard for the dollar, creating severe problems on Wall Street and in the banking community. In theory, the dollar was backed by both silver and gold, although no one actually took the silver backing seriously. The bill was passed mostly to placate the western states, which saw an opportunity to raise themselves to a new level of financial importance.

But questions began to arise about the dollar's value, and the prospects of inflation frightened investors. The stock market experienced a severe sell-off. Foreign investors were frightened by the prospect of the dollar's losing its traditional gold backing. When combined with the tariff issue, the whole matter became highly combustible. The economic uncertainty became a strong motivating force behind further industrial combinations. The issue was further clouded when apologists for the tariff argued that the increased revenues gained from it would help the government in its effort to replace the gold reserves, which were rapidly dwindling. The real issue remained, however, the gold controversy. Even though the silver legislation was repealed in 1893 after a short but disastrous performance, the trusts could still hide behind the tariffs, and their protection from foreign competition was ensured.

Labor problems also created difficulties for the image of big business. The steel industry in particular witnessed an especially ugly incident that cast a long shadow over one of the more enlightened industrialists, Andrew Carnegie. Falling steel prices caused Henry Clay Frick, the manager of Carnegie Steel, to offer the workers at the Homestead plant, near Pittsburgh, a pay package that was substantially lower than the one that had just expired. When workers rejected the contract and became rancorous, Frick closed the Homestead plant and called in armed Pinkerton detectives to guard it. After several pitched battles in which numerous shots were fired, seven detectives and eleven workers lay dead in one of the bloodiest confrontations in American labor history. Frick himself was shot by an immigrant anarchist but survived. The matter finally went to the courts, and the plant opened a year later, in 1893, and resumed normal operations, but not without leaving an indelible mark upon American industry. Subsequent magazine articles described the conditions at the plant and the surrounding area in graphic terms. The general public became aware that the coal mining areas of Pennsylvania were bleak, desolate places to begin with, and began to understand the plight of the workers who fought so hard to maintain a meager standard of living in the face of Frick's cost-cutting measures. Carnegie was criticized as an absentee landlord with a plantation mentality, since he had been not in Pennsylvania at the time of the strike but at his baronial home in Scotland. He

The Public as Castaways Among the Sharks, artist unknown.

apparently regretted the entire incident, confessing that "the works are not worth one drop of human blood," but he had known of the contract negotiations that led to the strike in the first place.

The troubles of 1893 led to a severe depression, the worst in twenty years. Over five hundred banks failed, 30 percent of the railroads were in bankruptcy, and over fifteen thousand businesses failed. Social discontent began to emerge in the West, and there was even talk of some states seceding from the Union. The finances of the United States were in jeopardy when the gold reserves fell to unacceptable levels. Treasury finances finally were stabilized when a group of banks led by J. P. Morgan and August

Belmont & Co. helped the Cleveland administration sell bonds to foreign investors, restoring gold to the Treasury's reserves. Despite the operation, bankers still were severely criticized for profiting on the transaction at the expense of the Treasury. And the mood of the country was turning distinctly ugly. Tensions between the industrial East and the agrarian West were exacerbated by the depression, prompting the talk about secession. The silver controversy provided a genuine source of regional tension that was to linger for some time and provided the conspiracy theorists with ammunition for years. By the time McKinley ran against Bryan in the 1896 election, prosperity was again emerging, and his administration was characterized by a general improvement in the standard of living. A precedent was also established. His administrations would be the first, but certainly not the last, Republican presidencies to suffer charges of favoring monopoly consolidations; similar charges of being soft on monopolies would be leveled at Republicans for the rest of the twentieth century.

ROUGH RIDING

Bringing the trusts to court began in the 1890s almost immediately after the ink on the Sherman Act dried. The financial crisis began about the same time. First in its sights as government attempted to prove that the economy was coming under the stranglehold of large corporations was the sugar trust. The American Sugar Refining Company already controlled a sizeable proportion of the country's sugar refining capacity. It was the successor to the older group of refiners organized by Charles Havemeyer. V. I. Lenin claimed that "Havemeyer founded the Sugar Trust by amalgamating fifteen small firms whose total capital amounted to $6.5 million. Suitably watered, as the Americans say, the capital of the trust was declared to be $50 million."[3] One of the lawyers who worked on its formation was John Dos Passos, whose son would make his mark on American literature in the next century. The new company acquired even more capacity when it bought several Philadelphia refineries, extending its control to almost 98 percent of total U.S. production. One of them was the E. C. Knight Company, which lent its name to the suit, *United States v. E. C. Knight Co.* The government sued in federal court in Pennsylvania, alleging that the buyouts were unlawful combinations designed to restrain trade and create a monopoly in the sale and manufacture of sugar. The lower court did not agree, however, and the United States appealed to the Supreme Court. In 1895 the Supreme Court upheld the lower court's decision, deciding that the Sherman Act was not applicable in this case. Chief Justice Fuller, writing for the majority, stated that the Sherman Act "struck at combinations, contracts, and conspiracies to monopolize trade and commerce among the several states or with foreign nations; but the contracts and acts of the defendants related exclusively to the acquisition of the Philadelphia refineries and the business of sugar refining in Pennsylvania. . . . There was nothing in the proofs to indicate any intention to put a restraint on trade or commerce."[4]

Fourteen years later, revelations came to light that would have changed the Court's mind. Much of the sugar trust's business came from imported sugar; tariffs protected the American industry, but the company found a simple way around the duties, bribing New York customs officials to look the other way concerning the quantities imported. In 1909 the *New York Sun* ran an exposé of the company's methods on its front page, claiming that this method saved the company at least $30 million in tariffs over the years. It went on to say that the company bribed officials and anyone who discovered its methods. The whole fraud had been accomplished "with the assistance and connivance of powerful and petty politicians all of whom shared in the plunder."[5] But before all this came out, the Court's decision was nevertheless a shock to all of those who believed that the Sherman Act would be effective in dealing with the growth of the trusts. It seemed to hark back to the Granger cases of the 1870s, when the interstate commerce clause was rendered almost ineffective by the rapid growth of the railroads and the courts' literal interpretation of the existing law in *Wabash Railway Co. v. Illinois*. William Howard Taft remarked that "the effect of the decision in the Knight case upon the popular mind . . . was to discourage hope that the statute could be used to accomplish its manifest purpose and curb the great industrial trusts which . . . were making every effort to restrict production, control prices, and monopolize the business."[6] But as Taft also noted, the government's case was not well prepared, and much evidence that might have proven its case was not included in its argument. The attack upon monopolies would have to wait for another day.

VOL. 5.

No. 118.

THE JUDGE.

ENTERED AT THE POST OFFICE AT NEW YORK AS SECOND CLASS MATTER. COPYRIGHT 1861 BY THE JUDGE PUBLISHING CO.

Price

NEW YORK, JANUARY 23, 1884.

10 Cents.

THE MONEY-BAG SENATE.
Mr. Payne has all the requisites for a good Senator.

Money Influences Elections, by Hamilton. *The Judge*, 1894.

Balancing Capitalist and Socialist Interests, by Wales. *Puck*, n.d.

McKinley Gorging Himself on the Spoils of Office, artist unknown.

Another major case soon came to the Court. The United States filed suit against eighteen railroads for fixing rates west of the Missouri River in *United States v. Trans-Missouri Freight Association* in 1892. The railroads responded by claiming that the Interstate Commerce Act implicitly gave them the right to establish common rates, but the Court did not accept the argument. In a somewhat controversial majority opinion, Justice Peckham wrote, "We think, after careful examination, that the Statute [Sherman Act] covers, and intended to cover, common carriers by railroad."[7] After years of wrangling with the railroads at both the state and federal levels, the Court finally decided that that they were subject to the same law as other industrial companies.

Several other noteworthy cases followed the *Trans-Missouri* decision. In *Addyston Pipe and Steel Company v. United States* (1899), six companies had conspired to fix the price of cast-iron pipe that they manufactured and

King Monopoly's Insatiable Appetite, by Dalrymple. *Puck*, 1890.

sold interstate. Effectively, a cartel was created in which the companies
involved pooled their interests in the name of greater economies. They
claimed in their defense that Congress did not have the authority to interfere with private contracts between companies that were involved in interstate commerce. But the Court found that Congress indeed had the
authority to do so and ruled against the company. Nevertheless, the ambi-
guities in the justices' opinions and the Republican administration gave
many corporations the heart to continue the fight against the government.
Pooling arrangements like the one in the *Addyston* case were becoming
fairly common, with the companies involved taking advantage of them
until they were struck down. The *Knight* decision showed that the government's case would not always prevail. Between 1896 and 1901 the number
of mergers negotiated rose exponentially, showing that the battle was
hardly won from the government's position.

The popular cause against monopolies was embraced in the later 1890s
by none other than Andrew Carnegie, the steel baron from Pittsburgh. In
1902 Carnegie began to renounce the consolidation trend in big business
as antithetical to American ideals. Throughout Theodore Roosevelt's
administrations, the industrialist continually sided with the president on
progressive reforms, jettisoning his earlier conservative views on social
Darwinism and free competition. Previously he had discussed competition

in terms that left little doubt that industrialists were in charge of the economy: "The price which society pays for the law of competition . . . is also great but the advantages of this law are also greater still than its cost," he wrote in *The Gospel of Wealth* in 1889. Twenty years later the expatriate Scot remarked that "to leave monopolists in control would not be tolerated by the people, therefore there must be control and that control . . . must be in the hands of the general government." Critics who witnessed this metamorphosis charged that Carnegie could well afford to change his views. He had sold his interest in his steel company to J. P. Morgan in 1901 for slightly less than $500 million, making him the richest man in the world. Perhaps he remembered the flap created twenty years earlier when William Vanderbilt assumed the same title with a fortune estimated at about $100 million; at the time, the British prime minister remarked that no one should be allowed to keep that much money because he posed a threat to the financial system. Keenly aware of the change in public sentiment, Carnegie entered the debate over the trusts squarely on the side of the emerging Progressive movement.

The clash between big business and the federal government entered a distinctly harsher phase when Theodore Roosevelt became president. After McKinley's assassination, the new president began an active policy of trust-busting. Assuming that big business was essentially rotten to the core, his first administration sought to dissolve the trusts. Popular opinion was certainly on his side. The disparities between the wealthy and the poor had grown wider and wider since the 1880s, and public sentiment was against the industrialists, especially those whose fortunes were the subject of widespread discussion. Andrew Carnegie became a benefactor of public causes, especially libraries, in response to the tenor of the times. Many others followed suit, hoping to be seen as sharing part of their fortunes with those who had helped them earn them in the first place. One who appeared to champion the consumer did not share in the same display of public generosity. William Woolworth, founder of the chain of retail stores that bore his name, was one of the few business magnates who left his entire fortune to his family rather than share it with public causes. Yet Woolworth made his fortune by selling goods at low prices, and he was seen as someone who served the public rather than exploited it.

Roosevelt's attitude toward business recognized the pitfalls that critics of the trusts could fall into. "The greatest harm done by vast wealth is the harm that we of moderate means do ourselves when we let the vices of envy and hatred enter deep into our own natures," he stated emphatically. Critics countered by openly wondering how he could included himself in the class of those of "moderate means" since his family was one of the oldest and most established in New York. His ideas were not warmly received by the business community. He favored a "square deal" for the workingman and opposed the long reach of the modern corporation and holding company. He made this clear in his first annual message to Congress, stating that "in the interest of the whole people, the nation should, without interfering in the power of the States in the matter itself, also assume power of supervision and regulation over all corporations doing an interstate business. This is especially true where the corporation derives a portion of its wealth from the existence of some monopolistic element or tendency in its business."[8] This was part of his "big stick" policy, which he promised to use against large corporations that did interstate business.

Roosevelt won the first round of his battle against the monopolists. Of *United States v. Northern Securities Company*, Roosevelt recalled that "just before my accession [to the presidency] a small group of financiers desiring to profit by the governmental impotence to which we had been reduced by the Knight decision, had arranged to take control of practically the entire railway system of the country. . . . Not long after I became President, on the advice of the Attorney General, Mr. Knox, . . . I ordered proceedings to be instituted for the dissolution of the company."[9] The Supreme Court obliged by handing down a decision in 1904 that upheld the Sherman Act and helped to dismember a holding company that had extensive railroad interests. The Northern Securities holding company was charged with monopolizing railroad lines in the Pacific Northwest. It was an amalgam of Morgan, Harriman, and Hill interests that controlled the bulk of the rails west of the Mississippi River. Justice John Harlan, writing for the majority, said, "If such combination be not destroyed all the advantages which would naturally come to the public, under the operation of the general laws of competition . . . will be lost and the entire commerce of the immense territory in the northern part of the United States . . . will be at the mercy of a single holding corporation."[10] Roosevelt remarked that the case's success "definitely established the power of the Government to deal with all great corporations. Without this success the National Government must have remained in the impotence to which it had been reduced in the Knight decision."

The power of the pen continued to put pressure on Standard Oil. In 1902 Ida Tarbell's *The History of the Standard Oil Company* was published. Unlike Lloyd's more polemical *Wealth Against Commonwealth*, little criticism was leveled against the book, which proved to be one of the more enduring corporate histories ever written. Tarbell was one of the first woman muckraking journalists. She graduated from Allegheny College and studied at the Sorbonne before becoming editor of *McClure's Magazine*. She was raised in the heart of Pennsylvania oil country, where her family was in the oil production business before being forced out by Standard Oil. As a result, she had firsthand knowledge of the tactics used by the giant company in its quest for dominant market share. This was a trait she shared with other muckrakers and reformers, notably Louis Brandeis. She was already well known for her articles on Lincoln and Napoleon and was one of the highest-paid journalists of the day. Articles written for the magazine on Standard Oil eventually led her to the book-length study, in which she systematically documented the growth of Standard Oil and the tactics used by Rockefeller to build his empire. In her conclusion she put the case emphatically: "So long as railroads can be persuaded to interfere with independent pipe lines, to refuse oil freight, to refuse loading facilities, lest they disturb their relations with the Standard Oil Company, it is idle to talk about investigations, or antitrust legislation or application of the Sherman law. So long as the Standard Oil Company can control transportation as it does today, it will remain master of the oil industry and the people of the United States will pay for their indifference and folly."[11]

Tarbell's remarks served to remind the public that the country was indeed at the mercy of one corporation. Executives of the company had different views, however. In what financial analyst John Moody described as the Standard Oil view of the universe, S. C. T. Dood, counsel to the company, enunciated the benign view of social Darwinism when he said, "But men whose integrity is such as to permit them to be entrusted with the management of large capital, whose intellectual grasp of principles and details is such as to command with their products the markets of the world are those who will soonest realize that the policy which succeeds is that which accords fair treatment to all." Nevertheless, the company most prominent in the minds of congressmen when the Sherman Act was passed was enjoying record profits almost every year. After Watson's suit in Ohio had ordered the company dissolved, with much foot-dragging the stock was transferred to other Rockefeller-controlled companies. Ohio filed contempt charges against Standard Oil for not heeding its order, but the company had shifted all of its capital to New Jersey by that time. That it continued to pay record dividends only heightened the general impression that it was flouting the law. In 1906, at the behest of Roosevelt, the Justice Department filed suit, charging that the company engaged in monopoly practices by attempting to control trading and commerce in petroleum and its by-products. The stage was set for the first epic battle between government and big business.

A decision was handed down against Standard Oil by a Missouri circuit court in 1909. Rockefeller himself testified in a well-rehearsed performance, but to no avail; the court ordered the breakup of the trust. The company immediately appealed to the U.S. Supreme Court but lost again, by an 8–1 vote, two years later. The Court noted the extent of the previous case, consisting of twenty-three volumes of printed material comprising over twelve thousand pages and covering a forty-year period of the company's history. Standard Oil was affirmed a monopoly, engaging in restraint of trade. Justice White, writing for the majority, stated that "one of the fundamental purposes of the statute [the Sherman Act] is to protect, not to destroy, rights of property."[12] But Standard Oil's sins were too great when weighed against its benefits to continue to exist as it had. The company was ordered to break up, liquidating its stock and returning the funds to its shareholders. The individual companies went their respective ways, free to compete against each other when the holding company no longer existed. The federal government had successfully dissolved the largest and most profitable business enterprise ever created. Whether it had weakened the Rockefeller empire was not yet clear.

Although the company was physically broken up, its grip was maintained through the newly created individual companies. And Rockefeller was still the main beneficiary, if no longer the major force behind the company. He was the owner of about one-quarter of the shares of the old trust, and now found himself a one-quarter owner of the thirty-odd new companies created by the decision. How all of this affected competition was clear: Upon hearing of the decision, J. P. Morgan was said to have remarked, "How the hell is any court going to compel a man to compete with himself?"[13] The public relations value of the breakup was monumental, but Rockefeller's wealth actually increased, and the new set of companies continued to dominate the markets. The more radical approach—making Rockefeller and other major shareholders divest themselves of their holdings—was never a viable option.

In its decision, the Court applied a principle that would become a hallmark of antitrust decisions thereafter—and in which fundamental common law reared its head again, despite the fact the common law usually bends in the face of federal statutes covering a specific area such as the Sherman Act. In the opinion, Chief Justice White used the term "standard of reason." In assessing Standard Oil's record as regards the provisions of the Sherman Act, White stated that it was intended that the "standard of reason which had been applied at the common law and in this country in dealing with subjects of the character embraced by the statute makes it certain that its purpose was to prevent undue restraints of every kind and nature."[14] The lone dissenting voice of Justice Harlan demurred on the grounds that it smacked of "judicial legislation."

The Republican Party quickly split into two distinct factions. Those who favored Roosevelt's policies were branded socialists by the old guard of the party, which favored the "Stand Pat" policies of Mark Hanna and Nelson Aldrich of Georgia, among others. Large corporations and business combines had contributed much to the national wealth, and this faction of the party favored the status quo rather than radical change. The alignment was remarkably similar to the opposition that Franklin Roosevelt's New Deal would face from the old guard of the Democratic Party in the 1930s. As a result, the second Roosevelt administration took a different tack on trust-busting. After the election of 1904, a more recalcitrant Congress refused to simply stamp its approval on attempts to dissolve the trusts outright, putting more reliance on federal agencies designed to monitor and curb holding companies. Roosevelt later noted, "Monopolies can, although in rather cumbrous fashion, be broken up by law suits. Great business combinations, however, cannot possibly be made useful instead of noxious industrial agencies merely by law suits. . . . I at once began to urge upon Congress the need for laws supplementing the Antitrust Law. . . . I strongly urged the inauguration of a system of thoroughgoing and drastic Government regulation and control over all big business combinations engaged in inter-state industry."[15]

Congress obliged, passing the Hepburn Act in 1906. This new law gave increased power to the Interstate Commerce Commission, which had quietly been slipping into obscurity. In the first decade following its founding, the ICC had taken upon itself the power to decide rates for the railroads. This was challenged in an 1897 court case. The Supreme Court ruled that the ICC did not have the authority to set rates because "there is nothing in the act fixing rates . . . the grant of such a power is never to be implied."[16] For the next ten years the authority of the ICC was greatly reduced and its power was open to question. In his second administration Roosevelt realized that renewed power in the hands of the ICC would be necessary in his fight against monopolies. In his fifth annual message to Congress he told it, "I regard this power to establish a maximum rate as being essential to any scheme of real reform in the matter of railway regulation. The first necessity is to secure it; and unless it is granted to the commission there is little use in touching the subject at all."[17] The Hepburn Act was designed to restore the commission to a central position in the fight against big business. Roosevelt openly advocated its passage, but the legislation had its detractors, Senator Nelson Aldrich being the most notable. The act enabled the ICC to determine maximum rates for the railroads when petitioned. It permitted appeals to the federal courts, but now the rail carriers would be forced to show that their rates were fair and nondiscriminatory. Roosevelt was able to claim later that "we were able to put through a measure which gave the Inter-State Commerce Commission for the first time real control over the railways."

Although the victory was significant, the battle was far from over. The Justice Department next tackled the second largest trust in the country, the American Tobacco Company. The monopoly was headed by James B. Duke, who had consolidated a number of smaller companies, including Lorillard, into the American Tobacco Company in 1890. Born and raised in North Carolina, Duke had witnessed his share of poverty and outside interference in his own state, ranging from natural disasters to the dark carpetbagging forces of Reconstruction. The Duke family became one of the wealthiest in the country. Duke reportedly gave away over one-third of his fortune to charitable and educational causes. His best known gift was $40 million to Trinity College in North Carolina, which subsequently changed its name to Duke University. Duke's trust reportedly controlled over 90 percent of cigarette production, and during the years that followed it extended its domination to other tobacco products as well. After the Northern Securities decision, it reorganized itself, but many of its transgressions were outlined in a lengthy report later issued by the U.S. Commissioner of Corporations in 1911.

When the suit was first filed in 1908, Duke was interviewed at his home in New York because he was too ill to go to court to testify. For three days he was questioned by his own attorneys about the company's organization and finances. Present was James McReynolds, of the Justice Department and later attorney general. Unlike Rockefeller's testimony in the Standard Oil suit, Duke was so forthcoming that McReynolds did not cross-examine him. His forthright testimony about his company only strengthened a point that the government made in its suit, however. It claimed that Duke acquired other companies secretly, allowing them to continue to operate under their names with the same management. He claimed he did it to maintain the various companies' profitable continuity rather than hide the ownership from critics. "We don't gain anything by getting rid of competition," he said. "If we started to buy them with that idea they would start to build them faster than we could buy them," he asserted, recalling the problems the railroad barons had had with upstart organizations like the Nickel Plate. Denying that his company was a monopoly, he asserted, "We want the competitors to go on. I think we make more money that way than if we had a monopoly."[18] But the lower courts were not convinced and found against the company. The case was appealed to the Supreme Court and was decided two weeks after the Standard Oil decision. The same reasoning was used as in the Standard Oil case, with the Court noting that "the ground of complaint against the American Tobacco Company rested not alone upon the nature and character of that corporation and the power it exerted . . . but also upon the control which it exercised over the subsidiary companies by virtue of stock held in said companies." It noted that it was giving the antitrust law a broad interpretation when it stated that the "law will be given a more comprehensive application than has been affixed to it in any previous decision."[19] American Tobacco was indeed a monopoly and in restraint of trade. The standard of reason was applied, and again Justice Harlan was the lone dissenting voice. American Tobacco was found to have monopolized the trade in tobacco products and was ordered dissolved.

Some of the actions taken against trusts never got to the Supreme Court. In one of the more unusual cases, the government filed suit in 1912 against the International Harvester Company. Harvester was formed in New Jersey in 1902 as a trust made up of five smaller companies that when combined controlled about 85 percent of the market for harvesting machines. The company was created by J. P. Morgan & Company partner George Perkins, who earned the bank a $3 million fee in the process. Morgan's influence was so great that Perkins was able to boast, "The new company is to be organized by us; its name chosen by us; the state in which it shall be incorporated is left to us—nobody has any right to question in any way any choice we make."[20] The government thought otherwise and filed suit to dissolve the company. A lower court found in its favor. Harvester appealed to the high court but then suddenly withdrew its appeal, accepting the decision of the lower court. The lower court had already found the company to be an unreasonable restraint of trade, violating the Sherman Act. More significant, the opinions of the judges in the circuit court drew a line of distinction that would become widely accepted across the board. A distinction was necessary to separate "good" trusts from "bad" ones. A good trust was one that did not exercise its considerable powers to the detriment of the public by stamping out competition or by rigging prices in its favor. Those that did were the bad trusts, which were much more clearly in violation of the Sherman Act. Although the Harvester case did not receive a Supreme Court ruling on the matter, the terms "good" and "bad" came into use thereafter, trying to make a distinction between size and the exercise of market power.

The victories over the two "bad" trusts were not as substantial as they appeared. Although the two giant companies split into smaller ones, operating mostly on a regional basis, the smaller companies shared the same stockholders. Rather than market on a national basis, they did so on a regional basis. But in the case of Standard Oil, the individual companies each had almost total market control over their local areas, so for all practical purposes the monopoly remained intact.[21] Many smaller companies against which proceedings were brought signed consent decrees, agreeing to refrain from engaging in monopoly practices in the future, and as a result the government did not order their dissolution. The net effect of such steps was mixed, but one clear fact was emerging: Trust formation was no longer in vogue. As U.S. Steel discovered, even a nod or a wink in the right direction could easily be misinterpreted. In the future, large business combinations would take a different tack.

IMPERIALIST DREAMS?

The conspiracy theories characteristic of the Populists found fertile ground in the pre–World War I years. The international cabal often suspected of running the country for its own ends seemed to be operating at full steam, supporting an arms buildup that would eventually lead to war. There was considerable fear among Populists and Progressives that monopolies were extending themselves internationally as well as domestically, making them even harder to control. Naturally, their chief motive was assumed to be profit, but the process by which they extended themselves was imperialism. Expansionist governments' favorite way of extending influence was gunboat diplomacy. By keeping close ties with their governments, monopolies could rely upon them to enforce business contracts for them overseas in times of trouble. Similarly, Marxists saw imperialism as the highest stage of capitalism and the great industrialists as imperialists.

One of the nineteenth century's greatest critics of imperialism was the Englishman J. A. Hobson. A self-proclaimed heretic from his university days at Oxford, Hobson wrote in the muckraking tradition, although his topics were broader than those of his American counterparts. In 1902 Hobson wrote that "it was this sudden demand for foreign markets . . . which was avowedly responsible for the adoption of Imperialism as a political policy and practice by the Republican party to which the great industrial and financial chiefs belonged, and which belonged to them."[22] While echoing American sentiments about McKinley and Mark Hanna especially, his probe was international in scope, in keeping with the imperialist phenomenon he feared.

Hobson's writings appealed to cabalists who would make connections between politicians, bankers, and industrialists that proved tantalizing. Even Theodore Roosevelt fueled that suspicion when he wrote in his memoirs that one of the reasons the United States went to war with Spain in Cuba was because "our own direct interests were great, because of the Cuban tobacco and sugar, and especially because of Cuba's relation to the projected Isthmian canal," a surprisingly frank admission from a trust-buster. The First World War also proved a boon to American capitalists in general, as exports more than tripled after American involvement began. But this was true of all wars in the industrial age. They made money for the financiers and manufacturers who supplied the belligerents. Even some avowedly antitrust politicians beat the war drum, including Teddy Roosevelt, paradoxically fanning the same flames he sought to extinguish through his antitrust policy. "The adventurous enthusiasm of President Theodore Roosevelt and his 'manifest destiny' and 'mission of civilization' party must not deceive us," Hobson wrote. "It was Messrs. Rockefeller, Pierpont Morgan, and their associates who needed imperialism and who fastened it upon the shoulders of the Great Republic of the West."[23] Roosevelt understood his own ambivalent position clearly. He stated unequivocally, "We have not the slightest desire to secure any territory at the expense of our neighbors." He was splitting hairs, because the monopolists did not seek to add overseas possessions to their empires, only markets where they could sell their products. The Spanish-American War certainly fit the mold. Dewey's victory over the Spanish fleet in Manila Harbor benefited the bankers. "The public financial arrangements for the Philippine war put several millions of dollars into the pockets of Mr. Pierpont Morgan and his friends," Hobson said, becoming one of the first commentators to make such a blanket assertion. He may also have been aware that the war was a millionaires' war. The New York *Daily News* reported that no fewer than nineteen sons of millionaires were serving in the conflict. Perhaps, like Teddy Roosevelt, they found the war a way of expressing their patriotism at a time when big business ruled supreme.

Analyses of this sort, peppered with Marxist ideas, gave rise to all sorts of criticism. The bankers and industrialists had to tread lightly for fear of arousing public indignation, and possibly another congressional hearing. And the more traditional old guard was even able to jump on the same bandwagon without playing any of the Marxist tune. Henry Adams railed about the foreign Rothschild interests influencing American policies during the financial crisis of 1893, when August Belmont joined Morgan in the financial package that rescued the Treasury. Adams' brother Brooks later became an intimate of and advisor to Roosevelt. In everyday politics, not everyone thought of lumping Roosevelt in the same category as Morgan or Rockefeller, but Hobson's sweeping ideas created a new category of imperialist that cast everyone associated with American politics and big business under the same shadow.

American protective tariffs provided ammunition for the critics of imperialism. Industrial societies, according to the critics, had excess capacity: The markets at home were not large enough to absorb the goods produced by capitalists, so exports naturally became the way that capitalism expanded. Tariffs protected industries at home so that foreign competition would not hamper their ability to produce—and to rig prices when necessary. Since all capitalists behaved the same way, imperialism became the answer to their dreams. When an underdeveloped country agreed to buy from an industrialized nation and then reneged on the deal or could not pay, gunboats from the more developed nation would usually help settle the matter. While manifest destiny was sold at home as a natural process whereby the United States would expand from sea to sea, foreigners saw it as another belligerent way of extending American domain and markets. The Monroe Doctrine was nothing more than an official notice that European competition was not wanted in the Americas.

Hobson's criticism struck the public in Britain and the United States like a thunderbolt and further tarnished the image of big business. World War I soon became a laboratory for anti-imperialist critics, since it revealed so many links between big business, finance, and government, as well as the fine line between patriotism, good business, and war profiteering. While American industrialists were selling their wares to their Allies, financiers naturally operated behind the scenes to provide money and exports for the combatants. The House of Morgan came under fire for its role in helping supply Britain with arms and materiel, for a price.

When the war began, the British and the French sought a huge amount of materiel from the United States. Their agent became J. P. Morgan & Co., which supplied the Allies with the required resources.

Morgan hired Edward Stettinius, president of the Diamond Match Company, as head of its export department. He began a frantic program of purchasing that easily became the largest in history. In a little over a year he purchased about $3 billion worth of goods for the Allies. Morgan's commission for the work was 1 percent of its value, $30 million. This operation put an inordinate amount of power in the hands of the bank, and the British recognized it. Criticisms abounded that Morgan was giving contracts for the supplies to Republican-led companies and those companies in which Morgan had interests profited handsomely.[24] But once the United States entered the war, Morgan gave up its role as agent, partially to avoid criticisms that it was profiting from a war that the country had become enmeshed in.

There were other visible signs of industrial self-interest. In the decade prior to the war, navy leagues had been organized in many industrialized countries, ostensibly dedicated to the principle that strong navies protected strong democracies. In 1907, the United States, in an amazing display of both naval power and naivete, sent its fleet of battleships around the world on a public relations cruise to show foreign governments its military strength. It was dubbed the Grand Fleet but later became sarcastically known as the Great White Fleet because the steel ships were all painted white—making them very good targets. Upon their return they were all painted the now familiar battleship gray. Theodore Roosevelt was one of the more vocal advocates of a strong navy in his years as cabinet member and vice president. In 1908 he commented that "if we did not have a foreign possession; if we abandoned the Monroe Doctrine . . . it would still be necessary for us to have a navy, and a strong fighting navy." The American version, called simply the Navy League, was certainly no different. Its members included Morgan, Rockefeller, Henry Clay Frick, Charles Schwab, Senator James Phelan of California, Elihu Root, and Theodore Roosevelt, many of whom had a vested interest in a strong navy because of their holdings in the steel industry. Roosevelt always maintained that a strong naval force was the best defense the country could have. Senator Henry Cabot Lodge of Massachusetts put it more bluntly in Congress when he said that "battle ships are made to be used."[25]

Prior to the United States' entry into the war, the league put strong pressure on Woodrow Wilson's administration to join in the conflict by aiding the Allies. Along with other interest groups, they began an internal propaganda campaign to pressure the administration to increase American naval capacity. After the *Lusitania* was sunk by a German submarine in 1915, the movement picked up considerable momentum. The Navy League immediately responded by asking Congress to allocate $500 million for improvements in the fleet. The political pressure was not confined to lobbying; the propaganda element was also strong. Books and pamphlets were produced bemoaning American naval weakness. Popular movies such as *The Fall of a Nation* parodied D.W. Griffith's *The Birth of a Nation* by depicting a foreign invasion of the United States by what appeared to be German troops. The pressure eventually paid off when Wilson succumbed and asked Congress for funds to expand the navy in 1915, prior to American entry into the war. The league issued a resolution at the Union League Club in New York that stated "a large bond issue of, if necessary, $500,000,000 should be authorized at once. These bonds would be rapidly absorbed by the American people for such a purpose."[26] Steel prices, which had been relatively steady since the turn of the century, increased over 50 percent during the war, providing its producers with handsome profits. The organizations proved to be highly successful lobbies for the interests of the top echelon of bankers and industrialists who were for war, against prohibition, and would later challenge Franklin Roosevelt and the New Deal. The Navy League's secretary was William Stayton, who would later lead the Association Against the Prohibition Amendment (AAPA) in the 1920s as well as the American Liberty League in the 1930s.

Being identified with the arms buildup was not without its risks. After J. P. Morgan died in 1913, the House of Morgan was headed by Jack, his son. A gunman invaded the Long Island home of Jack Morgan in 1915, bent upon stopping the sale of arms to the Allies. After shooting Morgan twice, he was subdued and arrested. The gunman, a former university lecturer in German at Cornell, also attempted to blow up the Capitol in Washington. He eventually committed suicide in jail. Morgan recovered without serious injury. A year later German agents blew up Black Tom, a munitions dump in Jersey City, within sight of New York City, causing over $20 million in damages. Acts of sabotage and terror were becoming commonplace as U.S. financing to the Allies increased.

The strenuous lobbying on behalf of a stronger navy combined with the extremely harsh terms imposed on Germany by the Allies after the war gave many the impression that the war was fought for economic reasons. Bankers, especially the Morgan men, played an important part in the reparations talks. Their hold on key positions in and out of the administration helped them maintain their grip on the financial system. Morgan led a huge bond issue for the Allies in 1915, dubbed the Anglo-French loan, that became the largest single bond issue in history, with generous fees to match. It would achieve fame again thirty years later in an antitrust suit. Despite the revelations of the Pujo hearings, convened in 1912 to investigate the financial system, and the various antitrust hearings prior to the war, business continued as usual for financiers. Although a connection clearly existed between the industrial trusts and the financiers, the country was still at the mercy of Wall Street, and many critics were intent on bringing the connection into the light.

"INVISIBLE TRUSTS"

After Roosevelt's administration ended, his successor, William Howard Taft, continued the pursuit of big business. The track record of the Navy League and the suspicions about imperialism were leading many in Congress to inquire into the affairs of bankers as never before. For the previous thirty years J. P. Morgan had been considered a government within a government, and it was apparent that the government on the outside would have to take a look at the one within.

In 1909 Taft was roasted at the annual affair run by the Gridiron Club in Washington, an annual meeting of journalists and politicians that became a Washington tradition. The trusts were the subject of one of the many skits satirizing politicians. In it, Attorney General George Wickersham, an avid pursuer of the trusts, was implored by them to relent a bit, to let them sleep:

> Come Georgie, come
> Bid us good-night,
> And do not fill our hearts with dread.
> We're tired now, and sleepy too;
> Come put us in our little bed.[27]

But there was no sign that was going to happen. During Taft's administration, a new twist occurred in the investigation of trusts. Borrowing a term coined by Congressman Charles Lindbergh, Congress began investigation of the "money trust." This purported trust consisted of the big banks, mostly in New York, that controlled credit and finance in the country.[28] The broad allegation against them, as Senator La Follette put it, was that the trust's "power is unlimited. In large affairs, it gives or withholds credit, and from time to time contracts the volume of money required for the transaction of the business of the country, regardless of everything excepting its own profits."[29] Equally important was the matter of control. By controlling the access to money, the bankers could catapult themselves onto corporate boards and in many cases eventually seize controlling interests in these companies. The argument went that this was as much a trust combination as U.S. Steel or American Tobacco. Actually, it was more of an ad hoc cartel that formed over the years to arrange large financing deals for industry. While the *Addyston* case blocked most industrial cartels, it was much more difficult to do so with one that provided mainly invisible services such as banking and securities underwriting. And there was nothing in the existing banking laws to prevent the larger banks from forming syndicates for underwriting. In any other industry, this form of pooling was forbidden. In banking, it was de rigueur. The best that Congress could do at the time was investigate it.

The money trust investigators owed a sizeable intellectual debt to Louis Brandeis, the crusading lawyer whose investigations into J. P. Morgan's insurance and railroad empires revealed the tentacles of financial power. Born to Jewish immigrants, Brandeis graduated first in his class from Harvard Law School in 1877. His preoccupation with what would become known as Progressive causes can be found in his own family history, much as with Ida Tarbell. His family was temporarily forced to leave the country while he was still in secondary school and return to Germany. His father had incurred serious losses after the market crash in 1869 and the depression that followed, attributable to none other than the already infamous Jay Gould. Brandeis became known as the "people's attorney" for espousing public causes and practiced law privately in Boston for a number of years before being appointed to the Supreme Court in 1916. His book *Other People's Money and How the Bankers Use It* (1913) became the financial bible of the Progressive movement. Brandeis argued that bankers merely used depositors' funds to aid their own causes by extending credit to companies. Being in central positions of control, they were able to exercise power out of all proportion to their original functions. This criticism was the first serious one leveled at bankers from a reforming angle as well, following Brandeis' earlier writings and activities as a champion of workingmen's causes. While the Populists and Progressives differed in some of their goals and platforms, both groups claimed Brandeis as intellectually one of their own. One of his best-known activities prior to the First World War was an examination of the New Haven Railroad and the power that J. P. Morgan exercised over it.

The management of the New Haven Railroad, more properly known as the New York, New Haven & Hartford Railroad, was one of the sloppier affairs embarked upon by the Morgan bank. The affairs came to light shortly after the death of Pierpont Morgan in 1913. The railroad had acquired a local Massachusetts line a few years earlier and had also been acquiring local streetcar services in a violation of state law. A newspaper fired the opening salvo against Morgan's influence in 1910 by publishing an editorial calling the banker a "beefy thick-necked financial bully, drunk with wealth and power who bawls his orders to stock markets, directors, courts, governments and nations."[30] The Senate approved an investigation of the line, and the ICC began a probe into Morgan's dealings. The results were startling. Over $200 million of the railroad's funds had been used for outside investment purposes, mainly acquisitions. In 1913 the ICC recommended that the railroad divest itself of its local shipping and trolley businesses, and Jack Morgan, succeeding his father at the helm of the bank, promptly fired Charles S. Mellen as its president. Mellen was suspected of shady financial dealings during most of his tenure at the railroad. The line acquired a monopoly over rail transportation in five states, but it was being systematically looted by its directors and its stock price eventually collapsed. Mellen always claimed that he redirected funds only on Morgan's orders. The missing money was never adequately accounted for; the assumption was that it indirectly found its way into the directors' pockets.

Brandeis' more general criticism of bankers attracted many followers who also believed that too much power resided at the corner of Broad and Wall Streets, the headquarters of J. P. Morgan & Co. And with good reason. The United States had existed without a central bank for the better part of the nineteenth century and early into the twentieth, ever since Andrew Jackson refused to renew the charter of the Bank of the United States. The constant debate about states' rights and the role of the federal government vis-à-vis the states had prevented the creation of a central institution. The lack of a central bank that could exercise control over money and credit creation had caused numerous stock market panics and severe economic slowdowns. When the Treasury found itself in difficult positions, it often had turned to private bankers for help. Over the last quarter of the nineteenth century that increasingly meant employing the services of J. P. Morgan & Company. Critics maintained that Morgan was the unofficial central banker to the United States, an intolerable situation that could not be allowed to continue. And Morgan was not alone. Other New York bankers also exercised similar powers, unaccountable to the public.

Brandeis' views about bankers, especially investment bankers, were some of the strongest yet expressed about the financial oligarchy he claimed was running the country. "Though properly but middlemen, these bankers bestride as masters America's business world, so that practically no large enterprise can be undertaken without their participation or approval . . . the key to their power is Concentration—concentration intensive and comprehensive."[31] Brandeis quickly made the connection between banking and monopoly. The money trust was a reality that could not be easily challenged. But unlike in the railroad or oil industries, rates charged by bankers were private. It was difficult to show how the fees they charged actually harmed the public. At the time, the big banks rarely dealt with individuals. Most of their business came from their corporate customers. Brandeis' criticisms became the standard for the Progressive movement, the successor to the Populists.

The collapse of the Trust Company of New York and several New York brokers in 1907 caused a severe financial crisis, and Morgan raised funds to provide liquidity for the market. But his generosity came at a price, and Progressives accused him of profiting from national economic woes. Similar criticisms had been raised in the past, going back as far as the Civil War. As long as the country lacked a central bank, the criticisms would continue. There needed to be an institution that could match the need for money with the supply in the country. Roosevelt acknowledged this early in his presidency when he admitted that "it is necessary that there should be an element of elasticity in our monetary system." But he stopped short of advocating a radical overhaul of the financial system, preferring to leave that power in the hands of the banks. "It would be unwise and unnecessary at this time [1902] to attempt to reconstruct our financial system," he said during his first administration.[32] Finally, when tangible discussions began about instituting a central bank during Taft's presidency, it was generally agreed that given its increasing role in the world economy, the United States could no longer afford the luxury of lurching from one financial crisis to another. The real question would concern the role of the extraordinarily influential private banks in any new system.

In 1910 a group of bankers and politicians met secretly at Jekyll Island in Georgia at the behest of Nelson Aldrich, a Republican senator from that state. Banking interests were divided about the need for a new regulator of any sort, but the wind was blowing toward the establishment of a European-style bank like the Bank of England. Wall Street interests were anxious to know how they would be affected, since they had had things much their own way since the Civil War. The antimonopoly spirit had finally passed from the industrial and railroad holding companies to the banks, and their influence on the economy was similar, if less visible. Proving that banks were consolidating to gain monopoly power was difficult, however.

Democrats in Congress pressed for hearings on the putative money trust. The hearings began in December 1912 in what was billed as one of the greatest public gatherings of bankers in recent memory. The major figure in the hearings was not the chairman, Arsenee Pujo of Louisiana, after whom they were named, but the chief counsel, Samuel Untermyer, a New York lawyer. All of the alleged members of the money trust were called to testify, including J. Pierpont Morgan and George Baker of the First National Bank of New York, along with the chief executive officers of National City Bank, Kidder Peabody & Co., Lee Higginson & Co., and Kuhn Loeb & Co. Untermyer's questioning was designed to show the relationships that the bankers had built up over the years and how they exploited them. Morgan, for example, had used his banking powers to build the General Electric Company after having acquired it from Thomas Edison. When added to his acquisition of what became the U.S.

Steel Corporation from Andrew Carnegie, his empire benefited substantially. His holdings and directorships in other banks and railroads were also extensive. He also effectively dominated the three largest life insurance companies in the country. But it was his control of over half a million miles of rail lines by 1910 that was most telling. Together, he and George Baker controlled much of the coal transportation in the country and thus effectively controlled the vast coal deposits owned by the railroads. In 1900 the price of coal was raised by 10 cents a ton, representing an increase of about 8 percent. That alone raised the ire of the U.S. Industrial Commission and journalists alike. Gustavus Myers, one of the better-known muckraking journalists of the day, wrote that "the population was completely at the mercy of a few magnates; each year as the winter drew on, the coal trust increased its price. . . . Housekeepers were taxed $70 million in extra impositions a year, in addition to the $40 million annually extorted."[33] Louis Brandeis asked in 1913, "Can full competition exist among the anthracite coal railroads when the Morgan associates are potent in all of them?" Yet Morgan ingenuously disavowed any knowledge of controlling coal transport in the country.

The Pujo hearings were also notable for actually bringing Morgan into the public eye. The tycoon always maintained a low public profile. His testimony, along with that of Baker, rivaled Rockefeller's performance in the antitrust case for being well rehearsed and played very close to the vest. Bankers had become aware of the sentiments against monopolies and bigness in general among the public, and they were careful not to reveal much that Untermyer did not already know about their businesses. In addition, industrialists and financiers were turning to public relations specialists as they attempted to put forward a kindly, benign image. Part of that image was that they were too important to be familiar with the everyday details of their businesses. In the new age of managerial capitalism, the industrialists professed to leave detail to their subordinates in their various companies, although it was widely assumed that Morgan, like Rockefeller before him, knew exactly how his business was being run by his professional managers.

Another industry that developed in these years was automobile manufacturing. As early as 1895 the magazine *Horseless Age* appeared, presaging what was to become the great American industry and preoccupation.

Henry Ford introduced the Model T in 1908 and sold twelve thousand units. At the outbreak of World War I, his annual sales exceeded half a million cars. And while Ford was perhaps the most familiar name in automobile production, General Motors quickly became the actual industry leader.

The company was the brainchild of William Crapo (Billy) Durant, who started it the same year that Ford went into production. Hailing from Flint, Michigan, Durant was a flamboyant and outspoken salesman and organizer who fused several companies into GM. Almost from the beginning, auto production was extremely competitive, crowded by numerous small companies of all sorts. After the stock market panic of 1907, financing became difficult for many of the small firms, which existed mainly on lines of credit from their bankers, and quite a few people in the nascent industry became convinced that consolidation was needed if stronger, more competitive companies were to emerge. Benjamin Briscoe, one of Durant's early collaborators in designing General Motors, portrayed the necessity to consolidate in no uncertain terms: "In this year 1908 many of us thought that the industry was beset with difficulties and so came the desire to some of us to form a combination of the principal concerns in the industry . . . for the purpose of having one big concern of such dominating influence in the automobile industry as, for instance, the United States Steel Corporation exercises in the steel industry."[34] After tortuous negotiations with J. P. Morgan & Company, General Motors was assembled as a combination of Buick and Oldsmobile. Later Cadillac and other divisions were added. At the time of its inception, Henry Ford was also involved in the merger talks, though his demands for a cash-only deal could not be met and he eventually dropped out of the consolidation. But Durant soon ran into financial difficulties and was forced out by a syndicate of bankers who were his creditors. He responded by organizing the Chevrolet Motor Car Company with the Swiss industrialist Louis Chevrolet. The new company was so successful that Durant repurchased a controlling interest in GM. He ran the company successfully until 1920, when the postwar recession severely damaged the company's finances. He was ousted a second time and succeeded at the helm by Pierre du Pont, a Morgan ally. Within a year, du Pont reorganized GM, revamping its management and production processes. The company emerged much stronger as a result, able to successfully challenge Ford. This accomplishment, along with the success of DuPont itself, made him one of the country's most famous industrial managers.

Like many of the other smaller auto manufacturers, Durant was not much of an adversary for the bankers upon whom he would ultimately depend. A convincing salesman, he was a high school graduate—not common at the time—but he was still facing bankers whose educational pedigrees were as good as their family blood lines and their ability to rely on the old boys' network. Much suspicion surrounded Durant at the time because he had a reputation as a speculator in the stock market, an unsavory position for the bankers with whom he dealt to publicly accept. Thomas Lamont of J. P. Morgan & Company remarked that "several times we said to the du Ponts that Durant was interested in speculations in Wall Street and each time they denied it because Durant denied it to them. . . . By [finally] corkscrewing it out of him . . . it was disclosed that he owed $27 million and that three banks and twenty one brokerage houses were involved."[35] That reputation came to haunt him in his dealings with Morgan and no doubt had something to do with his dismissal. Yet Durant went on to make one of the most sizeable fortunes of the 1920s on Wall Street while still ostensibly the president of Durant Motors. In later years GM, the company he created, would come under investigation as American auto production became more and more consolidated, eventually with only three companies.

Linked to the automotive industry was the DuPont chemical company, which bought a sizeable block of GM stock in order to solidify its position as a leading supplier of parts to the company. The cost of the purchase eventually totaled $49 million and came from DuPont's expansion fund, suggesting that it was more than just an "investment."[36] But of course auto parts were not DuPont's main business. The company profited handsomely by selling munitions to the United States and its allies during the war, grossing over a billion dollars between 1915 and 1918. The company was subject to charges of profiteering, although it claimed that much of that money went to pay excessive profits tax, a fact that the du Pont family would use later in the decade to support the anti-Prohibition movement. But the profits enabled the company to expand into chemicals and paints. It was aided immeasurably by the American government's seizing of German patents during the war as alien property, opening the door to DuPont's entry into the business. The investment in GM was financed with those profits. The 23 percent stake purchased would return to haunt both companies in forty years in a famous antitrust case.

BAD TIMING

After Woodrow Wilson won the presidency in the election of 1912, Progressive ideas dominated the major antitrust legislation passed by Congress. Finally, many tenets of the Progressive credo were to become law, including additions to the Sherman Act in the Clayton Act. Although Taft's administration was mostly conservative, his antitrust policies were very much in line with those of his predecessor, and the same can be said of Wilson's. Indeed, Wilson's public pronouncements on trusts and trust-busting were stronger than those of Taft or Roosevelt. Both Democrats and Republicans had included antimonopoly rhetoric in their platforms for the 1912 election, although the Democrats were more determined. They called for the "prevention of holding companies, of interlocking directorships, of stock watering, and control by any one corporation of so large a proportion of industry as to make it a menace to competitive conditions." The new administration kept its campaign pledge, attacking business on all fronts.

The Populism of the nineteenth century faded from national politics and was succeeded by Progressivism. But conspiracy theory was still one element of the movement. Robert La Follette, the reforming Republican from Wisconsin, was a particular proponent of such theories; he believed, for instance, that the panic of 1907 was instigated by Morgan for his bank's gain. A strongly built but short man who favored pompadour-style haircuts, La Follette was a family man who had graduated from the University of Wisconsin after working his way through at a series of odd jobs. He was elected governor of Wisconsin three times before entering the Senate in 1906. He ran for president on the Progressive ticket in 1924 and garnered almost five million popular votes. His son Robert Junior succeeded him in the Senate after his death in 1925, and his son Philip became governor of Wisconsin. La Follette followed in the tradition of favoring practice over theory in politics and economics, a trend found at the university in his youth. Clearly from the anti–Wall Street and anti-big-business contingent, he was known as someone especially well informed in economic affairs, lending credence to his conspiracy theories. Louis Brandeis once described him as knowing more about the railroads than anyone in the country. Brandeis himself was named to the Supreme Court in 1916 by Woodrow Wilson, a crowning achievement for the activist lawyer. Now he was in a position to sit in judgment on those organizations created by the previous generation of industrialists.

The major piece of antitrust legislation that followed the principles of the Democratic platform was the 1914 Clayton Act. The act made it difficult to create new horizontal mergers, prevented interlocking directorships, and proscribed price discrimination. The ban on interlocking directorships was aimed at investment bankers who often sat on more than one board. In particular, Morgan's control of U.S. Steel and the profits made by investment bankers in forming the new company figured prominently in the minds of lawmakers. The act was hailed as a new weapon in the antitrust battle, but time would show that its bark was fiercer than its bite. Unfortunately for trustbusters, the wording of the act contained the seeds of its own circumvention. It stated that "no corporation engaged in commerce shall acquire, directly or indirectly, the whole or any part of the *stock* or other share of capital of another corporation engaged also in commerce where the effect of such acquisition may be to substantially lessen competition between the corporation whose stock is so acquired and the corporation making the acquisition."[37] But it did not mention assets, and so companies wanting to acquire the assets of another could do so because the act did not specifically prohibit it.

The act also exempted organized labor from many provisions of the antitrust laws, providing the labor movement with a much-needed boost at a critical time in its own history. Samuel Gompers, the president of the American Federation of Labor, actively lobbied on behalf of this part of the act, considered to be something of a bill of rights for the labor movement. But the labor leader's assertion that unions should be exempt because there was a philosophical difference between a man's labor and what he labored over did not hold much water with those who did not always sympathize with organized labor. The *New York Times* was critical of what it called "objectionable class legislation" and Gompers' support for it, opining that "the purpose of the Clayton bill's clause is to make a distinction between bad unions and bad trusts which good unions and good trusts neither need nor ask for."[38]

In 1915 the Federal Trade Commission was established to examine corporations that were thought to be restraining trade and creating monopolies.[39] If unfair competition could be proven, then the five-member commission created by legislation had the authority to refer the problem to the attorney general. But the term "unfair competition" was criticized for being too vague. "The depth and breadth of the law are not clear from its text," mused the *New York Times,* and the paper argued further that the idea of unfair competition was moot. "Everybody knows what 'unfair competition' is, but some know better than others," it said, referring to the bill's framers. "In the legal sense [it] is only fraudulent competition, such as selling substitutes, things 'just as good' as others, or one man's goods instead of another's. If the lawmakers intend anything broader than this, just what do they mean?"[40] The first head of the commission was attuned to the meaning, however. Joseph E. Davies had previously been a commissioner of corporations and went on to become ambassador to the Soviet Union. However, the FTC met with only limited success until after World War II, showing that the *New York Times'* original doubts were right on target.

The last great battle between the Justice Department and big business before the 1920s boom began was the suit brought against the United States Steel Corporation. Since its creation in 1901, U.S. Steel had grown to become the largest company in the world. After the initial purchase of Carnegie's company, J. P. Morgan continued to purchase other companies until the company became the largest in the world. Much of the consolidation came during a period of trust-busting by the Roosevelt and Taft administrations, with "Big Steel" and its president, Judge Elbert Gary, after whom Gary, Indiana, was named, operating under the assumption that it was exempt from antitrust action. The assumption ultimately proved to be a mistake. Parts of the reorganization of the company became classics of investment-banker greed and showed the problems associated with having financiers controlling companies. When U.S. Steel was organized, Wall Street was employed to sell securities in the new entity. The U.S. Commissioner of Corporations estimated in 1911 that over $90 million in fees was realized by the syndicate of investment bankers that led the sale, headed by J. P. Morgan & Company. That bank turned a profit through its newly won control of the company as well as its role in underwriting securities in it. That enormous gain would become the rallying point in later attempts to bring trust financiers to heel. Brandeis remarked that "the standard for so-called compensation actually applied, is not the 'rule of reason,' but 'all the traffic will bear.'" Ignored in the criticisms, however, was the fact that investors' expectations about U.S. Steel's prospects were what helped fill the underwriters' wallets.

One of U.S. Steel's major acquisitions was that of the Tennessee Coal, Iron and Railroad Company during the financial panic of 1907. Moore and Schley was a medium-sized Wall Street house that was in danger of failing. Most Wall Street banks were concerned about the failure, fearing that it would have a domino effect on other firms as well. Part of Moore and Schley's holdings was a majority stake in Tennessee Coal, which possessed a large amount of natural resources. Morgan arranged for U.S. Steel to purchase Moore and Schley's stock in Tennessee, providing the Wall Street firm with the funds it needed to survive; in return, a number of financiers agreed to provide funds to save the banking system, quelling the panic.

When the bankers agreed to Morgan's plan, Gary and Henry Clay Frick were dispatched to Washington to get Roosevelt's blessing for the deal; the administration needed to be placated, since U.S. Steel's acquisition of Tennessee's resources certainly smacked of monopoly concentration. Without a friendly Justice Department, the deal would have been inconceivable. They got the approval they wanted, but they may have misled Roosevelt about what the deal involved. Roosevelt received them at the White House with Elihu Root, the secretary of state, also attending. The attorney general was not present, so the president dictated a note to him immediately after the meeting in which he stated that "Judge Gary and Mr. Frick informed me that as a mere business transaction they do not care to purchase the stock [of Tennessee Coal], that under ordinary circumstances they would not consider purchasing the stock, because but little benefit will come to the Steel Corporation from the purchase."[41] The two claimed that they were merely making the proposal to save the stock exchange and the banking system from the panic. Roosevelt accepted their statements and concluded, "I felt it no public duty of mine to interpose any objections."

The president claimed that this meeting was an example of his "square deal" policy; trying to help business when the big stick was inappropriate. But it symbolized a shift in his policy toward business as well as a change in the tenor of Progressive reforms in general. Eliminating monopolies was a difficult business and appeared to be a losing battle; in contrast, the notion of "square deal" implied a policy of cooperation rather than belligerence. But the meeting with the financiers seemed to backfire on Roosevelt. He was accused of being soft on Wall Street and of having been duped by Morgan. Roosevelt was well aware of the criticisms. At the 1907 Gridiron Club dinner, normally an occasion for merriment and roasting of the guest speaker, Roosevelt proved to be an ungracious guest, turning the evening on its head by attacking a group of financiers who were present, including Morgan. One of the journalists present remembered the evening in vivid terms. "He began rather cordially . . . and then turned squarely toward the eminent financiers sitting not thirty feet from him. He became emphatic at once. With accusing finger he pointed at these astonished plutocrats and told them what he had in store for them. . . . I remember Mr. Morgan, with a big cigar clenched in his teeth, glaring at him as he talked."[42] What was in store was intense scrutiny of Morgan's vast holdings. The Bureau of Corporations began a study of U.S. Steel, and the House of Representatives began a second investigation. The House investigation especially was surrounded by controversy because most of the members of the committee formed by Rep. Augustus Stanley of Kentucky, bearing his name, were hostile to big business. The committee's reports, eventually published in 1912, were critical of U.S. Steel on many counts.

The pivotal point in the criticism concerned the failure of the Trust Company of America, a New York bank, during the panic of 1907. The bank was also a major holder of Tennessee Coal stock. The report concluded that George Perkins, a Morgan partner, had precipitated the run on the Trust Company so that its stake in Tennessee Coal would have to be sold. This interpretation of the facts dovetailed with similar accusations made by Senator Robert La Follette of Wisconsin that the entire panic of 1907 was precipitated by the money trust, and especially Morgan, in order to take advantage of certain anomalies that he saw in the marketplace.[43] In 1911 the Justice Department filed suit against the company, seeking Big Steel's dissolution.

Then came some embarrassing revelations about the information made available to the Stanley Committee. David Lamar, a Wall Street trader with a particularly predatory reputation, purported to have knowledge of the transaction as well as other dealings on the Street that would embarrass the legendary bank, and he admitted to being the real author of the Stanley resolution. He had written the bulk of it several years earlier in order to embarrass his enemies, the Morgan interests, but when it reached Stanley, the congressman was more than happy to introduce it in the House. When it became clear that Lamar's story apparently was true, the Stanley committee's findings fell under a pall.[44] But the Justice Department did not withdraw its suit against U.S. Steel.

However, before all of this scandal emerged, Augustus Stanley and Robert La Follette, two of the strongest opponents of big business, introduced an antitrust bill in Congress in 1911 designed to fine-tune the Sherman Act. They had realized that antitrust cases such as the ones against Standard Oil and American Tobacco could not be won in a real sense because the companies would simply reorganize differently, maintaining their holds on their respective markets. Essentially, the La Follette–Stanley antitrust bill sought to place the burden of proof on the accused rather than the accusers. Companies would have to show that their actions did not violate the law. Senator Moses Clapp of the Interstate Commerce Committee began hearings on government policy toward business shortly thereafter, and two of the notable witnesses were Louis Brandeis, a particularly strong ally of the bill, and George Perkins, representing Morgan, who was opposed. Their testimonies gave clear views of both sides of the monopoly issue.

Perkins testified that big did not necessarily mean bad and that the major benefit of size and consolidation in business generally was increased efficiency. But one of the reasons that Brandeis was called to testify was Senator La Follette's desire to get at the heart of the money trust. Brandeis criticized the bankers as well as the industrialists. He argued that the money men became interested in industry because of the huge commissions they could generate by sitting on corporate boards and carving themselves into every deal that passed in front of them. U.S. Steel was a prime example. Conservative estimates were that over half of its capitalization was pure water, meaning that shareholders had been issued worthless stock, and that Morgan was responsible for it. Brandeis questioned Perkins' contention that the steel trust was efficient, citing defective steel rails as examples. "I am so convinced of the economic fallacy in a huge unit," he maintained, "that if we make competition possible, if we create conditions where there could be reasonable competition, that these monsters would fall to the ground."[45]

When arguing theory versus practice, Brandeis usually held sway over his opponents. He concluded his remarks to the Clapp committee with an impassioned plea that legislators consider the social implications of the trusts, not simply the economic ones. "When you do that," he concluded, "you will realize the extraordinary perils to our institutions which attend the trusts." But despite Brandeis' eloquence, the La Follette–Stanley bill did not pass. The Sherman Act remained the sole weapon the government could use against the trusts until the Clayton Act was passed.

Critics of big business were not heartened by two court decisions in 1918 and 1920. Both provided fuel for the merger trend that would erupt in the coming decade. In *United States v. United Shoe Machinery Company*, the Justice Department filed suit against the so-called shoe trust in 1911, claiming that a group of shoemaking-machinery manufacturers had combined to drive out competition. The company claimed that it had simply combined disparate businesses that had no effect upon competition. The case finally reached the Supreme Court seven years later. Two of the justices refrained from voting: James C. McReynolds because he was previously attorney general under Woodrow Wilson before being named to the Court, and the newly appointed Brandeis because of his appearance before Senate committees several years before. The vote without them was 4–3 in favor of the company. With them, the result probably would have gone in the opposite direction.

The U.S. Steel case also took years to reach the Supreme Court. In the fifteen years since its founding, the company had become the country's largest, with assets almost five times those of Standard Oil, the second largest. When the Court rendered its decision in March 1920, Brandeis and McReynolds again abstained. And again the Court ruled in favor of the company, saying that while U.S. Steel may have been organized to gain monopoly control over the steel industry, it had not actually done so. In fact, its domination of the steel industry had declined from Roosevelt's day. Gary and his associates had formed organizations, pooled interests with other companies, and even held joint dinner meetings with the intent of closer alliances, but did not achieve them. And when it caught a whiff of the government's case, the company quickly changed its tactics so it would not prejudice its own case. As a result, U.S. Steel was exonerated, judged a good trust. As in the shoe case, the decision probably would have gone the other way if the two abstaining justices had voted. These two antitrust cases were bitter for Brandeis. He later bemoaned the fact that "the Sherman Law was held in the *United States v. United States Steel Corporation* . . . to permit capitalists to combine in a single corporation 50 percent of the steel industry of the United States, dominating the trade through its vast resources."[46]

The Court's findings in favor of the steel and shoe trusts paved the way for the decade of merger and amalgamation that followed. Big business and finance did not fail to notice that two of the trust's most vociferous critics prior to the war had had to disqualify themselves from the most important cases in a decade, and the Supreme Court would not be a restraining factor in the development of larger mergers in the decade to follow. With Warren Harding's election to the White House, big business was in an even more enviable position. Friendly Republicans now controlled the once-antagonistic Justice Department. The way was clear for a decade of corporate expansion not seen since McKinley was president.

3

LOOKING
THE
OTHER WAY
(1920–1930)

The country can . . . anticipate the future with optimism.
—CALVIN COOLIDGE, 1928

THE 1920S WERE YEARS of great contradiction. Business, employing new technologies eagerly sought by the public, began to circumvent the antitrust laws as flagrantly as at any time in the past. It became the decade of the consumer, who was bitten by the urge to purchase automobiles, radios, and appliances as never before. Technology made new products available, and innovative production made them widely accessible. The same consumers became less demanding of their government than the previous generation. Several successive Republican administrations were characterized by scandal and a laissez-faire attitude toward business that bordered on neglect when compared with previous administrations. The feeling in the country was that things were all right and bound to get even better. Henry Ford stated confidently that permanent peace was almost here because "the present generation is too intelligent to be tricked into war." Will Rogers wrote that the climate even made politicians obsolete. "We lost Roosevelt TR, a tough blow. But here we are still kicking. So, if we can spare men like Roosevelt and Wilson there is no use in any other politician ever taking himself serious."

Yet amidst what appeared to be prosperity, the wages of the average worker were actually dropping. The rich got richer while the working class scraped to make ends meet. The F. W. Woolworth Company reported profit margins of 20 percent but actually lowered the wages of salesgirls in its stores, citing the need for belt tightening. Congress passed the Fordney-McCumber Act in 1922, strengthening the protective tariffs that had been in place for a generation. This bill gave the president the power to adjust tariffs on those imports deemed to be selling too cheaply in United States. This measure angered many allies, and some, such as France, rethought the repayment of their war debts to the United States. Why repay if the United States was hurting their ability to export cheaply?

The good times were marred by Prohibition, although celebrating was certainly not put on hold. Prohibition appealed to those who believed that the United States was on the straight and narrow, although the reality was quite different. Bootlegging became the largest underground business in the country. Herbert Hoover, secretary of commerce under Calvin Coolidge and an advocate of free trade, was also well known for his emphasis on American family values in his speeches and writings. It was not long before he became the butt of many jokes equating the seemingly good times with strong family values. He was parodied on many occasions. One of them ran:

> 'Twas the night before Christmas
> And all through the house
> Not a creature was sleeping,
> Not even a mouse.
> The glasses were set on the
> mantle with care.
> In the hope that the bootlegger
> Would soon be there.[1]

Xenophobia was on the rise, especially when foreigners were suspected of being Communists or anarchists. Sacco and Vanzetti were convicted of murder in part because they were suspected of unproven seditious activities. The Ku Klux Klan's membership soared into the millions, while in Tennessee the Scopes monkey trial pitted William Jennings Bryan, the former silver advocate, against Clarence Darrow. That was not the only appearance that Bryan made. He was also employed by Florida real estate developers to tout the virtues of buying a plot of land in that state. The Florida land bubble, and subsequent bust, was the first great speculative debacle of the decade.

While the country busied itself with numerous diversions, the decade witnessed the greatest growth in mergers yet. Acquisition-minded companies exploited the vague language of the Clayton Act to their full advantage. The number of companies swallowed by others increased almost twenty times over between 1918 and 1929. Of the top fifty mergers, almost half were between power companies. Railways and oil companies ran a strong second. The political climate certainly helped. Andrew W. Mellon was treasury secretary under all three Republican administrations of the decade. Before his appointment, Mellon and his brother Richard invested $150,000 and launched the Aluminum Company of America, dubbed the "aluminum trust," eventually selling it to Schwab's Bethlehem Steel for a profit of over $17 million. Andrew Mellon was the first "monopolist" to assume the job of treasury secretary, an appointment that would have been unimaginable during the administrations of Roosevelt and Wilson.

The 1920s became the decade of retailing, radio, and banking. Manufacturing certainly continued to grow, as did most sectors of the economy, but businesses linked to the retail sector witnessed the greatest growth. The public was better-educated, listened to their new radios, and read more than ever before. *Reader's Digest* and the Book of the Month Club both were founded to provide their subscribers with reading material at home. Fox Theaters swallowed up many smaller local cinemas to become the largest amusement business in the country. General Motors overtook Ford as the largest producer of automobiles, forcing Ford to cut prices on its somewhat dated Model T. By 1924 its price was only $290, almost $700 lower than it had been in 1910. Over thirteen million autos were registered by 1923. Car manufacturers with names like Whippet and Hupmobile offered a full line of models, advertising in the national newspapers. In 1925 Dillon Read, a New York investment bank, helped finance a $140 million cash offer for the Dodge Brothers auto company, a deal notable for the absence of watered stock and other noncash incentives. Significantly, between 1922 and 1929 little activity occurred on the antitrust front. After

By Ding. © *Des Moines Register*, 1927. Reprinted with permission.

the economy rebounded from the severe recession of 1921–22, not much effort was made to curb business growth; instead it was encouraged as an antidote to the effects of the war and the slowdown. A boom developed unlike any before it. The more rancorous arguments about who was controlling the reins of production were temporarily put on hold.

The good times unfolding in the 1920s were not the only reason that antitrust activity began to slow. Other than the Sherman and Clayton Acts and some interpretations by the Supreme Court, which were quickly circumvented by big business, the Progressive movement and other critics of business combinations had fallen short in their quest to control the direction of American business in general. The period was one full of writings on the new subject of management. Hundreds of new books appeared concerned with productivity and efficiency in business, but the political movement had no real response. It was still committed to fighting the inequities of big business with precept only—a risky proposition in a period of industrial and technological advances. Many of the Mugwumps, Populists, and Progressives were theoreticians of a new age, but they remained mostly critics of the status quo in society rather than present a blueprint for reform accompanied by a specific plan of action. In the mid-1930s Thurman Arnold, later to head the antitrust division of the Justice Department, wrote of the Progressive Age that "the reason why these attacks [against big business] always ended with a ceremony of atonement, but few practical results, lay in the fact that there were no new organizations growing up [on the reforming side]. . . . The opposition was . . . well supplied with orators and economists, but it lacked practical organizers. Preaching . . . simply resulted in counterpreaching."[2]

In 1922 a Supreme Court case resulted in an extraordinary bit of good luck for America's pastime, helping set the tone for antitrust activity—or rather, the lack of it—for the rest of the decade. The Federal Baseball League, a new rival to the established American and National Leagues, sued the National League, claiming that professional baseball monopolized the market for players, violating the Sherman Act. Once a player signed on with one of the teams in either league, it was difficult if not impossible for him to jump leagues. The Federal League saw this as restraint of interstate trade, in violation of the antitrust law. But the Supreme Court saw it differently. In a unanimous decision, the Court ruled that players who crossed state lines to play for different teams were not engaged in production, only in playing. As a result, their actions did not involve interstate commerce and did not fall under the scope of the Sherman Act. The decision was unanimous and delivered by Oliver Wendell Holmes. Somewhat unexpectedly, the decision stood for decades, exempting major league baseball from the antitrust act. While not one of the Court's most important decisions, it certainly became one of its best-known.

Other 1920s cases had more of an impact upon business. In the 1925 case *Wolff Packing Co. v. Kansas,* the Court broke a trend established by the Court nine years earlier in *German Alliance Insurance Co. v. Kansas.* In that case, the Supreme Court ruled that Kansas indeed could regulate insurance rates within its boundaries. The case established that insurance was in the public interest. This case established a broad definition of a "public utility." Following this doctrine, Kansas in 1920 declared food manufacturing and preparation an industry in the public interest. Wolff objected, declaring that it was just a private business. The Court unanimously upheld the verdict in favor of the company, declaring that no monopoly existed and therefore there was no reason for state regulation. A state legislature could not regulate an industry simply by declaring that a "public interest" existed. The concept of public interest in the case was set forth by Chief Justice Taft, whose vague opinion left the definition of public interest wide open.[3] However, the result of *Wolff* was to discourage the idea that states could determine which businesses operated in the public interest. Not until the New Deal would industry be challenged on this front.

The state of business in the 1920s suggested to many that competition was on the wane. The merger boom and the emergence of mass retailers and advanced production techniques put considerable pressure on small businessmen, many of whom folded their tents. The number of companies with huge capitalizations increased dramatically from 1900 to 1929. Standard Oil of New Jersey was still among the top five largest industrial companies, along with AT&T, the Pennsylvania Railroad, and U.S. Steel. Most were industrial companies, but public utilities also were riding the merger trend as well. Those opposing consolidation and big business in general had not fallen entirely behind, but they had changed their method of attack. They became more sophisticated and now used more analytical economic arguments than they had in the past. The prices charged by large-scale producers and their productive capacities were also being examined as never before.

Despite these critiques, Congress contributed to the emerging consolidation trend by reversing a trend toward more competitiveness in the telephone industry. Alexander Graham Bell invented the telephone in 1876, but he lacked the capital to develop his invention into a system and so sold licenses to other companies to operate local phone systems instead. The local Bell phone companies had virtual monopolies in their respective home areas, and in 1884 Bell established AT&T to provide long-distance services. Independent phone companies complained to the Justice Department and the ICC during the First World War that AT&T was in violation of the Sherman Act. As a result, AT&T entered into an agreement with the regulators not to purchase competitors and to provide connection services for companies not in the Bell system. Then in 1921 Congress passed the Willis-Graham bill, allowing AT&T to purchase competing exchanges subject to regulatory approval. The number of independents had already begun to drop during the war, and this move continued their decline. The importance of the telephone during the world war convinced many that a telephone monopoly was in the country's best interests. Clearly, the Progressive era was at an end, with officially approved consolidation taking its place at center stage.

While the economy continued to expand and companies consolidated, one group was in danger of being left behind. The plight of farmers had become an important policy issue during the Progressive era. Farming was thought of as a noble profession, tied to the nineteenth century's most valuable possession, the land. Unfortunately, it was also tied to penury in many cases, since cash flows for farmers were not particularly strong. Boom-and-bust cycles were common in farming, in part a result of crop losses due to bad weather and pests. The recession of 1921–22 hit farmers especially hard. When the rest of the economy rebounded after 1922, the agricultural sector remained in the doldrums for the rest of the decade. Many of the gains made in industry had not yet been realized by farmers, whose finances and organization were two steps behind the industrialized parts of the country. Congress stepped in on the farmers' behalf. The Capper-Volstead Act was passed in 1922, exempting agriculture from the antitrust provisions of the Sherman Act. Farmers were allowed to form cooperatives to produce and market their products. The very idea of a cooperative seemed to clash with American ideas about competitiveness and fair play, but farmers argued that big business engaged in the same practice under the table through suppliers' agreements and transportation deals with railroads, and the government was powerless to refuse the farmers' demands because of the central role that agriculture played in the economy. The Progressive movement also backed farmers—one of the few major political movements to do so—but it too had changed, evolving into a liberalism attracting the urban middle class rather than representing agrarian ideas associated with the Midwest. The old Progressives, such as William Jennings Bryan, had lost their influence. As Richard Hofstadter noted, "The pathetic postwar career of Bryan himself, once the bellwether for so many of the genuine reforms, was a perfect epitome of the collapse of rural idealism and the shabbiness of the evangelical mind."⁴ Fortunately for business, that collapse of evangelical spirit also meant there were fewer ridiculing cartoons and acerbic journalists out to make a reputation at the expense of capitalists.

During the Taft administration a system began to be put into place to provide farmers with more equitable access to capital. The measures were long overdue. In the past, farmers had paid more for their mortgages than did city dwellers, and the rates varied widely nationwide—the closer a farmer was to the East Coast, the cheaper his mortgage was. Finally, during Wilson's second administration a credit act was passed to make farm financing more uniform through a federally financed board called the Federal Farm Bank. The Farm Credit System was also established. Wilson noted that "the farmers . . . have occupied hitherto a singular position of disadvantage. They have not had the same freedom to get credit on their real estate that others have had who were in manufacturing and commercial enterprises." When the bill was signed into law, that disadvantage began to disappear. The bonds sold by the new Farm Credit System required government help because Wall Street was not interested; the government provided a guarantee and made the bonds tax exempt to entice investors. However, another problem loomed on the immediate horizon that would quickly test the new system's resources. A severe drought triggered a farm crisis that did not abate for years. By the early 1930s, the farm belt would be eroded by a severe drought that created the images used by John Steinbeck in *The Grapes of Wrath*.

Treating farmers in a favorable manner set a precedent that would be repeated during the Depression years and again after World War II. Farming also became an issue in the struggle over the future of the Wilson Dam at Muscle Shoals, Alabama, when nitrate production and hydroelectric power for the Tennessee Valley was discussed during the Harding administration. The groundwork had already been laid for government-recognized monopolies that would dominate certain sectors of the economy, although at the time it appeared to be nothing more than another chapter in the battle against monopolists intent upon extending their reach into new and promising areas for profit. Farming itself was not a target for monopolists, but there were other issues surrounding it that made alluring targets for business consolidators. Although these issues would combine to form the major political preoccupation of the decade, other consumer-oriented affairs captured the public's imagination—and the attention of big business.

GONE SHOPPING

At the time of World War I, most shopping in America was a local affair, with consumers buying the necessities of life from local merchants in relatively small shops. Retailing on a large scale had begun to develop after the Civil War, but it was not until the 1920s that the industry began to merchandise on a massive scale, with stores opening branches and crossing state lines to capture other markets. John Wanamaker, Rowland H. Macy, Aaron Montgomery Ward, and Richard Sears and Alvah Roebuck all opened merchandising establishments in the nineteenth century, and they slowly began to grow larger over the years. Their strategies were different, but they all achieved huge success. Macy's became New York's best-known department store, while Wanamaker served Philadelphia. Montgomery Ward was based in Chicago and added a new dimension to selling by expanding into the mail-order catalogue business, selling to farmers who could not regularly come to town to shop. It billed itself as the "original Grange supply house," evoking a familiar farm name, and shipped goods to its customers via the railroad, ironically evoking other not-so-fond memories of the past. Sears Roebuck, also located in Chicago, sold via catalogues as well. Soon operations like these accounted for over 25 percent of retail sales in the country. The department stores and direct mail merchandisers revolutionized the way selling was done by buying in large lots, and their profits showed the strategy to be a smart one. In one of the most widely read analyses of American economic life in the 1920s and early 1930s, Adolf Berle and Gardiner Means argued in *Modern Corporation and Private Property* that "the rate of growth of these chain stores is so far in excess of the growth of total retail sales as to represent a noteworthy encroachment of corporate upon private enterprise in distribution." Retailing was only one of many industries that would come under scrutiny for the effect they were having upon American everyday economic life.

The department stores were not the only ones showing great growth. The Great Atlantic & Pacific Tea Company bought up thousands of smaller grocery stores to become the first great supermarket chain. Its success spawned dozens of others. Piggly Wiggly stores dotted the South, traditionally a stronghold for family-run businesses. Woolworth's continued to expand, bringing the five-and-dime concept nationwide and reducing prices in the process. Chains of tobacco-related stores, such as the United Cigar Stores company run by George Whelan, opened nationwide, often with initial help from the big tobacco companies. They became the forerunners of the convenience store of later years. Whelan became very wealthy as a result and often spent his leisure time aboard his yacht with Billy Durant. He attributed over 70 percent of his sales to tobacco products and the rest to chewing gum and safety razors.

The distribution of goods had changed substantially, and the mundane retailing business suddenly became one of the most profitable in the country. But even in retailing, an element of speculation was never far from the surface. Expanding stores meant finding land to put them on. Often that was an excuse for simply buying land for a quick gain, not for a store location. Land speculation was the first great bubble of the 1920s, followed by the stock market rally. George Whelan's United Cigar Stores were engaged in the speculative bubble that surrounded Florida real estate. Clearly, investors of all sorts, from the uninitiated to professional swindlers, were having a try at Florida property. "We are cashing in on real estate in Florida and will have a profit there of $4 million or $5 million," Whelan boasted.[5] The bubble burst in 1927, leaving many penniless, after a couple of hurricanes swept the state.

Marketing, previously confined to the newspapers, grew to have a national scope, as it paid to advertise nationwide now that customers could find many goods in their favorite chain store. Advertising became a $3 billion industry for the first time in 1925, a level that would not be seen again until 1946. General Motors spent $15 million on ads in 1926 alone. Just how ingrained promotion had become was shown in the success of adman

Bruce Barton's 1925 book *The Man Nobody Knows,* in which he portrayed Jesus Christ and his apostles as the first true success stories in selling. In a country strongly influenced by fundamental Christian principles, no one seemed to take offense. Senator George Norris of Nebraska recognized the phenomenon when he said that "the early twenties brought the American people to their knees in worship, at the shrine of private business and industry."

The new selling methods among the retailers also brought suspicions and charges of price collusion. The large stores and chains were able to offer better prices to their customers than the smaller, local retailers. The concept of economies of scale took on a new application. Producers clamored to supply chains such as Sears and Montgomery Ward, but suppliers often were forced to deal exclusively with the chain or risk losing their contracts. It was unreasonable to accuse the new store combinations of monopoly concentrations at the marketing level, but the stores were suspected of making unreasonable demands upon their suppliers. However, it would take another ten years for Congress to react to this new method of reducing competition. In the interim, the country reveled in the new consumerism, and a new economic fact of life became entrenched. Two-thirds of the economy was driven by consumption. In order for it to remain at that level, selling needed to become an even more advanced art, and consumer access to the stores was vital.

The advertising and selling phenomenon was not confined to retailing. Financial services began selling their message of riches through the stock market to a new army of investors. Capitalizing on a wave of mergers that joined quite a few brokers to large banks in the war years, many banks now had their own brokerage subsidiaries. The National City Bank of New York, through its subsidiary the National City Company, began an all-out assault on the public's increasing appetite for securities. The bank ran ads in the major newspapers and magazines with captions like "I Shouldn't Have to Do It Alone," meaning that the investor had plenty of help available from a National City broker. Many of the banks produced literature designed to educate investors on the intricacies of stocks and bonds. What was less apparent, however, was the fact that many of those investors were sold securities that the banks had a vested interest in, namely, securities underwritten and held by the banks themselves. Investors were not aware that the banks were selling them their own inventories, many times at greatly inflated prices. At other times the risks associated with many of the bonds sold by bank subsidiaries were not made clear to their buyers.

THE MAGIC BOX

Selling to the public was aided immeasurably by the widespread use of the radio. The "wireless" became the first great communications breakthrough of the century. In many ways, it was also one of the most improbable. Technically, the invention owed its direct origins to Guglielmo Marconi, the Italian engineer who did the most to develop the concept. But on the industrial side, it owed at least as much to a Russian Jewish immigrant whose vision for a "musical box" never wavered. As a result of David Sarnoff's idea, the radio became the great technological breakthrough that combined scientific ingenuity with organizational expertise. It quickly became the most popular item on the household's list of must-have items, and it revolutionized life in the 1920s.

Sarnoff came to the United States from Russia as a child. After settling with his family in New York, he took a job with the American Marconi Wireless Telegraphy Company around the turn of the century as an office boy for $5 per week. He progressed through the ranks until fate vaulted him into the public eye in 1912. He was the first person on land to pick up radio signals from the sinking *Titanic* in the North Atlantic, and he promptly conveyed the message around the world. For a brief time he was the sole source of information about the sinking and the rescue of survivors as he manned his radio in New York. He duly reported the names of the survivors as they were pulled out of the ocean and transmitted by rescue ships. That alone was significant because the *Titanic*'s maiden voyage carried many well-known industrialists, politicians, and members of British and American society. John Jacob Astor was one of its many victims.

After the war, radio telephony (as it was then known) came to the attention of the Defense Department. Of equal strategic interest was the possibility that the British Marconi Company was actively seeking a worldwide monopoly on wireless transmission. If it succeeded, the United States would be at the mercy of a foreign power. An all-American company was needed to develop the technology for the United States. As a result, General Electric took over the development of the necessary technology from AT&T and became the early industry leader. But in order to do so, it would need help on technical and production matters. The Radio Corporation of America was established in 1919, and its major founding shareholders were the former American Marconi Company, Westinghouse Electric, General Electric, and AT&T, as well as the United Fruit Company. The chairman of the board was Owen Young. Sarnoff was a manager of the company. United Fruit, an improbable member of a technology pool, contributed capital because it saw radio communications as an efficient way of keeping in touch with its far-flung empire in Central America and the Caribbean. RCA was able to gain an enormous advantage almost from the start because it pooled its own patents with those of its partners and used them to its technical advantage. But despite all of the talent of the companies involved, the new company relied heavily upon Sarnoff's vision of a new wireless product that possessed far greater commercial potential than military applications alone—a wireless device that could receive broadcasts of music and other events. The technology was already generally known, but it was his insistence that RCA produce it on a mass scale that gave the idea its impetus. The first broadcasting station was improvised in 1920 by Westinghouse from its own engineers' designs to report the presidential election. This became station WDKA in Pittsburgh. The first truly important broadcast was the report of Warren Harding's victory in the 1920 presidential election. Shortly thereafter, Sarnoff proposed that RCA broadcast the heavyweight title fight between Jack Dempsey, the reigning champion, and French challenger Georges Carpentier in Jersey City. Sarnoff quickly improvised by erecting temporary broadcasting facilities in Hoboken, New Jersey, at the last minute, allowing the broadcast to proceed. The event was a great success and the first sporting contest ever broadcast. In 1920 the first licensed radio broadcasting station began operating, WWJ in Detroit. Coverage of the World Series and college football soon followed. By the summer of 1922 the first commercial was broadcast over WEAF in New York City, touting apartments in Queens. The Scopes trial in Tennessee was carried nationwide, making it the most celebrated trial of the decade.

Within three years, radio's phenomenal growth was apparent. The *American Review of Reviews* stated that "it would be a commonplace to say that when wireless telephoning became practical, about the year 1914, no one dreamed that its use would ever be general or popular." Yet within a three-year period over five hundred stations had been licensed, and more were on the way. Consumers bought over two and a half million radios within a four-year period. RCA, by now producing radios called Radiolas, grossed almost $200 million during the decade and reaped profits of nearly $20 million. The first great communications revolution of the century had begun, and no one was quite sure of where it would lead.

Wireless technology developed at a stunning pace. RCA sent the first wireless telegraph transmission of a photograph in 1924. Two years later it teamed up with the British post office and AT&T to conduct the first transatlantic telephone conversation. Shortly thereafter the first national broadcasting network was established by the National Broadcasting Company in 1926. The Columbia Broadcasting System followed in 1927. Recognizing that federal control of the airwaves was necessary, President Coolidge signed the Radio Control Act into law in 1927, creating five zones in the country, each with a commissioner at its helm.[6] In 1928 merger talks between RCA and the Victor Talking Machine Company of Camden, New Jersey, began with an eye toward producing recording equipment for the broadcasting company. The *New York Times* reported that "the Victor Company has entered into contracts which make available the cooperation of the Radio Corporation, the American Telephone and Telegraph Company, the Western Electric Company, the General Electric Company, and the Westinghouse Electric and Manufacturing Company. All of which are reported to be in force at the present time."[7] The pooling arrangement was the sort that was well known in antitrust circles but was politically difficult to prosecute. By combining their various strengths, these companies came close to creating a vertically integrated structure that caused suspicion among the regulators. That radio was integrally involved in the national defense made it difficult to pursue the pool. RCA was later sued by the United States and agreed to end the pooling practice, but it helped the company establish itself as the industry leader from the beginning.

Sarnoff was another in a long line of immigrants to leave an indelible imprint upon American business, a line that included Alexander Graham Bell and Andrew Carnegie, among others. Radio would continue to grow rapidly until another new product, only at its very beginning in the 1920s, began to make inroads as well. When television became the next major technological breakthrough, RCA would again be in the forefront. Both industries began to attract antitrust attention as they grew, but their appeal to both consumers and the military insulated them from some of the criticism that other businesses attracted.

TURN ON THE POWER

While retailing, broadcasting, manufacturing, and a myriad of other businesses were merging to serve the new, affluent nationwide market, the greatest consolidation of the decade came in the utilities that provided electric power. Still a luxury before the world war, power came into its own in the 1920s. Electric power production followed the same pattern as other industries. In the forty years since Edison opened the first power generating station at Pearl Street in New York City, near Wall Street, the industry had been transformed. In order to be competitive, it had to grow in terms of size and efficiency. But power production clashed with government interests on more than one occasion. Who should provide this source of energy and at what cost? Should rates be uniform or vary? The idea of "public" began to creep into the utility realm. The Federal Power Commission was created in 1920 but, due to the political climate, found itself with little to do. It may have been slightly ahead of its time, since the great power company consolidations still lay ahead. Nevertheless, the 1920s witnessed an increasing debate over the rates charged to the public and the amount of power generation concentrated in a few hands.

A stronger government presence changed the complexion of the debate. In the fifty years since the railroad debate began, government's increased presence meant that the issue was no longer *whether* big businesses, especially those that were particularly capital-intensive, should be regulated. The newer question was how much they should be regulated and even whether the federal government should be a direct partner or simply a watchdog. The idea that government should somehow participate in enterprises was anathema to the business community, but the idea had much support in Progressive political circles. Experiences from the past were playing a real part in determining how to deal with the future. There was much agreement that a recipe for regulation was needed, but the exact mix still had not been agreed upon. The later 1920s would help settle the question.

Prior to World War I, electric power was produced by small companies. The vast utility empires were formed in the early and mid-1920s, amalgamating the smaller companies under umbrellalike holding companies. Like the railroads before them, the utility holding companies were organized simply as shell companies that owned others. This was done in order to circumvent the restrictions placed upon them by the FTC. Holding companies could not be directly accused of restricting competition simply because they held the stock of competing companies. A holding company normally issued capital in the form of stocks, bonds, and nonvoting preferred stock, and sometimes there was as little as several thousand shares controlling a vast utility empire. A Federal Trade Commission study revealed that the Associated Gas and Electric System controlled over two hundred operating companies with capital of over $1 billion. Two men ran the entire operation.

During Coolidge's administration, the FTC acquired Republican commissioners who were not sympathetic to the idea of an active agency intruding into business. One of Coolidge's appointees, William Humphrey, a Republican congressman from Ohio, considered the FTC an "instrument of oppression" and quickly set out to ensure that it took a less active affair in pursuing business combinations. The commission began to undertake "studies" of alleged violations rather than prosecutions. One of them, a seven-year probe into the public utilities industry, would lead to radical changes in the way power was produced in the 1930s, but only after Humphrey's tenure had ended. The new force behind the study was Robert E. Healy, who became chief counsel to the FTC in 1928.

The greatest growth for utilities was in providing power to homes rather than businesses. The average customer was using more electricity every year, and residential use, which once had lagged behind business use, accounted for half of all demand by the late 1920s. Also in this decade Congress passed bills designed to improve public health by raising housing standards. One section of the country was in particular need because of low per capita income of its population and decades of governmental neglect. This was a vast tract of land in the South around the Tennessee River basin, commonly known as Muscle Shoals, named after a town in

Alabama. Its history was one of poverty and exploitation since the days of Reconstruction. But it was also rich in natural resources, especially nitrates, which had wartime applications in explosives and a peacetime use in fertilizers.

Muscle Shoals was the site of a nitrate plant built during the war. Also at Muscle Shoals was the Wilson Dam, a government project begun during World War I but never completed. The original cost to the government for both was almost $85 million, and the maintenance costs were very high as well. For several years they sat idle while the political football was passed around Washington. Then in the early 1920s activity began again as some elements in Congress wanted to use private interests to develop them in order to provide cheap electricity and fertilizer for the area. Former secretary of war and one-time presidential aspirant Newton Baker emphasized its importance when he said, "I would rather control Muscle Shoals than to be continuously elected President of the United States." Governor Al Smith of New York, when accepting the Democratic nomination for president in 1928, recognized the importance of Muscle Shoals when he asserted, "It will be the policy of my administration while retaining government ownership and control, to develop a method of operation for Muscle Shoals which will reclaim some fair revenue from the enormous expenditure already made for its development and which is now a complete waste."[8] The area thus became a battleground for government and the private sector in a classic confrontation over who knew what was best for whom.

The Harding administration put the projects up for public bids soon after taking office. The Republican philosophy at the time was that private industry, not the federal government, should take up projects in the public interest, and big business was definitely interested. Liberals in Congress felt the project should not be left in private hands. A chief advocate of government intervention in Muscle Shoals was Senator George Norris of Nebraska, who was also instrumental in exposing the Teapot Dome scandal that plagued the Harding administration, and who sponsored numerous bills in the 1920s designed to provide for government operation of electric power plants.

In 1921 Henry Ford offered to operate the dam to provide electricity for the area; he claimed to be interested in the project for the good of rural farmers, who would benefit from the fertilizer to be produced there. Others saw a less altruistic motive. Ford's real objective, according to his critics, was not fertilizer production but the power facilities: He actually hoped to get into the power business through the back door with government assistance. A close ally of Norris, fellow liberal Gifford Pinchot, put it bluntly. "The Ford plan," he stated, "is seven parts waterpower, one part fertilizer." The type of nitrate production that Muscle Shoals supplied had become obsolete when the Germans developed an alternative, called the Haber process, during the war. But if Muscle Shoals represented outdated technology in fertilizer production, its capacity to produce electricity was enormous. Ford's offer aroused vocal opposition. He had requested a one-hundred-year lease on the properties, almost doubling the standard fifty years that the government normally considered. Norris responded by saying that "the most effective help to save the people from such a monopoly would be to have the federal government own at least some of the power producing elements that enter into such a system."[9]

Even others in the power business voiced their misgivings about Ford's offer, although it may have been out of fear of Ford as a competitor rather than because of economics. James B. Duke, the tobacco king who was then president of the Southern Company, a regional power utility, agreed with the auto magnate when he said that "the trouble with Muscle Shoals is that it is in no situation to reach or establish industries to absorb its power and pay interest on the investment under fifty years of development . . . but I would not take it as a gift today. . . . I would take it on Ford's basis, where the Government gives him $50 million and he pays only 5 percent on $28 million a year."[10] Duke certainly understood the economics of producing power. He had been involved with hydroelectric plants in the South since 1904, before the breakup of American Tobacco. Originally introduced to power production in South Carolina by his family physician, Duke hired a young engineer and provided 50 percent of the money originally needed to finance a power production facility. Within a year, his investments expanded and the Southern Company was founded. The investments in power appeared to be the desire of an active business mind to seek new areas for investment, not to extend monopoly practices into other areas. The engineer, W. S. Lee, recalled that Duke was able to make decisions about spending millions of dollars on capital developments without blinking an eye. "I do not recall that there were ever any formal or written instructions given me during my many years of association with Mr. Duke," Lee remarked. "It was his policy to designate one man to begin with and complete a thing rather than start a debating society or hold a town meeting over it. His friends often said that 'action was his middle name.'"[11]

Ford's bid was supported by both the Republican House and the Senate but died when a conference committee run by Norris failed to act upon it two years later. Ford finally withdrew his bid in 1924. Ford himself said in 1926, "We don't want Muscle Shoals now because we can produce power elsewhere just as cheaply," a tacit acknowledgment that nitrates had been a secondary objective. This was confirmed elsewhere: In 1927 the peripatetic publisher of the *Wall Street Journal*, Clarence Barron, was in Florida talking to a vice president of the Corn Products Company who bragged that his company was a better investment than that of its competitor Allied Chemical. The journalist disagreed. Barron wrote that "after ten years of experiment [Allied] is now to build a giant plant that will make nitrogen from the air [the Haber process] cheaper than the government or anybody could make it with Muscle Shoals as a gift."[12] As a nitrate producer, Muscle Shoals literally was on the rocks.

The property speculation in Tennessee that developed around Ford's bid was bubblelike. When the first hint of private ownership was suggested, a land boom developed similar to the one raging in Florida. Real estate hustlers hired special trains to bring potential buyers from as far away as New York City to show them the virtues of country living. Swindles abounded as a result. Senator Norris said that he did not blame Henry Ford for the fiasco, but others were not as certain. Many who lost money in the deals did blame Norris for his opposition, however. On one of his visits to Muscle Shoals, the man who escorted the senator happened to be carrying a pistol. When Norris asked why the man needed a gun, his escort replied, "I know of these land sales and I would be distressed beyond words, if, while you were under my guidance, some fool should take a shot at you in order to have what he feels to be his revenge." But Ford still remained correct on one score that would come to be borne out in several years' time: "The destiny of the American people for years to come lies here on the Tennessee River," he commented while his bid was still being

ANOTHER "GEORGE W." TRYING TO CROSS THE DELAWARE.

By Berryman. *Washington Evening Star*, 1931.

considered. He could not have foreseen the development of the Tennessee Valley Authority during the New Deal, however.

The lack of progress made on Muscle Shoals plus suspicions about a "power trust" finally led to a congressional investigation. In January 1928 the Senate Committee on Interstate Commerce opened hearings to discuss a resolution introduced by Senator Thomas Walsh of Montana calling for an investigation of the light and power industry. Senator Norris gave the hearings his full support. He stated that "the charge has been made . . . that there exists in the United States today a trust of gigantic proportions which controls the generation and distribution of electricity by water power." The claim was also made that this group was responsible for blocking specific corrective measures for Muscle Shoals because of their narrow self-interests. Indeed, the industry unleashed fierce propaganda in the 1920s against Muscle Shoals as well as state attempts to block consolidations in smaller utilities. Everywhere that private interests were involved in power production, the result was the same: They either produced specious arguments designed to kill off unwanted government intrusion or charged higher costs than municipally run utilities. Norris cited the examples of Los Angeles and San Francisco in 1924 to make his point. Los Angeles was supplied by municipally generated power, while San Francisco's came from private sources. Despite the fact that Los Angeles was in a desert environment, its power was cheaper than that supplied to San Francisco. His conclusion in supporting the hearings was clear. Speaking of Los Angeles, he stated, "We have seen this vast combination in the public utility industry grow from a 13 billion kilowatt hour proposition in 1914 to one of 59 billion kilowatt hours in 1925. . . . We have watched its gross revenues from the sale of electrical energy jump from $336 million in 1914 to $1.47 billion in 1925. . . . Nothing more clearly indicates the vast importance of the problem."[13]

Congress responded by passing two bills providing for public ownership of Muscle Shoals, but both were vetoed, one by Coolidge and the other by Herbert Hoover. When officially blocking the second bill in 1931, Hoover said, "I am firmly opposed to the government entering into any business the major purpose of which is competition with our citizens. . . . If the preoccupation of its official is to be no longer the promotion of justice and equal opportunity but is to be barter in the markets . . . that is not liberalism, it is degeneration." Hoover intervened in a conservative manner to block government-owned utility production when Franklin Roosevelt was governor of New York and a leading presidential contender for the Democrats in the 1932 election.

Roosevelt's battle with the utilities groups in New York symbolized the nationwide contest between government and the giant utility holding companies. As the 1920s began, the states carried the banner in the fight with the utility monopolies, just as they had done several decades before in the battle with the railroads. Once again, industry leaders and financiers bonded together to form monopolistic combinations while the state governments struggled to keep up. New York was a prime example. Earlier in the century it had granted the Aluminum Company of America the rights to power production on the St. Lawrence River. Over the years, the Mellon-led company did not develop the river or add any value to it, as it was mandated to do by the agreement. Eventually a Democratic New York state assembly, with Franklin Roosevelt as a member, revoked the company's rights. That began a long and often arduous battle between the Democrats, including the future president, and the trusts operating in and around the state. By the presidential election of 1932, the issue still was not resolved.

When he became governor, FDR inquired about the feasibility of state ownership and operation of power stations based upon hydroelectric power from the St. Lawrence. He was also interested in transmitting that power directly to users to counter the large power monopolies being formed in the state. The Niagara-Hudson Power corporation was being formed with capital of over $500 million, and he feared that the new company, which was financed by Morgan interests and was to become a part of the mammoth United Corporation, would be able to dictate rates charged for electricity. Roosevelt studied the rates being paid by New York residents and discovered they were among the highest in the country. A family living in Manhattan paid on average about $17 per month, while in Albany the charge was $19. In Buffalo, just across from Canada, the rate was $7.80, while a family in Ontario, where the provincial government took a role in electricity generation, paid only $2.79.[14] The conclusions were clear: Power provided by state and municipal authorities was cheaper than that from private sources.

There was also suspicion of a personal vendetta between Franklin Roosevelt and power companies in particular. Some utility company executives noted that Roosevelt seemed to be attacking holding companies more than the power industry itself. A common rumor at the time held that before he decided to run for governor in 1928, Roosevelt had asked his friend Howard Hopson of Associated Gas and Electric for an executive job. Hopson had turned him down. Hopson was one of the two men who oversaw some two hundred utility companies. Roosevelt, it was said, never forgave him for the slight, and this formed the basis for his attacks on the holding companies thereafter.[15] Generally, however, Roosevelt's position on utilities was consistent prior to the presidential election of 1932 and helped advance his credentials as a liberal reformer and enemy of big business. Walter Lippmann remarked that FDR's position "exhibited, it seems to me, an exceptional grasp of the main principles."

The public utility structure certainly appeared to be monopolistic. Giant companies dominated power production. The Southern Company, headed by James B. Duke, and Middle West Utilities, led by Samuel Insull, were two of the largest power companies in the country. The Morgan group included Niagara Mohawk, Consolidated Edison, and Public Service of New Jersey. For years Insull had been known as being in favor of monopoly in the power industry at the expense of competition. He was on record as having said that "regulation must be followed by protection and . . . regulation and protection naturally lead to monopoly."[16] Remarks like that tipped the balance against him early in the battle with Congress. Senator Norris reflected upon his battle with the power trust and categorized it as "the greatest monopolistic corporation that has been organized for private greed. . . . It has bought and sold legislatures. It has interested itself in the election of public officials, from school directors to the President of the United States."[17] Norris was referring mainly to Insull, whom he suspected of influencing dozens of elections around Chicago. New Deal figure Harold Ickes once referred to Insull as a "great and colorful figure from the American stage . . . even if he was dangerous to our economic well-being and a threat to our American institutions." That was something of a compliment from someone whom Insull once referred to as "an unsuccessful newspaper reporter who married money."

The examination of the power trust was based mainly upon hearings that the FTC held over a seven-year period ending in 1935. An amendment was added to the Walsh bill directing the FTC to conduct the investigation rather than the Senate, as originally proposed. Matters were exacerbated by some anti-utility propaganda disseminated by Gifford Pinchot as the FTC investigation began. In a pamphlet he had produced, Pinchot claimed that the power industry was dominated by a monopoly that controlled most of the power production in the country. The problem with his exposé, widely printed in the national newspapers, was that his case was overstated and did not quite coincide with the facts. Added to that was the anti-Insull position taken by the Hearst newspapers, which regularly reported on the FTC hearings. An example of the inflammatory reporting was found in an article written by M. L. Ramsay, a Hearst reporter, about an apparently benign attempt by the Insull organization to present its views on Muscle Shoals to Senator Carter Glass of Virginia. The article ran under the headline "Senator Glass Threatened by Power Trust," suggesting that sinister forces were being used by the Insull group.[18] As time wore on and the hearings proceeded, the newspapers tended to sensationalize them. Utilities, and especially those run by Insull, were accused of all sorts of machinations, from sponsoring the publication of school textbooks that treated them favorably to the wholesale buying of state politicians. Senator James Reed's committee investigating campaign finances questioned Insull at length about his generous contributions to Republican politicians during the 1920s. Insull freely admitted that he was extremely generous with many of them but also disingenuously claimed that he was often not clear about what policies they supported. After the Reed committee revelations, one recipient of Insull's largesse, the chairman of the Illinois Commerce Commission, was prevented from taking a U.S. Senate seat he had won.

In 1935 the Public Utility Holding Company Act was passed and the Tennessee Valley Authority was created, but not before some acrimonious exchanges and investigations had taken place. The power trust was linked historically to the General Electric Company, founded by Thomas Edison with the assistance of Samuel Insull in the nineteenth century. But Edison sold out shortly thereafter and Insull moved west to Chicago, leaving Morgan in control of General Electric. Duke's position at the Southern Power Company helped strengthen the fears that the old-guard monopolists had simply found other areas to pillage and plunder. There was a fair amount of evidence that this was indeed the case. The FTC stated in a report on utilities in 1927 commissioned by Congress that the General Electric Company was the largest single utility in the country, producing about 12 percent of the nation's power. No other utility came close to that amount. But the report noted that concentrations of utilities were increasing in all regions of the country.

Insull was the utilities baron of the Midwest, where he controlled Middle West Utilities from his Chicago base. An immigrant from Britain, Insull had gone to work for Edison as a business assistant before the

By McCutcheon. *Chicago Tribune*, 1927. Reprinted with permission.

inventor became famous. He turned to the Midwest when the Morgan coup forced him out of Edison General Electric in the 1880s. For the remainder of his career, which lasted until the Depression and the Senate hearings into stock exchange practices in 1933, he remained in Chicago, although his power companies were widespread. His vast empire and his largesse made him a legend in the city. He even built an opera house reminiscent of one built in New York in the nineteenth century by Jay Gould and Jim Fisk. Most of his financing came from local sources rather than from Wall Street, which he learned not to trust after the Morgan experience. Much of his investment banking was done by Halsey Stuart and

Co., a firm not considered an insider on Wall Street. He shared a distrust of New York finance with Henry Ford, who also thought Wall Street was conspiring against him at times. Insull's power plants were extremely efficient, producing electricity at less than half the competition's prices, and his business expanded rapidly as a result. He was also generous with his employees. The holding company that he headed had relatively little common stock in existence, and most of it was closely held by the top directors. The rest of the capital was supplied by borrowing. Thus only a few people controlled this vast business. Insull bought back shares of the stock on one occasion when they were for sale and distributed them to his employees, largesse that also ensured that the company remained in local hands rather than fall into those of unfriendly predators.

The FTC hearings began to turn up clear signs of monopoly. Insull's Middle West, J. P. Morgan's United Corporation, formed only in 1928, and the Electric Bond and Share Company, a truly national system spanning over thirty states, controlled almost 50 percent of national electric production between them. The *New York Times* found enough concentration of power to imagine that in the "end will be one gigantic corporation, which will furnish power from coast to coast." Insull's companies supplied power to most western states and several Canadian provinces. Alone, they produced about 12 percent of the country's power. A power trust indeed existed and threatened to be the same sort of monopoly railways had been in the previous century. For a brief time the utilities were more powerful than the railroads had been, but the approaching Depression would put an end to their short, monopolistic rule.

REVERSING GEARS

Investing in companies via large amounts of borrowed money became a signature of the 1920s boom. It also became the signature of the bankruptcies that followed. Those not considered Wall Street favorites—Billy Durant and Samuel Insull—were among the first to fall. That fact would not be lost on the Senate investigators and other policy makers who later studied the nature of the crash and its consequences. When times became tough, bankers certainly did not always extend a helping hand to those in financial trouble.

Billy Durant's fall from grace was indicative of the frailties of the decade. It also did irreparable harm to the reputation of the businessman as the average citizen's friend. Like Insull, Durant portrayed himself as a capitalist with a human face. After his summary dismissal from GM by the du Ponts and John Raskob, he rebounded quickly and founded Durant Motors, which introduced several new auto lines within a few years and appeared successful, at least on the surface. But his sources of capital did not originate with Wall Street. He sold shares in the company directly to small investors, many of whom considered him the workingman's champion because of his well-publicized falling-out with GM. However, Durant himself took up another pastime: speculating in the stock market. He quickly became one of the largest margin traders of the decade, buying and selling large positions on borrowed money. While his gains were impressive, his losses and interest charges were also staggering. At the same time Durant Motors, although apparently successful, was heavily in debt. By the late 1920s the company's stock had dropped substantially from its original price, and Billy Durant's critics became more vocal. Many who had faith in Durant became disillusioned. One unhappy shareholder wrote from Norristown, Pennsylvania, on the stationery of the Dixie Theater, an establishment dedicated to "high class vaudeville." He wrote, "The 225 shares of the stock which myself and family hold is only a drop in the bucket but it is all we could afford and have paid for it out of hard earned money and not through speculation. . . . What advice can you offer a man who has done all in good faith whereby he might recover what is possible?"[19] After the 1929 crash, Durant himself would be asking the same question.

Toward the end of the decade, many American businesses appeared to have expanded too rapidly. Automobiles, boots and shoes, cement, newsprint, locomotives, wheat milling, and coal production were just a few of the industries that had excess capacity.[20] But the overcapacity came crashing down with the stock market in 1929, creating unemployment—and with it a banking crisis—faster than anyone would have imagined. The economy in 1929 was more closely integrated than in the past. It now had the benefit of a central bank that could allocate credit evenly, and the railroads and advances in communications helped information flow more consistently. When the crash came, it spread through all sectors with astonishing speed, becoming the first modern market crash.

Banking acquired its notoriety during the last days of the 1920s. Many competitors and upstart rivals fell upon hard times when attempting to compete with a Morgan-led or -influenced institution. Samuel Insull and John D. Rockefeller before him clearly avoided Morgan, preferring other banks for their financings instead. Insull had assiduously avoided the New York banking coterie since his experiences with Edison in the late nineteenth century. Journalist M. L. Ramsay noted the distinct difference between Insull and other utilities barons reliant upon their bankers: "Where many huge power companies and systems became virtually branches of big financial houses, with Insull his office was the main office, and the financial houses were *his* branches."[21] As a result, hostility began to brew just below the surface. As one of his bankers recalled years later, "these New York fellows were jealous of their prerogatives, and if you wanted to get along you had to be deferential to them and keep your opinions to yourself. Mr. Insull wouldn't, and that made bad blood between them. Real bad blood."[22]

As it turned out, the bad blood was the beginning of the end for Insull and his empire. Fearing a takeover of his companies by Cyrus Eaton, a financier based at Otis and Co. in Cleveland, Insull began to pyramid his companies so that he and his close associates could maintain a tight control. Initially the stock markets took a liking to the new company and bid up the price of its stock to new but unsustainable highs. It continued to perform well even after the crash in 1929, but Insull needed to borrow money to fight off Eaton and thwart his threat. The cash was pledged by the Continental Illinois Bank in Chicago, but when it came time to put up the actual cash, Continental and the other Chicago banks admitted that they had to invite other banks and Morgan interests into the deal because they found themselves short of cash. Once the New York bankers were in the deal, the handwriting was on the wall for Insull. The stock of his companies was put up as collateral for the loan, and once he was in their net they refused to let him go. Then the stock became a target during the "great bear raid" that was conducted in the 1932 market in New York.[23]

During that brief but crucial time period, the bears (those who profited on declining stock prices) took control of the New York Stock Exchange. They sold short the shares of many companies, hoping to profit from the many stocks that precipitously declined in price. Once the stocks collapsed, it was easy to take over the companies involved because creditors did not extend fresh credit to companies in poor shape. In Insull's case, his creditors moved in swiftly—in fact, some of them had conspired with the bears to drive down his stocks. From that point, Insull's empire was effectively finished. He was personally vilified by many politicians, including Franklin Roosevelt. He fled the country in 1932 for Greece, which did not have an extradition treaty with the United States. As a result, his guilt on state and federal fraud charges appeared to be proven, although he returned home a year later because of political pressure. He was eventually exonerated of the charges brought against him. The collapse of his companies represented the greatest victory that one group of monopoly capitalists had waged against another since the battles between the railroads in the nineteenth century. But the affair was not portrayed as such at the time. Being mostly invisible to the public, financiers were still able to accomplish privately what Progressives feared most—pillaging the economy without regard for the consequences, all in the name of private profit.

The utility issue never quite became the contentious issue its critics hoped for. Calling the conflict between Roosevelt and the holding companies a "war," as some writers did at the time, overstated the issue considerably, and the unraveling of Insull's empire after the crash took some of the wind out of the critics' sails. The FTC hearings continued but were eclipsed in importance by the Senate hearings studying stock market practices, dubbed the Pecora hearings after Ferdinand Pecora became their chief counsel in early 1933. But the FTC labored on. Its voluminous findings about all aspects of utility finances and organization led directly to the passing of the Public Utility Holding Company Act in 1935 by a Congress no longer willing to countenance wild pyramid structures and the looting of utility companies. If the affair could be called a war, it was a quiet one. More important for the future of the economy was the fact that the government was not willing to let utilities develop as the railroads had. Regulation was on its mind, and official legislation was just around the corner. Equally important for the development of business in general was a study that would have remained much more obscure in less turbulent times.

COUNTERATTACK

Since the 1870s, muckraking had been a popular method of bringing the activities of monopolies and trusts to the surface. The late 1920s and early 1930s were no exception. Matthew Josephson's *The Robber Barons* appeared in 1932, and Gustavus Myers' *A History of the Great American Fortunes* was reprinted in a new edition, as it had been periodically since the turn of the century. But times had changed. No one doubted the presence and the power of the trusts, but the crash proved that the fundamental American economic problem was larger than the individuals at the head of these entities, and the cult of personality surrounding business was coming to an end. The federal agencies waging regulatory battles were doing so no longer against John D. Rockefeller or Pierpont Morgan but against a group of brilliant corporate strategists who were able to fend off government incursions onto their business turfs. For every apparent government victory, business merely reorganized and continued to consolidate its grip on the economy and society. What was needed was an exposé that outlined the problem in both economic and political terms. Monopolies were difficult to argue against when they provided a superior product. But when they could be shown to pose a threat to society at large, public sentiment shifted against them.

When the counterattack came, it originated from unlikely quarters. Two Columbia University academics, Adolf A. Berle Jr. and Gardiner Means, began work on a book that was to have a profound impact upon the New Deal and American social and economic affairs in general. In 1932 they published *The Modern Corporation and Private Property*, a wide-ranging study of the effect of consolidations and mergers in industry. While their revelations were eye-opening, their ability to show the links between business and politics gave the work an appeal wider than most economics books. They effectively collected the data revealed in the Pujo hearings twenty years before and made the political connections only vaguely suggested at the time. The astonishing conclusion that the economy was still consolidating despite the antitrust laws and the birth of the federal agencies was perhaps the book's most lasting contribution to economic and legal analysis at the time.

Berle was the son of a Congregationalist minister from the Midwest.

He graduated from Harvard at the precocious age of eighteen in 1913 and went on to receive a law degree. Brandeis' reforming zeal was certainly apparent at the law school, where many future reformers were exposed to the master's antagonism toward the bankers' coterie. After graduation, he joined the Boston law firm of Brandeis, Dunbar, and Nutter. Working for Brandeis' firm provided another link between the newly appointed Supreme Court justice and those younger analysts who were to later become part of Roosevelt's New Deal Brain Trust.[24] Berle went on to become an advisor at the Versailles Peace Conference in 1919. Later he became a professor at Columbia University's law school, where he teamed with a young Harvard Ph.D. student, Means, to begin working on the book.

They argued that the consolidation of industry was changing the nature of private property. Small businesses were forced to the wall by larger corporations. The individuals who had once owned businesses had been replaced by a new generation of shareholders and professional managers. It was clear from the outset that the managers who ruled corporations did not think themselves accountable to the vast new army of shareholders. They operated as a class apart and continued to wield power over industry without any serious check upon their powers. Berle and Means wrote that "there exists a centripetal attraction which draws wealth together into aggregations of constantly increasing size, at the same time throwing control into the hands of fewer and fewer men. The trend is apparent, and no limit is as yet in sight."[25] This accrued influence was called the "concentration of economic power," a term that would reappear time and again in antitrust issues over the next two decades.

Even for the individual who sat at home unconcerned by public affairs, the concentration of economic power was something that could not be ignored. It clearly affected his everyday life. As the authors put it,

> His electricity and gas are almost sure to be furnished by one of these utility companies: the aluminum of his kitchen utensils by the Aluminum Company of America. His electric refrigerator may be the product of General Motors Company or . . . General Electric and Westinghouse. The chances are that the Crane Company has supplied his plumbing features, the American Radiator and Sanitary Corp. his heating equipment. He probably buys

at least some of his groceries from the Great Atlantic and Pacific Tea Company—a company that expected to sell one eighth of all the groceries in the country in 1930—and he secures some of his drugs . . . from the United Drug Company.[26]

Clearly the effects of the consolidated industries were extensive. Mellon, Durant, the du Ponts, and especially Morgan had an influence upon the fortunes and lives of the average citizen more penetrating than that of many politicians and other public leaders. But they were not elected, even by the shareholders of many of the corporations they effectively controlled. Yet Berle and Means rarely mentioned any of the personalities that had forged the corporate leviathans; they discussed only the companies and the extent of their influence. They concentrated upon the "cartelization" of life that went hand in hand with big business. The muckrakers had made a point of singling out industrialists such as Rockefeller or Gould, but expository writing in the 1920s was more subdued. The only contemporaries mentioned by name in the Berle and Means book were the Van Sweringen brothers, Oris and Mantis, railroad barons from Cleveland. Their railroad empire, which collapsed with the onset of the Depression, rivaled Insull's utility empire for its complexity—holding companies were piled upon other holding companies, spiced with a wide array of subsidiary companies. But for the most part, Berle and Means saw institutions, not individuals, as the problem.

Unlike many studies of monopoly and trusts that preceded theirs, Berle and Means never once used those terms but concentrated on the more general term *property*. Shareholders had become estranged from their wealth and the power that supposedly went with property, whereas the ruling class (corporate heads and managerial ranks) were separated from owners and wielded true control of property. Severe economic downturns made this obvious. Berle and Means also used statistics to a greater extent than many of their predecessors and contemporaries to prove their point, constantly emphasizing the close relations between industrial concentrations and investment banking—without ample investment banking advice, many of the mergers would not have been possible, and often investment bankers took a portion of new securities they had underwritten as compensation for their services, automatically giving themselves equity positions that they could use to influence the companies' governance. The authors' Brandeisian ax appeared to be well sharpened. Rapidly breaking events made their book an instant classic among academics and policy makers. When many of them went on to join Roosevelt's brains trust in his first administration, including Berle, the intellectual continuity previously missing in antimonopoly battles finally was provided.

The proportion of corporate wealth held by the two hundred largest nonbank corporations was very high. They controlled about 50 percent of corporate wealth and almost 25 percent of national wealth. The 150 largest corporations grew at an average rate of 7 percent per year between 1919 and 1928, with gross assets increasing from $38.7 billion to $63.4 billion. Their growth rate exceeded that of smaller companies by a wide margin.[27] The number of shareholders jumped dramatically as well. AT&T saw the size of its shareholder list increase five times over, the Pennsylvania Railroad saw its grow twice over, and U.S. Steel's increased twice over as well. In both U.S. Steel and AT&T, the largest shareholders held less than 10 percent of the combined stock. That would suggest that each company was free of undue influence by any one party. But examining the shareholder roles of large companies did not give an adequate indication of how companies were controlled, because it revealed nothing of behind-the-scenes machinations, or what Berle and Means called the "regrouping of rights." Each company was actually Morgan-influenced to a great degree: AT&T was a perennial Morgan investment banking client, while U.S. Steel was a Morgan creation. Immediately after the crash in 1929, Richard Whitney of the New York Stock Exchange strode across the floor of the New York Stock Exchange and put in a buy order for "Big Steel" in an effort to stabilize the plunging stock market. He was acting for J. P. Morgan & Company as well as for the NYSE itself, although the support operation proved short-lived. FDR's irascible secretary of the interior, Harold L. Ickes, called Whitney "an errand boy for Morgan & Company."

The largest companies, especially U.S. Steel and Standard Oil, were able to maintain a strong influence over prices that continued well into the 1930s. Because of their size and vast network of suppliers and distributors, the prices that they set for their industries became the norm. Smaller competitors broke ranks only at their own peril. In many ways, the situation had not changed much since the days of John D. Rockefeller at Standard

Oil although now the price leadership had become institutionalized. The concentration of economic power became even more evident when the banking arrangements behind these big companies were exposed. U.S. Steel, International Harvester, and AT&T, as well as many of the utility mergers of the decade, used Morgan for financing, and most had Morgan partners on their boards of directors. The publicity-shy New York bank was clearly the most powerful institution in the country.

Berle and Means' study proved to their supporters that the financial power structure needed to be attacked. Traditional antitrust legislation and regulations had not been terribly successful, and new measures were needed to prevent the country from moving into a dangerous political and economic situation where the rich would become even richer while the small shareholder and average citizen lost influence.

The mood became somber as it was clear that someone needed to pay for the country's ills. It was reasonable to assume that big business would become the scapegoat, and indeed American business and society were on the verge of the most radical transformation ever seen—but the extent of the coming reaction was never anticipated by business. In 1931, the mood was somber but not without its light side. George and Ira Gershwin wrote a musical comedy satirizing presidential politics called *Of Thee I Sing*. It ran for over four hundred performances. Its record outlasted that of many Republicans who ran for reelection the following year. Soon, many industrialists and their Wall Street bankers would be singing to salvage their reputations in the wake of the crash and the early years of the Depression.

4

COLLAPSING
EMPIRES
(1930–1940)

*The enforcement of free competition is the least regulation
business can expect.*

— FRANKLIN D. ROOSEVELT

WHEN THE STOCK MARKET CRASHED in 1929, it put an end to the
dreams of more than one industrialist who had entertained notions of
empire. In quick succession, the organizations built by Clarence Hatry in
Britain, Ivar Kreuger in Sweden, Europe, and the United States, Samuel
Insull, and the Van Sweringen brothers all collapsed in a tangle of holding
companies and overextended finances. Get-rich-quick notions had
seduced the average investor, but the fall of these highly leveraged industrial empires caused a serious deterioration in national savings. But one
group seemed to be immune to the economic distress swirling around
them. In what Walter Lippmann called the paradox of poverty and plenty,
the upper middle class and the wealthy seemed hardly bothered by the
economic slump, while average citizens struggled to make ends meet.

Commentators wondered aloud if a new dark age was bound to follow
the "New Era," the nickname given to the period of prosperity that lasted
until the 1929 crash. Capitalism was on trial. Its test would be to weather
the storm and emerge triumphant despite record unemployment and

falling prices. *Business Week* noted that "the purchasing power of consumers in the lower income brackets . . . was too low in 1929 to buy and pay full cost value plus normal profit for the goods and services they consumed." After the Depression set in, their plight worsened considerably. Workers who only a few years before were having cars, radios, and other consumer products marketed to them at an unprecedented rate were now going door to door begging for work. George Soule, writing in *Harper's*, said that "as long as people wait for the downtrodden and the hopeless to produce a revolution, the revolution is far away. Revolutions are made, not by the weak, the unsuccessful, or the ignorant, but by the strong and the informed. . . . An old order does not disappear until a new order is ready to take its place." The combination of a new administration and labor unrest in the first years of the New Deal ensured that those most affected by the Depression would be heard.

By the mid-1930s it was obvious that monopolists still dominated the economy. The toy company Parker Brothers introduced Monopoly in 1935, and it quickly became one of the most popular board games in the country. Because of the Depression, certain industries were commonly known among the public to be monopolies, and the game reflected it, using utility companies as one of its monopolist industries. On the corporate side, despite all the well-publicized failures, most of the large industrial empires that were not highly leveraged remained intact, although the arguments for big companies, increased efficiency, and economies of scale did not seem quite as appealing as they had prior to the 1929 crash. Capital spending continued at many American companies, although sometimes in smaller amounts than before the Depression. RCA continued its research and development plans and did not cut back on expenditures. David Sarnoff said in a speech to the Investment Bankers Association in 1933 that the current economic climate "should serve as a basis for still further progress along lines that will assure not only the maintenance but further improvement of the American standard of living."[1] But even those who believed in the essential health of the economy were not prepared for the length or depth of the Depression. Big business had to wait almost a decade before seeing the sort of economic activity it had been accustomed to in the past.

Banking followed the same general trend. Banks began to fail nationwide at an astonishing rate, and many more tottered on the brink. They became weighted down under poor-quality property and business loans made during the boom years and later, under loans made to stock speculators. While the average citizen originally attributed the failures to the Depression in general, the fact was that the relationship between the stock market and the commercial banks was too close for comfort. Banks regularly loaned their deposits to brokers for further lending to customers on margin accounts. In many cases, the brokers were actually subsidiaries of the banks, so they were really lending money to themselves. What was lacking was a firewall, a structure that would prevent a stock market collapse from destroying the banks at the same time. Customers reacted in a predictable manner: They began to withdraw their money from the banks and hoard it, not trusting their bankers with the funds. Banks of all different types failed, but the bulk of the failures were among those that dealt with individual customers. The wholesale or institutional banks fared much better, though this very fact would inflame the suspicions of those who believed there was another Wall Street conspiracy afoot designed to fleece the public.

Compounding the problem was fraud. Many of the bankers used customers' deposits in unsavory schemes that hastened their own demise. The largest bank failure in history was that of the Bank of United States, located in New York City. Its two top executives defrauded depositors in order to fund their own get-rich-quick schemes. Within the first hundred days of Franklin Roosevelt's administration, Congress passed new, radical legislation designed to regulate the securities markets and resolve the banking problem. After a series of short bank holidays, the banks reopened stronger and leaner than before, but they still had to win back the respect of the public. The crisis, coupled with the continuing Pecora hearings, brought financiers into an unaccustomed and negative spotlight. Father Charles Coughlin, the "radio priest," railed against bankers as late as 1936 when he fumed in a nationally broadcast radio address that "neither Old Dealer nor New Dealer it appears, has courage to assail the international bankers, the Federal Reserve bankers. . . . In common, both old parties are determined to sham-battle their way through this November election with the hope that millions of American citizens will be driven into the no-man's-land of financial bondage." The reputation of bankers took a severe beating after 1929, and the damage lingered for years.

Public Swamped by Events, artist unknown, *White Plains Republican*, 1932.

The banking problems also inflamed social divisions simmering below the surface, and they only underscored what the workingman already knew—the rich were getting richer while his real wages were declining. Organized labor, which had been on the decline, took heart from a provision of the National Industrial Recovery Act (NIRA) of 1933 guaranteeing collective bargaining and began to push for better working conditions and better salaries. A bloody coal miners' strike occurred in Harlan County, Kentucky, and workers at Ford's Dearborn, Michigan, plant went on strike protesting Henry Ford's decision to drop wages in 1932 after having raised them in the 1920s. There the result was four dead and scores injured after police and plant security guards opened fire with automatic weapons on the crowd. Strikes were organized in Minneapolis and San Francisco as well. The San Francisco strike was the first European-style general strike in American history. Longshoremen shut down the West Coast ports. The violent strikes, Hoovervilles, and breadlines reinforced the widespread opinion that society was coming apart at the seams. The upper middle class and the wealthy began to talk of the coming "revolution," and many escaped the cities looking for a safe haven during times of trouble.

The great disparities in wealth were discussed in Congress on numerous occasions, much to the distress of Republicans. In 1934 Representative Samuel Pettengill of Indiana introduced a measure proposing an increase in federal estate and inheritance taxes. The Democratic congressman was armed with volumes of detail about the discrepancies in wealth in the country. According to his statistics, five hundred men reported taxable incomes that exceeded the gross incomes of 8 million farmers and their families by $100 million, although the dates were somewhat vague. By the mid-1930s, almost three million former tenant farmers had been forced off their farms and were wandering the country in search of homes and work. Citing reports like those helped Pettengill's bill sail through the House. When the bill reached the Senate, the proposed taxes were actually increased. Its champion in the upper house was Senator Robert La Follette Jr. of Wisconsin, who stated that "a concentration of wealth such as has taken place in this country" needed to be corrected soon. In order to remedy the situation, he said, "it is necessary for us to increase our revenues, the justice and equity of levying increased taxes upon estates is beyond argument." British inheritance taxes were the models for many Democrats' plans, although the revised Senate rates were still lower than those in Britain. A year later, Senator George Norris was still warning the wealthy and the upper middle class about disparities in wealth. Speaking at the University of Nebraska in 1935, he warned that although the Depression had been severe in 1933, "one of the sad facts staring us in the face was that it created 26 more millionaires than it had in 1932."[2] Congress was intent on using the increased taxes from these individuals to fill the void in the public coffers left by so much unemployment and bankruptcy.

Extremist political movements quickly sprang up to capitalize on the problems. Many felt the New Deal was not doing enough to protect the average citizen. The extremists also associated Roosevelt with the international banking cabal they blamed for most of the country's problems. Father Coughlin and Huey Long both made ample use of bankers in their fiery rhetoric. In California, Upton Sinclair ran for governor in 1934 on his End Poverty in California (EPIC) ticket, striking a chord by advocating government takeover of idle land and factories. Unemployed workers would be allowed to run them for their own use, bringing an end to hunger and idleness. The idea became very popular, spreading throughout the state, and Sinclair won the primary for governor on the Democratic ticket, although he did not take the election itself. After an intense campaign of false information and scare-mongering, his opponents were able to defeat him with a steady barrage of falsehoods and allusions to his Communist background. The opposition even had campaign posters of him designed showing a hammer and sickle in the background. It was not the first or the last time that massive campaigns of misinformation would be used in the 1930s to discredit an opponent.

Huey Long's campaign for a U.S. Senate seat was less idealistic than Sinclair's and more politically motivated. The premise of his social ideas was found in a pamphlet entitled *Share the Wealth,* which outlined his plan. In order to spread wealth around more evenly, the rich would be limited to keeping no more than $15 million each. Any accumulated wealth beyond that would be redistributed to the less fortunate. Long's ideas were talked about around the country, and he became mentioned as a contender for the presidential spot on the Democratic ticket in 1936. But his assassination in 1935 brought an end to the political side of the argument, although the popular notion lingered along with his reputation as the champion of the poor and disenfranchised. Long's ideas about limiting inherited wealth were picked up by left-wing journalist Gustavus Myers, author of a *History of the Great American Fortunes,* who published *The Ending of Hereditary American Fortunes* in 1939.

The Communist Party also made inroads by organizing workers, appealing to those who felt they had been disenfranchised by the capitalist system. Many of the strikes were organized by splinter groups that broke away from traditional American unions and united with the Communists. The party also joined with many celebrities and writers in the defense of the "Scottsboro Boys," a group of young black men accused of raping two white women who were traveling on the same train in the South dressed as hobos to avoid notice. The charges were clearly trumped up, but it took several years of appeals and political pressure to have the death penalty that was imposed on them dropped. Discontent raised its head in other less acceptable places as well, with the Ku Klux Klan remaining strong in the South and the West.

All the popular movements of the period shared a theme: Big business and the rich were in a world apart from the average workingman. Antimonopoly sentiments found a welcome audience as a result and would be capitalized upon during the 1930s by the New Deal. But the complicated times sometimes called for complicated answers to what appeared to be simple questions. In 1938 Douglas "Wrong Way" Corrigan decided that he wanted to fly to Europe à la Lindbergh but was refused a flight permit. Undaunted, he set out for Dublin; he later claimed that he had been headed for California but had misread his compass. Some later New Deal legislation appeared to achieve results in a similar manner. In order to defeat monopoly, government would begin encouraging cartels and other closely related trade associations.

ICON SMASHING

The crash helped solve the problem of the money trust in a way no one would have imagined a few years before. Ever since the Pujo hearings prior to the passing of the Federal Reserve Act twenty years before, the presence of the money trust had been generally acknowledged in political circles, but little had been done about it. Given the state of the banking laws, or the lack of them, little could have been expected. Applying antitrust laws against it was not feasible because proving that price rigging and squeezing the competition had occurred in a services-related business was almost impossible. Invoking the Clayton Act served little purpose because it was also difficult, if not impossible, to prove that all of the investment bankers who sat on numerous boards of directors did so for any reason other than to lend their financial expertise. But the crash proved a milestone for policy makers. As the Pecora hearings unfolded, they shed light on banking and brokerage practices, and gave Congress "conclusive" proof that the money trust was inimical to the public good.

By proving that it had caused and profited from the crash, the government could find ways to regulate its activities that would have been unheard of in better times.

The Pecora hearings did more than simply expose banking practices. They also served to debunk some of the myths surrounding bankers. J. P. "Jack" Morgan was a legendary figure in banking circles, as was his father before him. The same was true of George Baker and his son after him at First National Bank of New York. Sitting before congressional committees was not something that these bankers were accustomed to. Since the days of John D. Rockefeller, appearances by the great figures in business in public to testify about their business practices always drew a great audience. The Pecora hearings were no exception but the circuslike atmosphere surrounding them certainly showed that times, and attitudes, had changed. While the hearings often relied upon the sensational and Pecora made good use of theatrics at times, the underlying theme had to be one of bankers' abuses of the system they had dominated for so long. Without it, there was little to question them about. They had violated the public trust but clearly had not broken any specific banking or securities laws.

Part of the reason for the general interest in the hearings was the clash of styles and backgrounds of the participants. The hearings were originally called by Herbert Hoover in 1932. After a few undistinguished chief counsels had come and gone, Ferdinand Pecora assumed the reins in early 1933. The son of immigrants, Pecora, who had gone to law school at night and worked to support himself during the day, found himself face to face with some of the best-known figures in American finance, many from the country's oldest families. The questions about their personal finances, among other things, irritated the bankers, who felt that the committee hearings had gone beyond their original intent. But Pecora quickly established a reputation for calm probity when dealing with those who believed themselves superior to an Italian immigrant lawyer who was paid only $250 a month for his services to the committee. He interviewed dozens of witnesses, including Jack Morgan and Charles Mitchell, the chairman of National City Bank.

The two notable laws passed during the first hundred days of the New Deal, the Securities Act of 1933 and the Banking Act of 1933, have both been described mainly as laws designed to prevent investors and savers

A Real Test for You, Mr. President.

Artist unknown. *Denver Post*, 1933. Reprinted with permission.

from further abuses by unscrupulous bankers and brokers. The proof can be found in their main provisions. The Securities Act requires issuers of new corporate securities to register them with the (now) SEC. This intruded upon bankers' private domains, requiring companies to divulge their financial statements in a standard accounting manner. The Banking Act (Glass-Steagall Act) provided deposit insurance for bank accounts so that withdrawals need no longer occur because of panic. But both laws, especially the Banking Act, went far beyond protecting investors and savers and extended themselves into the realm of antitrust. In defining what commercial banking was, the act also stipulated who could and could not practice it. As Arthur Schlesinger noted, the banking and securities laws looked very much like nineteenth- rather than twentieth-century legislation. Rather than establish cooperation between government and business as the National Recovery Administration (NRA) was meant to do, the two pieces of legislation served to police the malefactors in the banking business. However, since no meaningful legislation existed to curb bankers and brokers, the two acts were steps in the right direction. And if viewed as antitrust legislation, then they certainly made more sense than some of the legislation that was to follow.

The Glass-Steagall Act gave bankers a year to decide which form of banking they would continue to practice, investment or commercial banking. The two were separated so that commercial bankers could not use depositors' funds to make loans to stock market subsidiaries or underwrite securities. That appeared to be a necessary separation given the antics of bankers in the 1920s. But such a separation was much more devastating to the money trust than any investigation into its activities. Technically, Section 20 of the law stated that a bank could derive no more than 10 percent of its revenue from market-related activities. That was an impossible figure for Morgan; Kuhn, Loeb, Kidder, Peabody, and the other major securities houses to achieve, and as a result, the securities houses opted to remain in the securities business, giving up any commercial banking activities, while Morgan chose commercial banking, handing over its investment banking business to the newly founded Morgan Stanley and Co., run mostly by former Morgan employees. Other people's money was to be deployed prudently while investment banking had to go its own separate way. Touted as a major restructuring of the banking business, the bill also put an end to the money trust. Whether the bankers' coterie would survive in another form was yet to be seen.

The Securities Exchange Act of 1934 dealt another serious blow to those who remained in the securities business. All stock exchanges had to submit to the regulations of the newly founded Securities and Exchange Commission (SEC). Five commissioners were created to oversee the stock exchanges and administer the Securities Act of 1933. Rules were drawn up to prevent all types of financial abuses, from short selling to nonexistent financial reporting. Joseph Kennedy, one of Wall Street's most adroit operators in the 1920s, was appointed its first chairman. The SEC was one of the most reviled of the New Deal agencies in its early days. Wall Street was furious at the regulations aimed at stock market practices, although investment bankers and brokers realized that yet more regulation was on the way. The behavior of brokers on the exchanges was a major topic of discussion in political circles and the handwriting was on the wall for the stock exchanges since Herbert Hoover began publicly complaining about brokers' behavior in 1932. Congress became less forgiving in its attitude toward those widely blamed for the crash and depression.

Casting a further shadow over Morgan's reputation was the collapse of the Van Sweringen brothers' empire. They were a reclusive, unmarried twosome who were consumed by their work. Short in stature and uneducated, they lived in Cleveland in a sprawling mansion but employed no servants and lived in only a few of the mansion's numerous rooms. Introduced to the Morgan bank by Al Smith, Oris and Mantis Van Sweringen amassed a sprawling railroad empire in the years prior to the crash. That included the infamous Missouri Pacific and a hydralike holding company called the Alleghany Corporation, which included the infamous Nickel Plate Railroad. Originally land developers, they got into the railroad business when they bought the Nickel Plate in order to serve their latest property development, Shaker Heights in Cleveland. Oris related to the Pecora committee in 1933 how they had come to acquire the notorious line. "We didn't have enough money to pay for it all. We arranged to defer a portion of the purchase price. . . . The purchase price was $8.5 million . . . the initial payment was $2 million." With the aid of a friendly bank in Cleveland they entered the railroad business and by the early 1930s had amassed an empire estimated at around $2 billion. The two eccentric brothers then used their Morgan connections to good purpose as the bank raised over $500 million in financing for them in the late 1920s. But their empire was highly leveraged and collapsed within several years. Morgan originally made over $8 million in fees on their securities offerings but finally lost over $9 million when they collapsed. Stock the bank originally sold at $20 sank to $5 per share.[3] The episode did little to enhance Morgan's reputation at a delicate time for bankers in general. By the time a congressional hearing was called to investigate later in the 1930s, both brothers had died and other matters became more pressing. The affair was another sorrowful tale in the history of railroads. From their early days to the era of the later barons, the railroad companies lurched from crisis to crisis, always seeming to attract the leverage artists and their willing bankers.

The railroads' problems were also problems for their bankers. But ingenious methods were used to limit the damage that the collapsing empires inflicted on the banks, especially J. P. Morgan & Company. Quite often the railroads would apply to the Reconstruction Finance Corporation (RFC) for assistance and then use the money borrowed to pay back their bankers. The RFC became an enduring New Deal agency but was actually proposed by Herbert Hoover and authorized by Congress in 1932. Its purpose was to provide government loans to sectors of the economy in need because of the Depression. Originally it was intended to aid small businesses, but quickly it became apparent that the largest companies were coming to the trough and receiving aid. Jesse Jones, a Texan who was its longtime chairman, acknowledged that the Van Sweringen enterprises applied for loans and were granted them, raising hackles in Congress in the process. Jones himself was also the object of much scorn in the press for overseeing loans made to railroad barons, among others, rather than small businessmen. He confessed, "I was not afflicted with any 'anti-banker' complex, but felt in this particular situation and others of a similar nature that the bankers had no right to unload their bad or slow debts on the government." But his views were not shared by the other members of the RFC, who frequently voted to give assistance to the banks through their struggling clients. The whole matter was finally brought to the attention of a Senate committee in 1937, but by then it could interview only the bankers—the Van Sweringen brothers had already died.

Though bankers themselves steadfastly maintained that they knew no more about a money trust than did their critics, and simply extended credit when requested to those whom they trusted, the years of arranging financings at high fees and their indelible imprint upon the economy during the 1920s made them a target. The bankers' grasp on the financial system was broken by a combination of laws that were put together at relatively short notice, based loosely on the principles of Louis Brandeis. Once the structure of their industry was changed, their influence quickly waned.

The Banking Act and the Securities Act were unquestionably effective. And although criticism of the New Deal abounded even before the first

Roosevelt administration was complete, *The Economist* remarked, "If it be compared with either the performance or the promise of its rivals, it comes out well. If its achievements be compared with the situation which confronted it in March, 1933, it is a striking success. Mr. Roosevelt may have given the wrong answers to many of his problems, but at least he is the first President of modern America who has asked the right questions."[4] One of those questions concerned the matter of industrial organization. How could people be put back to work, helping to ensure a recovery? The New Deal thought it could be achieved through cooperation between government and business, not two of the closest partners in the past. If the administration could appeal to business' civic side and provide something in return, then it could forge a working relationship that could help win the war. The thrust would not be legislation that restricted the activities of bankers. It would be a proposed partnership between two traditional antagonists.

EAGLES AND CHICKENS

In addition to the securities and banking laws passed quickly by the new administration, the farmers' plight was also addressed. In fact, the Agricultural Adjustment Act, passed by Congress in 1933, was the most radical of all the early New Deal legislation. Collapsing prices, unemployment, and crops decaying in the fields and in silos convinced the administration that radical new laws were needed to protect farmers. As a group, farmers fell outside organized labor and thus missed out on any economic benefits that labor organization might have brought. But Roosevelt was very interested in land use and moved quickly on plans to alleviate the farmers' bad fortune.

When Congress passed the new agricultural law, complaints that it smacked of Communism or socialism were heard from conservative elements everywhere. Even the newly installed president acknowledged that the legislation plowed uncharted fields. Critics certainly had a point. The law provided for payments to farmers to keep acreage out of use. That would help raise farm prices, then in a serious deflationary slump. The payments were funded by imposing a tax on food processing, which

Good News, by Clubb. Newspaper unknown.

amounted to a redistribution of wealth in a sense. And the law went even farther by providing farmers with interest rate subsidies on their mortgages. The entire package was part of a program by lawmakers from agricultural states to inflate the economy. It also offended those who still viewed the farmer as a rugged, noble producer of food who happily worked alone in relative obscurity.

On the nonrural end, the desire within the Roosevelt administration to forge an agency that would mold an industrial recovery resulted in the passing of the National Industrial Recovery Act (NIRA) in May 1933. The law created three agencies. One was the National Recovery Administration (NRA). Another was the Public Works Administration (PWA), and the third was the National Labor Board (NLB). The NRA was charged with promoting the organization of industry by fostering cooperation among trade groups. The PWA was charged with providing jobs through public expenditures on building projects. The NLB guaranteed collective bargaining to labor. Many detractors of the New Deal saw the NIRA as a significant step on the road to socialism because of its central planning aspects. Industry liked what it saw, however, and gave its wholehearted support to the NRA in particular. The part it liked the most was the suspension of the antitrust laws.

In order to foster a recovery, the law proposed that working hours be reduced and wages increased. The danger was that any employer that attempted to do so without the guidance of government would find itself quickly forced out of business by the competition. Similar businesses were urged to form trade associations and act in unison rather than independently. If they did so, they would be expected to maintain uniform costs in their businesses, prohibiting sales below cost. They would also have to observe certain social goals such as striving to improve labor conditions, increase wages, and abolish sweatshops and child labor. The hoped-for result of such a suspension of the antitrust laws was an improvement in the average worker's lot. More than seven hundred codes were drawn up for various industries. One of the most enthusiastic participants in this process was investment banking, which vigorously drew up its own code, partly to try to repair its image after the crash and the Pecora hearings. The trade group it formed led directly to the creation of the National Association of Securities Dealers by Congress in 1937.

A New Look for Farms, by Cargill. *Cortlandt Standard,* 1933.

The first head of the NRA was a retired brigadier general, Hugh Johnson. He had previously served as an aid to financier Bernard Baruch. Neither Baruch nor Harold Ickes, who headed the PWA, thought Johnson the best man for the job. Baruch thought he was a better second or third in command, while Ickes characterized him as "especially dictatorial and absolutely beyond control." Upon taking the job, Johnson recognized the sort of turmoil he faced. Of his appointment, he said, "This is just like mounting the guillotine on the infinitesimal gamble that the ax won't work." Nevertheless, upon taking command he devised a slogan and a mascot for the NRA. Any company that joined in the effort could display a blue eagle at their places of business and on their advertising. The slogan beneath it read "We Do Our Part." Many companies did join. Not to do so would have appeared unpatriotic. But some went against the tide; Henry Ford was one notable abstention, referring to the eagle as "that Roosevelt buzzard." Nevertheless, the public relations side of the effort was a great success. Blue Eagle parades were held in various cities, the biggest occurring in New York in September 1933.

Lost in the public relations hoopla was the fact that the antitrust laws had taken a backseat, although temporarily, to a concerted effort at economic stimulation. By allowing businesses to form trade associations and "collude" on prices, the government acknowledged that cartel-like associations did provide some benefits to society after all. The message was not lost on the large corporations that had been accused of exercising monopoly power in the past. Now there was some positive recognition, however slight, that they were good for the economy if properly harnessed. They accepted government demands because most felt that something had to be done to set the economy aright, even if that meant giving up some of their other traditional freedoms. But the opportunity to forge relationships with an eye toward the future made it worthwhile to cooperate with the Roosevelt administration.

Johnson acknowledged that the antitrust laws sometimes stood in the way of economic progress. At the very least, they did not prove particularly effective in times of crisis. Referring to the war effort in 1917, he said, "We did not repeal the Antitrust Acts. *We simply ignored them.*" The war effort required competitors to pool their resources, trade secrets, and facilities; the NRA was attempting the same sort of thing in 1933. He also offered one of the strongest public statements to date in support of the NRA: "NRA will have to move on a broad front and at terrific speed if it can beat that record of the destruction of individual enterprise made under the full force of the Antitrust Acts, the negative powers of the Federal Trade Commission, and the most active business period in our history," referring to the 1920s.[5] According to this view, which was shared by many in both the administration and the business community, the antitrust laws had done more to blunt competition than any other single factor. That competition led many smaller companies to fold or drop out of competing with the larger ones, eventually leaving the latter with a lion's share of their respective markets. In the heyday of the Progressive era, having one so antagonistic to the antitrust laws in a position of power would have been unthinkable. But what was good for business was paramount. Antitrust took a backseat. *Time* named Johnson its Man of the Year in 1933, putting his picture on the cover.

The NRA did not prove successful in its short lifetime, as the economy failed to respond. But what killed it was a legal challenge to the NIRA that reached the Supreme Court in May 1935. *Schecter Poultry Corporation v. United States* became one of the most oft quoted cases in the years ahead. The Schecter company, located in Brooklyn, New York, was charged with violating the NIRA code by ignoring minimum-wage and working-hours requirements. The company's defense was based on the question of whether the law's delegation of congressional authority to the executive branch was valid. By a vote of 9–0 the justices struck down the NIRA as unconstitutional, shattering the very foundations of the New Deal. The Court's judgment, in a unanimous decision read by Chief Justice Charles Evans Hughes, was that even the severe economic conditions of the time did not create the sort of conditions that justified enlarging the powers of the presidency at the expense of Congress. Immediately after the decision Louis Brandeis remarked to a New Deal lawyer that "this is the end of this business of centralization, and I want you to go back and tell the President that we're not going to let this government centralize everything. It's come to an end."[6] For monopoly concentrations, centralization was not the primary issue, however. A clear message had been sent by the Congress and administration that cartels would be tolerated if operating in the public good. As Johnson put it, "NRA came as a blessed alleviation of the dog-eat-dog rule of the Antitrust Acts . . . it means only that competition must keep its blows above the belt, and that there can be no competition at the expense of decent living." The message was contingent upon other principles embodied in the NIRA. But the antitrust battle was far from over. It had just been put on hold temporarily.

TURN OFF THE POWER

The spring of 1933 witnessed an end to the long battle between the government and private interests over the future of Muscle Shoals. Roosevelt's idea that power production should be in public hands clashed with

By Clubb. *Utica Dispatch*, 1933.

the opinion of corporate interests that Muscle Shoals was better off under their control. Southern politicians united with power company executives and Republicans to maintain that the battle was between big government and private enterprise, between good and evil. A congressman from New Jersey summarized the opposition to a government-operated facility best when he said it was "simply an attempt to graft onto our American system the Russian idea."

Clinging to the notion that publicly produced electricity was cheaper than privately produced electricity, the New Deal proposed a regional power-producing company called the Tennessee Valley Authority. The bill proposing the project met with difficulty in the House, but at Roosevelt's behest Norris led the charge in the Senate, which passed it overwhelmingly. Finally the House accepted a compromise and the Tennessee Valley Act passed in May 1933. The new agency became the greatest intrusion by government into the private sector since the farm legislation passed during Wilson's presidency, and conservative business elements continued to oppose it. The *Wall Street Journal* was among this group, as it had condemned the entire drift toward government ownership since the First World War.

The three-man commission at the head of the new authority included Arthur Morgan, a former president of Antioch College; David Lilienthal, a lawyer and disciple of Louis Brandeis; and Harcourt Morgan, former president of the University of Tennessee. (Neither of the Morgans was connected to J. P. Morgan.) The three did not work well together, largely because of the eccentric nature of Arthur Morgan, and the directors openly feuded with each other about the agency's goals, which was not characteristic of New Deal programs in any case. While Lilienthal was concerned with power development and Harcourt Morgan was more concerned with the development of new fertilizers, Arthur Morgan's interests were broader. Their conflicts began almost immediately and became legendary in Washington. The Gridiron Club satirized the directors at its 1938 roast with a skit narrated by a journalist disguised as a "mountain woman" in her cabin in Tennessee, telling a story to an assembly of children:

> Oh, the TVA directors, they were split in different sectors,
> And they took to New Deal feudin' when they'd meet.
> They'd accuse each other quicker than it took your eye to flicker.
> They would call each other, "liar Crook! and Cheat!"[7]

Unfortunately for the newly christened agency, Arthur Morgan began to alienate many with his comments about the nature of the people who lived in the Tennessee River basin, referring to them on more than one occasion as having "low levels" of personal character. He believed that great social and economic developments were lost on the locals, who, by implication, deserved their low social and economic status. As a result, he favored the development of local industry based mostly upon crafts, something that he felt the inhabitants could easily grasp. He even suggested that they use their own form of money. Those views earned him even less respect from his colleagues. He also suffered from physical problems that almost caused a nervous breakdown. In 1938 the president finally removed him from the job, recognizing that he was not suitable for the sensitive post. He was succeeded as chairman by Harcourt Morgan.

David Lilienthal proved to be the pivotal member of the TVA. Originally supported for the appointment by George Norris, among others, he was another "people's attorney" in the Brandeisian mold. Specializing in public power problems, he was the foremost advocate of municipally generated power and an ardent foe of the big utility companies. In many respects, Lilienthal was able to achieve in his generation what Charles Francis Adams Jr. had only dreamed of several generations before. Born in 1899 in Illinois to Austro-Hungarian immigrant parents, he studied at Harvard Law School, where he came into contact with Brandeis' ideas through instructors such as Felix Frankfurter, with whom he studied utilities law. From his student days, Lilienthal dreamed of achieving a reputation similar to Brandeis' by joining the ranks of public advocates—not the most popular field for a young man with high aspirations. After working in private practice for a few years, he took an enormous risk by accepting a job offer from the newly elected governor of Wisconsin, Philip La Follette, to join the state's railroad commission. The governor wanted to change the commission's mandate and broaden it to include all public services. The job was originally offered to James Landis, later to be chairman of the SEC, but he turned it down because of the meager compensation—Wisconsin offered $5,000 per year, a fraction of what a lawyer could make in private practice. La Follette then offered Lilienthal the job over dinner in Madison, the state capital. After sleeping on the offer, Lilienthal went back to see La Follette the next morning and told him that he had consulted with his wife by telephone. "Do you know what she said? . . . If this appeals to you, take it. So I am happy to accept."[8]

The choice proved to be a wise one. While only at the job for a short time, his performance came to the attention of national Democrats, and Roosevelt chose him for the newly created TVA. He was the only northerner selected for the job—a "carpetbagger" in the minds of some southern politicians, who wanted all three jobs for their own. But he would help the TVA quickly become the major vehicle for government-inspired capitalism during the Depression. Its dramatic increase in public spending appeared to give credence to the ideas of British economist John Maynard Keynes, who advocated fine-tuning fiscal policy to stimulate the economy. In reality, massive public projects such as the WPA were good politics in the face of desperate economic conditions that would have been attempted despite economic theories. Keynes himself met with a mixed reaction from FDR's advisors. Bernard Baruch distrusted him because of a feud that dated back to their participation in the Versailles conference after World War I. The programs the TVA financed gave rise to a new generation of entrepreneurs and builders who would become the first to embark upon major building projects without the aid of the banks or Wall Street. Lilienthal was later nominated to become chairman of the Atomic Energy Commission, although his political enemies charged him with being a Communist, something of a payback for his days at the TVA.

The early TVA became an experiment in social engineering as well as producing some of the great engineering feats of the twentieth century. It built several notable dams in the West. The agency taught farmers in the Tennessee River basin how to adopt new methods of farming, leading to greater productivity. New dams were built (one named after Norris), and the frequent floods that previously characterized the area were averted in many places. Traffic on the rivers within the Tennessee Valley increased five times over, and fertilizer production increased dramatically. More significant for the power industry, the TVA produced cheap electricity on a massive scale and so became a yardstick by which private producers around the country could be measured. Norris' and Roosevelt's premise that municipally generated electricity was substantially cheaper than that produced by private companies appeared to be borne out. But the birth, and subsequent success, of the TVA did not spell the end of the utilities' problems. Regulation was just around the corner.

Supplying power was another classic American industrial dilemma. Like railroads and telegraphy before it, electric power was vital to the development of the country. *The Economist* noted that the technical side provided the model by which electricity was produced in Britain. But the newspaper also noted, "The device of the holding company has been used more consistently and carried further towards its logical conclusion in the American electrical industry than in any other." No one doubted the technological superiority of the product, but the devices by which it was financed were another matter entirely. As *The Economist* remarked, "Pyramiding was carried to fantastic lengths, and in many of these pyramids the operating companies were 'milked' for the benefit of the holding companies. When carried to these extremes, holding companies contribute nothing to the efficiency of the industry, but positively endanger it."[9]

In the early years of the Depression, in fact, over twenty utility companies went into bankruptcy. Investors' funds were being lost as the leveraged companies began to groan under the weight of their debt burdens. The revelations of the FTC hearings, completed in 1935, dovetailed with the exposés of the Pecora hearings. But they also went beyond them by revealing, in direct testimony, propagandistic practices by the utilities that amounted to nothing less than an all-out war upon their perceived enemies, the goal being to ensure private ownership of power production in the country.

The utilities' propaganda machine was organized through trade associations. Their attack was carried out through advertising, newspapers, journalists, educators and schools, and the occasional movie aimed at fostering their belief that private ownership was in the best American tradition. Early in the hearings, George Oxley, the director of information for the National Electric Light Association, was questioned by Judge Healy of the FTC as to the extent of his association's efforts to bring the power story to the public. Previously, the comments of the most ardent of the utilities spokesmen, J. B. Sheridan, suggested that utilities should do as much as possible to "change and direct the economic thought and practice of the American people." Healy then posed this question to Oxley: "Do you know of any means of publicity that has been neglected by your organization?" Oxley's response was to the point: "Only one, and that is sky writing. I don't believe we have tried that with airplanes."[10]

Anyone who disagreed with the utilities' emphasis on private ownership was labeled a Communist or a socialist, also in keeping with an American tradition of the period. Detractors sardonically claimed that anyone who used the post office would be labeled a Communist by the propagandists because it was a government-owned operation. In any event, the hearings showed that the utilities had at one time or other attempted to buy major newspapers in keeping with their avowed aims. The *Cleveland Plain Dealer, Detroit Free Press, Minneapolis Star, Atlanta Constitution,* and

Boston Globe all received indications of interest from them. They were successful only in buying some smaller papers, however, of which the *Chicago Daily News* was probably the best-known.

The plot thickened when the FTC heard about the antics of two young men named Hall and LaVarre employed by the International Paper Company and supplied with huge amounts of money to buy newspapers in the Southeast. Their monthly expense accounts exceeded the average worker's annual salary, indicating that their task was to impress local newspapermen. At first glance, it would seem that paper companies and newspapers were a natural match. But soon it was discovered that International Paper was acting on behalf of the utility companies. As a large user of water-produced power, the paper company was keenly interested in centralizing power production. The FTC learned that the minutes of the company's October 1928 directors' meeting made mention of employing two young men and appropriating $2.5 million for them to purchase newspapers. When Healy subsequently questioned LaVarre about the ambitious buying program, he received a fairly frank answer. "That was a pretty large order for a beginner without any money wasn't it? . . . At any rate, you did not risk anything?" LaVarre replied, "No. As a matter of fact, the International Paper Company took all the risk."[11]

When the propagandists ventured outside business, their actions became even more sinister. Influencing textbooks and education was one sphere of activity very close to the power trust's heart. J. B. Sheridan, the director of the Missouri Committee on Public Utility Information, claimed, "I have recently completed a survey of standard textbooks upon civics and economics used in the public schools in several states . . . and I am irresistibly driven to the conclusion that the chief effort of the public schools appears to be manufacture and production of socialists and communists." Something would have to be done to correct the influence. Setting the record straight about private ownership was certainly a step in the right direction. But fixing a few facts about recent history did not hurt, either. A textbook used in the Illinois public schools, *Community Life and Civic Problems,* correctly stated that "as late as 1926 a man then serving as president of a number of electric light companies in the Middle West gave in a single primary election over $200,000 to the candidates of both parties," referring to the recent contributions made by Insull to the campaign of Frank Smith in his race for the U.S. Senate from Illinois. But when it was discovered that he had accepted money from Insull, Smith was prevented from taking the seat he had won. Later an executive of Middle West Utilities recommended that the passage be omitted from the next edition, and the publisher obliged.[12] The utilities had changed history to their liking.

At other times there were attempts made to influence a book even before it was published. The National Electric Light Association did not like certain material in a text written by a University of Wisconsin economics professor. When the offending material was removed by its author, the association professed to like it so much that it offered to underwrite the distribution of the text to every high school in Missouri. Similar attempts were made to curry favor with colleges and universities—the trade groups made grants of varying amounts to the University of Michigan, Northwestern, the Harvard Business School, and the University of Missouri, among others. Unlike other, more traditional gifts made to educational institutions, these were considered "indirect payments" made to foster their sponsors' own ideological point of view. Critics maintained that this came perilously close to using a monopoly position to subvert the democratic process.

The power industry's strong ideological stances and attempts to mold public opinion had precedent. Samuel Insull suffered bad press at the hands of the Hearst newspapers in the early 1930s, so journalists' power was still fresh in the industry's collective mind. Insull himself displayed a strong penchant for propaganda during World War I. He personally led the British propaganda efforts in the United States during the war and learned a great deal about molding public opinion, especially when painting the Germans as barbarians.

In the summer of 1934 the president appointed the National Power Committee. The result was substantial legislation designed to put an end to utilities' independent behavior. The committee's chairman was interior secretary Harold Ickes, and other members included Robert Healy, formerly of the FTC, and David Lilienthal, of the TVA. Ickes said at the time, "It will be our duty to consider power questions in a very broad way and recommend legislation, if we feel that legislation is called for on particular phases of this question." As matters turned out, that was something of an understatement, for utility regulation would prove to be as comprehensive as securities legislation and in some instances even more so.

The resulting Public Utility Holding Company Act was in all respects a typical New Deal document. Recognizing the power generation business as an interstate one, the new law required all utilities engaging in interstate commerce to register with the SEC. The commission was given the authority to regulate all securities issues of the utilities and had the power to refuse a new issue if it did not find sound reasoning behind it. This was also a direct slap at the investment banking community, which had made enormous fees over the years by issuing watered-down securities for the power companies. But another provision of the act, known as the "death sentence," proved even more controversial and raised the ire of utility executives and their bankers around the country. This provision allowed the SEC to limit holding companies to a "single system" and required some to break up as a result. In an interesting twist, the act's death sentence provision was in 1938 deemed applicable to the railways. Once again, railroad finances were the subject of congressional investigation given that the railway lines were again in desperate straits. The railroads usually raised prices when in need of cash, but the ICC thought that inappropriate. "No competitive industry can work out its salvation through a price-increasing policy alone," it stated.[13] The idea was to employ the death sentence provision to force some railroads to consolidate, thus lowering costs. That was exactly the opposite of the strategy used against the utilities and showed the long evolution the railways had undergone since the days of Gould and Vanderbilt. What was death for one industry was considered a lifeline for another.

The death sentence provision was a blow to Morgan's empire as well as Insull's, as holding companies that controlled more than one power system in different states were outlawed unless the holding company could prove that its possession of more than one system allowed it to operate highly economically or was vital to the public. While moves like this led some to claim that the Roosevelt administration was doing all it could to break up private enterprise, Brain Trust member Rexford Tugwell recalled that although "I felt that public ownership was necessary . . . I was surprised to find that Roosevelt thought it necessary only as a standard for private utilities."[14] The utilities were not going down without a fight, however, and mounted a massive public relations campaign against the bill and against the president himself. They sent out millions of telegrams and letters against the bill from fictitious parties, aimed mostly at congressmen. This tactic was reminiscent of a similar but failed ploy used at the 1932 Democratic national convention by the financial community and utilities companies to support the candidacy of Newton Baker for president.[15] The utilities also started a rumor that Roosevelt was not in possession of all his mental faculties. Why else would someone be in favor of such draconian legislation? The House consequently rejected the original death sentence clause as a result of the lobbying but later accepted a compromise.

The act was not fully supported by the first SEC chairman, Joseph Kennedy. He also objected to the death sentence provision but by then was on his way out of the SEC. His successor, James Landis, tried to calm the power community, inviting its executives to Washington in the spirit of what he hoped would be cooperation, only to be told that they were ready to do battle. He then tried a national radio address, broadcast on CBS, similar to the one that Joe Kennedy gave when the Securities Exchange Act was first passed. Kennedy's address smoothed the ruffled feathers of Wall Street, but Landis' effort was not successful. The SEC had to fight the power companies in the courts before they would register with the new body, though ultimately the Public Utility Holding Company Act was allowed to stand.

CONFUSING?

While many small businesses suffered during the Depression, quite a few of the larger ones managed to remain afloat despite the bad times. Small mom-and-pop grocery stores were closing, while the large grocery chains conducted their profitable businesses as usual. The suspicion was that the larger stores were able to control prices by either insisting that their suppliers sell to them at more advantageous prices than they did to the independent stores or forcing the suppliers into exclusive agreements. But the Clayton Act was not particularly effective against price discrimination. Section 2 of the act contained a proviso that made that section of the law inoperative against price discrimination if such discrimination was done "in good faith to meet competition." In other words, any company charged with price discrimination could simply claim that it was doing so because it was forced to do so by its competitors. Not one FTC complaint issued under the act claiming price discrimination ever resulted in action, either by the commission itself or by the courts. As a result, a movement was mounted to amend the act with more muscular language. As Wright Patman, chairman of the House Antitrust Subcommittee, put it, a law was needed to "protect the independent merchant, the public whom he serves, and the manufacturer from whom he buys, from exploitation by his chain competitor."

Patman was the perfect champion of the small against the large. Born in 1893 to a family of poor tenant farmers in Texas, Patman put himself through law school working as a part-time janitor. His first foray into politics came in 1920, when he won a seat in the lower house of the Texas legislature. He later became a district attorney and was at one time protected by Texas Rangers when it was rumored that a professional had been hired by organized crime to kill him. He was elected to the House of Representatives in 1928 and spent over forty-five years there. He became a foe of big business and monopolies over the years, sharing his advocacy of the people with a fellow Texan and member of Congress, Lyndon Johnson. He became involved in the anti-chain store movement when his constituents began to rail against what they saw as "outside" interests penetrating the local market, putting shopkeepers out of business. The affair had a distinctly anti-eastern ring to it. A local broadcaster in Louisiana, less than fifty miles from Patman's district, said over the airwaves that giving profits to the chains was tantamount to "sending the profits of business out of our communities to a common center, Wall Street, and closing this door of opportunity to those who entertain the hope of their children becoming prosperous business leaders."[16] Regional populism still had a profound impact on the way legislators responded, and Patman, who believed that eastern banking was dominated by monopoly, favored any attempt to protect the small merchant from the larger predators, who were all financed by Wall Street.

The Robinson-Patman Act, the second major piece of legislation directly attributed to an FTC report (the utility act was the first), was passed by Congress in June 1936. It sailed through the House with few opposing votes and passed the Senate unanimously. The legislation was an attempt to nip potential monopolies in the bud by proving price discrimi-

nation; in Patman's words, "price discriminations that are practiced frequently or regularly, and at will, with devastating effects, can only be
employed by a seller who has market power approaching monopoly control over prices in the markets in which he operates."[17] If Standard Oil had
been attacked that way thirty years before or even earlier, it would likely
have been more effective than breaking up the trust only to see it rise again
in a different form.

Unfortunately, the attempt to close the loopholes in the Clayton Act
only made the new act's language even more complicated. Commenting
on the law, the *New York Times* remarked that "it would require the combined efforts of our best economists and half a dozen Philadelphia lawyers
to predict the effects of the so-called Anti–Chain Store Act alone . . .
because it may encourage the formation of vertical trusts."[18] The fear was
that the prohibitions against interstate selling were not applicable within
the states. That had the potential to set off a wave of vertical combinations, where the companies in related businesses merge. But some businessmen saw advantages in the law, although not perhaps in the manner
originally intended. The president of the Remington Rand Company
commented that it was a step toward truth in advertising. He said that
since business had advocated truth as a policy for some time in advertising,
"why should we not, with equal reason and strength, advocate truth in
prices, and that, it appears, is what the Patman law seeks to accomplish."

Although the purpose of the Robinson-Patman Act was to strengthen
the language against price discrimination, it would be at least a decade
before the law was effectively used in the courts.[19] Applying it to various
instances of price discrimination proved very difficult; the sheer complexity of the problem was shown when Patman published a book of almost
four hundred pages explaining the law. But in the end the act was not as
radical as other planks in the Roosevelt administration's programs aimed
at abuses by big business. Although the Glass-Steagall Act was painted as
a banking law, by forcing the money trusters out of their comfortable
niches it did more than any other piece of federal legislation to break up
monopolies. Like the Public Utility Holding Company Act, it was aimed
at specific industries that had received considerable attention in the press.
The Robinson-Patman bill was much more general, aimed at an abuse
rather than the abusers. In a radical period in American history, the act

was mostly overlooked. Arthur Schlesinger later characterized the act as an "irrelevance to most New Dealers. Its enactment completed the major domestic record of an undistinguished congressional session."[20] When compared to the banking or securities legislation or the holding company act, it was only a lamb in wolf's clothing.

OUT OF THE CLOSET

In the few years since the Securities Act, the Banking Act, and the Public Utility Holding Company Act had been passed, a general suspicion grew that the economy was still in the hands of monopolists. Now arguments began to arise concerning the inequities involved in monopolistic formations in business and industry. Books published by Joan Robinson and Edward Chamberlain systematically outlined the theory and economics of imperfect competition, seeking to uncover its peculiar nature. The popular answer held that the economy was being harmed by the inequalities in income of the population. Beyond that, the rich were acting unconscionably by their actions throughout the crash and Depression.

Compounding the economic problems of the 1930s was the recession of 1937–38. Economic activity, which had been on the rebound, again slowed down, and the stock market followed suit. At first it was not considered particularly serious, given the economy's performance over the past several years. When asked if the stock market's fall in 1937 meant that a new depression was coming, almost three quarters of those questioned said no. The year was not a bad one by Depression standards. *Life* magazine's annual college issue portrayed happy undergraduates at play on campuses across the country. Cigarettes were touted as "aiding digestion," and other frivolous advertisements could be found in the magazines and newspapers. But within a year, attitudes changed. When asked if the current state of the economy was in recession or depression, 60 percent said depression. When broken down by party, the responses were more telling. Seventy percent of Republicans thought it was a new depression, while only half of Democrats believed that.[21] In the majority Democratic view, the rich still controlled the means of production. The fear was that by keeping prices artificially high, monopolists and oligopolists were thwarting an economic recovery.

During Roosevelt's second term the Antitrust Division of the Justice Department showed signs of coming to life again after a long period of dormancy. Thurman Arnold, of the Yale Law School, was appointed head of the division. The rumpled-looking Arnold, who was noted for his wit, had published a book entitled *The Folklore of Capitalism*. Its contents, while certainly witty and cynical, hardly recommended him for the job. Arnold was sympathetic to many of the industrialists whose names were anathema to the New Dealers and the Progressives and Populists before them. He argued that "actual observation of human society . . . indicates that great achievements in human organization have been accomplished by unscrupulous men who have violated most of the principles we cherish . . . yet they raised the level of productive capacity beyond the dreams of their fathers."[22] He claimed that breaking up large business combinations was about as practical as scrapping the automobile and returning to horse-drawn transportation. Yet under this acerbic critic of the antitrust laws the department was to make great strides in its perennial battle against big business.

Arnold's confirmation hearings before the Senate certainly proved that he was intellectually adroit enough to handle the job. Convincing Senator William Borah, a Republican from Idaho, whom he previously criticized, that he was fit for the job was certainly a feather in his cap, but other detractors remained. Journalist Joseph Alsop remarked that "he looks like a small town storekeeper and talks like a native Rabelais," referring to the lawyer's loquaciousness.[23] But Arnold was able to revitalize the department by doubling its staff, increasing its budget, and retraining its current members to be more effective litigators. Just about the time that he assumed the reins of the Antitrust Division, the administration opened its inquiry into monopolies on a broad front.

Arnold's attitude toward the Sherman Act and the future of capitalism had a distinctly futuristic ring. One of the first advocates of consumerism, he argued that the proper role of large business enterprises was to ensure that the consumer got a fair deal from industry. Coupling that with the antitrust laws, he argued that "most of the books in the past on the antitrust laws have been written with the idea that they are designed to eliminate the evil of bigness. What ought to be emphasized is not the evils of size but the evils of industries which are not efficient or do not pass effi-

Little Miss Muffet

FDR Unsettled by Stock Market, by Egli. *Columbus State Journal*, 1937.

FDR's Saber Rattling, by Parrish. *Chicago Tribune*, 1937.
Reprinted with permission.

ciency on to consumers."[24] As he saw it, the recession of 1937 was just another economic slowdown caused by poor distribution of huge inventories. Companies had increased their production but not lowered prices, so the surplus never found its way to the consumers. The recession was the result. The same thing had happened in Germany after the First World War, when monopolies dominated government; the implication was that rigid prices and an increasingly impoverished population could lead to the rise of dictatorship. This attack on big business for not being responsive to the needs of the individual consumer became one of the origins of modern consumerism. It marked a significant shift in antitrust thinking and would pick up steam in coming years.

One of the major cases that Arnold assumed after taking over the

Of All Times to Rake Leaves!

Bad Timing, artist unknown. *Rochester Times Union*, 1937.

Antitrust Division was the complaint that the Justice Department brought against Alcoa. In over a hundred separate charges, the government accused it of maintaining monopoly power over its industry on a broad front. As in many of the notable cases of the Progressive era, the company's chief executive was called to testify. Arthur Davis had spent his entire working life with Alcoa and was able to answer accurately and without notes most questions put to him. His testimony provided the continuity that helped lead to a decision. However, the case wound its way through the federal courts for almost eight years and outlasted many of the individuals who either brought it or tried it. A *New Yorker* writer remarked in 1942 that the case already contained "fifteen million words, or more than thirty times as many as *Gone With the Wind* . . . If the period of preparation is included,

Harold Ickes Beating Up Business, artist unknown. *Portland Press Herald*, 1937.

the Alcoa case outlasted the Civil War." By the time the case was eventually decided, it would almost outlast World War II as well, and was the longest in the history of American law to date.

An early warning shot in the battle against monopoly was fired by Harold Ickes, who in a radio address in December 1937 attributed the current economic problems to a battle between plutocracy and democracy. On one side were America's sixty wealthiest families. On the other was the rest of the population of the country, the slaves of the wealthy. He made his point dramatically when he said that "here in America it is the old struggle between the power of money and the power of democratic instinct. . . . it must be fought through to a finish—until plutocracy or democracy—until America's sixty families or America's 120 million people—win."[25] The reference to the sixty wealthiest families came from a recent book entitled *America's Sixty Families,* by Ferdinand Lundberg. Ickes carefully wove an account of their influence into his antimonopoly message. His speech was hotly debated, and he later recalled that "nothing that I have ever done before has been the cause of so much publicity. . . . After all, I think that the fight in this country today is one between the great mass of people and wealth. For some time it has been in the President's mind to make this the issue in the 1938 elections. If he doesn't, I don't know what issue we are going to run on."[26]

The rhetoric and the political implications were quickly seized upon by the Gridiron Club. At its 1938 dinner it portrayed the sixty families banished to a desert island in the Pacific. They sang in unison:

> We are the sixty
> Oh we're the sixty
> We're the families who had all the dough
> Won't it be funny
> Without our money
> For their taxes, where will they go?
> If you're a Rockefeller, Vanderbilt or—just a Gould
> Stay away from any place by Franklin ruled.[27]

The vast dichotomy between the rich and the rest of the population had the potential to make an interesting campaign issue in the 1940 presidential election. Alfred Sloan's salary as president of General Motors in 1938 was over $500,000, a figure often cited by critics of the rich as excessive even in good economic times. But he was not alone. Over fifty thousand individuals were said to have salaries exceeding $15,000 at a time when the average was less than one-tenth that amount. Hundreds of corporate executives made $50,000 or more. In April 1938 the president called for the creation of the Temporary National Economic Committee (TNEC) to investigate the monopoly problem. The overriding question was whether his intent was political, as Ickes suggested, or represented a genuine desire to determine the extent of monopoly concentration. The measure passed both houses easily, and the TNEC was officially created in June. Its brief was simple—to ascertain the extent of monopoly concentrations in the major industries and the ways in which they were maintained.

The TNEC was unique since it was composed of representatives of both houses of Congress as well as the executive branch. In that respect, it looked more like a federal agency than a committee. The Senate was represented by Senators Borah, King, and O'Mahoney, the chairman. The House members included Representatives Sumners, Reece, and Eicher. Executive appointees included William O. Douglas of the SEC, Garland Ferguson of the FTC, Thurman Arnold of the Justice Department, Isador Lubin of the Labor Department, Herman Oliphant of the Treasury, Richard C. Patterson of the Commerce Department, and Leon Henderson as executive secretary. Not all of them were avid New Dealers, but the majority shared the administration's views on business and competition.

The findings of the TNEC provided even more fuel for critics of monopoly than the Berle and Means study had ten years earlier. Public utilities, life insurance, copper mining, investment banking, building materials, dairy products, plumbing, chemicals, and other manufacturing were dominated by a handful of large companies controlling anywhere between 65 and 95 percent of their respective industries' assets. Apparently things had not changed much since the nineteenth century despite the efforts of trustbusters at the Justice Department and the FTC. And the lax antitrust atmosphere of the 1920s had not helped. The assets of the Metropolitan Life Insurance Company and AT&T individually were larger than those of all but the twelve wealthiest states. The Union Pacific Railroad

The Public Still Subjugated Under FDR, artist unknown.
New York *Daily News*, 1937.

had greater assets than the total asset valuation of Alabama, and those of General Motors outstripped those of Tennessee. Comparisons such as those were bound to stir up controversy, and they only added to the impression that big business dwarfed even governments in many cases. And since many of the wealthiest families were historically linked with big business, the numbers seemed to confirm the revelations of Lundberg and Ickes.

One of the ways by which monopoly control was maintained was by "price leadership." This was nothing more than the largest, dominant firms setting a price that the entire industry would follow. This was easy to detect in the investment banking industry, where a few large firms won the bulk of corporate underwritings by charging what appeared from the outside to be a very standard fee. Even when the smaller firms won an underwriting, they charged essentially the same fees. Recent practices among commercial banks also bordered upon price leadership. In the 1930s, when loans were difficult to make, Chase and the other large banks devised the prime rate of interest. The rate was set above that of Treasury bills and was standard among the large banks. Smaller banks had little choice but to follow when one of the large banks decided to change the rate. Other businesses followed the same general pattern.

One of the common types of price leadership gave an excellent indication of the extent of monopoly pricing. The TNEC heard from an array of witnesses about what was known as the "basing point system." This was setting prices by formula in an industry. All the large firms used the same formula, and prices charged to a customer were adjusted only for shipping from the local delivery area. Therefore, prices for big-ticket items such as steel were remarkably stable across the country. One of the expert witnesses testifying described the system as "the most successful single device that large American business . . . has hit upon in the last 75 years." On the surface, the practice seemed efficient. But when a smaller competitor tried to lower prices, collusion by the larger firms could be seen: Then the basing points were lowered and a new standard was set for the region. Everyone now charged the same as the aggressive competitor, and its advantage immediately evaporated. This was the method used by Carnegie Steel for years before it became U.S. Steel. In 1922 an executive of U.S. Steel admitted that such a "gentlemen's agreement" was in effect until about 1887; after that, pools became more common. And Judge Elbert Gary's dinners also played a role in price leadership in the steel industry, according to this interpretation.[28]

There were also elements of witch-hunting in the TNEC testimonies. Part of the lengthy proceedings were devoted to testimony about racketeering, although the avowed purpose of the hearings was to study the concentration of economic power. The connection was made, very tenuously, between monopoly and using force to avoid competition. In theory, a gangster who broke the legs of his competition was engaging in monopolistic collusion. Using force, or the threat of it, dated back to the early days of the Standard Oil monopoly. Applying the idea to the 1930s was a direct reference to the power of mobsters in New York and Chicago. Al Capone and his associates undoubtedly had a monopoly over the illegal production and distribution of spirits during Prohibition, but no one ever seriously suggested that they be prosecuted under the Sherman Act. Instead, charging tax evasion was the only way that the government could make a case against Al Capone. The same charge was used against many of the bankers who testified before the Pecora committee in 1933. At the time it seemed a natural consequence of their testimonies, in which several admitted under questioning that they had not paid any tax in recent years. Perhaps the best known was Charles Mitchell, until 1933 the president of National City Bank. Reviled as one of the bankers especially responsible for the country's economic problems, he was charged with tax evasion but acquitted in 1933. Once charged, however, many of the bankers found that public opinion held them in the same company as mobsters.

The recommendations made by the TNEC after it finished its investigation in 1941 were very broad and sometimes vague. The committee did not propose or endorse any specific legislation. Antitrust and monopoly measures were roundly approved by most members of the commission but remained unspecific. The real purpose of the hearings was to expose the structure of the economy more than to remedy it. There was also the political card. The administration used the monopoly investigation to fan the flames of indignation against big business, but not with the same strength displayed in 1933. The economy had entered the advanced industrial age, one in which large companies pushed the smaller to the side and workers were often displaced as a result. One TNEC staff member remarked, "We can't restore small units of production and force giant concerns to operate like thousands of individually competing small concerns or break them up without serious loss of economic productivity."[29] Events unfolding in Europe and the Pacific soon would prove that the large industrial firm was vital to the military effort aimed at the defeat of fascism.

By the time the TNEC finished its investigation, one fact had become painfully obvious for the antimonopolists: Business was being dominated by large organizations with the ability to set prices and consolidate as they wished. The New Deal measures helped curtail their power to some degree, in some industries more than others. The banking and utilities industries were affected the most during the 1930s. Those companies that produced tangible products fared much better and were able to avoid antitrust scrutiny. And within a few years, parties on both sides of the issue would be too busy with the war effort to worry about prices and concentrations of power.

5

CONCENTRATING
ON
FASCISM
(1940–1953)

There will be no war millionaires.
—FRANKLIN D. ROOSEVELT

UNTIL 1941 THE DEEP DIVISIONS between business, its East Coast financiers, and the rest of the country could still be clearly seen. Only the outbreak of war between the United States and the Axis powers rallied all around the common cause of defeating fascism. Ironically, the concentrated war effort begun by the United States on behalf of Britain and other allies assumed all along that the United States had the productive capacity necessary to defeat the Germans. As in World War I, large business organizations became a national asset rather than a danger to society as the unparalleled productive capacity of the country would be used to gear up the war effort. Many economic problems remained, but now the enemy came from without, not from within.

By the late 1930s, the attitude of the Roosevelt administration toward concentrations in big business was starkly clear. Any industry seeming to prosper during the Depression was suspected of having an unfair edge. The greatest victories of the decade were over the bankers, investment bankers, and utilities. Not everyone felt that the victories were complete, however. The behavior of the markets during the 1930s, heightened by the 1937–38 recession, led many within the New Deal to conclude that numerous restrictions placed upon the securities industry in particular were being circumvented. But the suspicions that prompted the TNEC inquiry began to be diverted by the buildup of hostilities in Europe. As the Democrats came to realize that they needed business as an ally rather than an adversary, the administration's rhetoric became more subdued, although its antimonopoly bent was still clear. The revelations of the hearings would not be forgotten, only put on hold until the end of the war was in sight.

The war years became an aberration in the constant tug-of-war between the government and big business. The Depression years had seen a swing toward Washington in the antimonopoly battle but the war years would see even more extraordinary developments in the decades-old battle. Because of the enormous costs associated with mobilization and fighting on two fronts, Washington had to begin to court big business; it had no other choice. Suddenly, bureaucrats began to construct organizations that would assume monopolistic power in their own right while industrialists would give up lucrative public service jobs to perform public service. The most powerful financier in the country would be a Texan employed by a government agency not known on Wall Street while followers of Louis Brandeis would assume the reins of industries, many of which had shown signs of being monopolistic in the past. War would turn the world upside down and make monopolists out of dedicated latter-day Progressives. Little of this could be foreseen in the late 1930s.

The TNEC hearings ended very tamely. Even Senator O'Mahoney of Wyoming, their chairman, remarked that they were basically "boring." They were not as antagonistic as the Pecora hearings and for the most part did not make the front pages of the newspapers. And monopoly concentrations and the evils of big business and family wealth did not become the big campaign issue that Harold Ickes had suggested in 1938. Despite the books by Lundberg and Myers, both picking up on Huey Long's original theme of confiscating inherited money, wealth was still admired. That is not to say that the TNEC did not have an effect on the antitrust movement. Its findings provided a veritable history book for suits to be filed by the Justice Department in the years ahead. Some suits were in their early stages when the committee was just being formed. Matters were complicated by the fact that many of the congressional committees and lawsuits themselves were profoundly affected by changes in staff as the years wore on. That was especially true of the Alcoa case, which spanned most of World War II, as well as the Pecora hearings and the TNEC itself. As new members came and went, the findings, presented in historical fashion, became a textbook on industry abuses as interpreted by the Justice Department. It would be easy for a future member of the Justice Department to pick up the TNEC record as well as those studies done by the FTC a decade earlier and resume a long-running case such as the Alcoa suit without much difficulty. The historical hangover would make itself apparent in the later stages of the war and especially during the Truman administration.

Although the United States took its traditional neutral stance in regard to the growing problems in Europe—the country had passed the Neutrality Act several years before—the news coming from faraway places such as Ethiopia and Poland clearly captured the imagination. Political cartoonists and muckrakers were quiet on the subject of big business, as they had been for most of the Depression years, when what economic-related criticism there was usually centered on the New Deal, not big business. Intellectually, it was almost a return to the distant past, when the state was being charged with holding increasingly centralized power over production. Big business was not out of the political doghouse, but it was no longer the center of attention the way it had been until 1929.

A Gallup poll in early 1940 indicated that only one in three surveyed believed that the United States would go to war again. The popular view was that the country had everything to lose and nothing to gain by intervening, but this started to change slowly after the Battle of Britain began in August of that year. Sympathy for Britain and France as well was strong, although most still clearly felt that it was not an American fight. Aid to the combatants without military interference was the most assistance that the public felt was justified. However, in another poll that proved to be a bad omen for Roosevelt's challenger in the 1940 presidential election, a majority of those polled said that if it came to a fight with Germany, they would prefer FDR as president to Wendell Willkie by a sizeable majority. In times of crisis, people wanted a proven leader.

Part of the reason for American indifference to European affairs could be found in the fact that the country was better off economically in 1940 than at any time in a decade. Income, production, and personal wealth were all higher than they had been in years. Unemployment was still at 15 percent in 1940, but that was the lowest rate in a decade. A statistic that made David Sarnoff smile was that over thirty million homes had at least one radio. Illiteracy was at an all-time low, and life expectancy had reached a high of an average sixty-four years. After years of hard times, society finally seemed to be returning to normal.

Another reason the public did not readily endorse war before the attack on Pearl Harbor was that the old Populist and Progressive notions about the origins of the World War I still held considerable sway. The general perception that the war was profitable for industrialists and bankers still dominated much popular thinking. Wendell Willkie, whom Roosevelt defeated in the 1940 presidential election, sounded the traditional battle cry of the Populists when he stated that the president "has dabbled in inflammatory statements and manufactured panics. . . . The country has been placed in the false position of shouting insults and not even beginning to prepare to take the consequence," echoing Robert La Follette thirty five years before. The sentiments for war and aiding the British were not universally popular, and many believed that FDR's agenda would lead only to unwarranted sacrifice. Charles Lindbergh said, "I have been forced to the conclusion that we cannot win this war for England, regardless of how much assistance we extend." People west of the Mississippi had decidedly weaker international leanings than those in New York and Washington and were strong proponents of neutrality; the isolationist leanings of Idaho's Senator Borah, one of Congress' most prominent Republicans, were well known and he had already been labeled "our spearless leader" by a political opponent years before. Robert La Follette described him as a man "who shook his lion-like mane, drew his sword, called for a charge on the enemy's breastworks, and stopped in his tracks before he got there." The only engagement with the Germans most people were willing to concede was in the case of an outright attack by the Third Reich. Still, when a Gallup poll asked whether people would vote for a "Keep Out of War" party headed by Lindbergh or other notable isolationists, an overwhelming 84 percent said no.[1]

Although the public was not convinced of the inevitability of war, politicians knew it was not far off. In 1939, at the urging of colleagues in

Midwestern View of the War, by McCutcheon. *Chicago Tribune*, 1939.
Reprinted with permission.

Princeton and elsewhere in the United States, Albert Einstein wrote to Roosevelt on the potential nuclear threat that Germany posed: "In the course of the last four months it has been made [clear] . . . that it may become possible to set up a nuclear chain reaction in a large mass of uranium. . . . A single bomb of this type, carried by boat and exploded in a port, might very well destroy the whole port together with some of the surrounding territory." Einstein had already been in the country for six years when he wrote to Roosevelt. His remarks proved correct but the United States was able to develop the bomb first. Hitler's version was widely reported to be the V-3 weapon. Winston Churchill said after the bomb was dropped on Japan in 1945 that "the possession of these powers by the Germans at any time might have altered the course of the war and profound anxiety was felt by those who were informed."

JOBS FOR THE BOYS

As the European war began to expand, FDR came to doubt neutrality's efficacy. In a message to Congress in 1939 he stated unequivocally, "I regret that the Congress passed that act [the Neutrality Act of 1935]. I regret equally that I signed the act." Supplying war materiel was not enough to bolster the Allies. Practically, the country could not afford to wait for Hitler to overrun Europe before deciding how to respond. Organizing the war effort, formally or informally, was a crucial matter.

The size of the task created many skeptics. Montague Norman, governor of the Bank of England, dropped by the American embassy in London for a chat with Ambassador Joseph P. Kennedy, and suggested that no less than "God Almighty" might be needed to run the operation. Norman was well aware that strong leadership was needed for an adventure that not all Americans supported.

The task of guiding the war effort fell to the president himself, who was as close to Norman's "God Almighty" as the country could find. Roosevelt was aware of the immense organizational problem facing a mobilization. While the public was unaware of the behind-the-scenes machinations, his administration was reshaped in 1939 to prepare for what some felt was an inevitable confrontation with Germany. Stockpiling began for certain vital war materiel such as rubber and cotton. Through a series of power shifts within the cabinet, the president managed to place the Treasury in the driver's seat for the war effort. That meant that the treasury secretary, Henry Morgenthau, would play a pivotal role in the conduct of the war. Additionally, in the summer of 1939 FDR created the War Resources Board (WRB). Its job was to advise on how best to mobilize the economy. For its civilian advisory head, the president chose Edward Stettinius Jr., formerly of General Motors and chief executive of the U.S. Steel Corporation. The prematurely white-haired and distinguished-looking businessman was the son of Edward Stettinius, who had managed J. P. Morgan & Company's export department during the First World War and later served as an assistant secretary of war. Like his father, Stettinius was close to Morgan and Wall Street because of his GM and U.S. Steel connections. Roosevelt realized that a huge effort such as mobilization needed to include big business and finance if it was to succeed.

As other members of the board, Stettinius chose Walter Gifford of AT&T, John Pratt of General Motors, Robert Wood of Sears, Roebuck, Harold Moulton of the Brookings Institution, and Karl Kompton of the Massachusetts Institute of Technology. The choices all were appealing to the business community, and it is clear that the entire group was chosen with political allegiances in mind. But the appointments came as something of a surprise to many commentators. Hugh Johnson wrote in his syndicated political column that the resources board represented "Morgan or Dupont financial interests" and that it was a "triple wonder that they accepted, that those interests permitted them to accept, and that the President appointed them."[2] Many chief executives had been members of the Liberty League and were not friendly to the New Deal. These were perhaps the most outwardly puzzling appointments FDR had made since putting Joe Kennedy at the head of the SEC, but it was also a master stroke by the president, for it extended a hand to business and Wall Street, both of which were feeling particularly persecuted by the New Deal.

Administration insiders were upset again, as they were when Kennedy's appointment had been announced six years before. The usually irascible Harold Ickes was particularly irritated. "We wondered how far the President would go or would permit others to go in abdicating in favor of big business, as Wilson did at the time of the First World War," he lamented later. "We had no illusions as to the celerity with which the 'big boys' would move in and take control if they were not rapped over the knuckles." Other close colleagues also complained. Jerome Frank, chairman of the SEC, feared that the war board would undo the gains made by the SEC in controlling Wall Street. At FDR's suggestion, Morgenthau assuaged Frank's fears. He also informed the French government, which was preparing to buy war materiel from the United States, that the administration hoped that they would not employ any American banks, notably Morgan, as brokers in their transactions. Roosevelt noted, "We have to be careful that J. P. Morgan does not get control, not that I have anything against J. P. Morgan because I am talking to him all the time . . . but the public need not know that."[3] The WRB was short-lived, however, and in 1940 FDR asked Stettinius to become commissioner for industrial materials. He immediately accepted. "That [same] afternoon, I wrote out my resignation as Chairman of the Board of the United States Steel Corporation and arranged to cut all my other business connections," he recalled. A rapid succession of other administration jobs opened for him as well. He was later to become secretary of state in 1944.

Congress passed legislation in the summer of 1940 shortly after the German army swept through France, Holland, and Belgium, empowering the Reconstruction Finance Corporation (RFC) to finance the war effort. Specifically, the agency was now able to build and lease manufacturing plants and finance the manufacture of any sort of war materiel it found necessary. Jesse Jones, as head of the RFC, became the czar of war finance and later was appointed secretary of commerce. This enabled the country's two strongest financial bureaucrats to direct the war effort directly in the shadow of the president. Morgenthau was involved with direct war financing, while Jones was charged with finding the money to build war plants and finance the production of materiel.

Jones became the dominant financial personality of the war era, with more public exposure than Morgenthau. Born in Texas in 1874 into a tobacco-farming family, the six-foot, two hundred-pound Jones was a natural businessman in the mold of Billy Durant and Henry Ford. He started his career in real estate, seeing opportunity in Houston, then only a small inland city fifty miles from the Gulf of Mexico. He envisioned the city as a great Gulf port. But in order to realize his dream, the local waterway had to be dredged and enlarged to accommodate oceangoing ships. With the help of local businessmen and government support, the engineering project was undertaken and successfully completed. He made a fortune by selling off the land and buildings he had bought before the project was undertaken. Not being content to simply sit and count his money, he became a banker. Eventually he was enlisted by Woodrow Wilson to serve as director of the Red Cross during World War I, a job that brought him into the national spotlight. His prominence and reputation as a prudent but insightful banker prompted Herbert Hoover to name him to the RFC when it was first established in 1932. Unlike many of the other members of FDR's team, Jones' business experience put him in the front line of the New Deal in dealing with businessmen and bankers. Never quite accepted as a dyed-in-the-wool liberal New Dealer, he nevertheless displayed many of the practical businessman's views that many other cabinet members and advisors lacked. Slowly he also began to accumulate the sort of power that financiers recognized well. Inadvertently, he became something of a financier of monopolies in his own right. As the major money man in the administration he was in a position to decide who received funds from the RFC and helped determine how they were used. His preferences were always for things practical rather than theoretical, and he displayed a strong party loyalty to the Democrats. He also displayed a strong "edifice complex" about buildings he had erected in Houston. His wife remarked that "he has great sentiment about all of his buildings. Every time he passes one, he pats and pets it."[4]

In 1940 Jones was requested to ensure that the United States had enough rubber to meet wartime demand. The price of rubber on the world market was about 20 cents per pound, but Jones would not pay the price; he wanted it cheaper. Jones claimed that he was advised by the country's rubber executives that he would be held hostage by rubber growers, who would use American demand to their own advantage. "Far Eastern rubber growers," he argued, "would begin to hold their stocks in the expectation of still higher prices."[5] While he dickered, the Japanese gladly paid the price and gained a corner on much of the rubber supply. Jones was well known for his antiwar sentiments, and his obstinance was interpreted as being politically motivated.

His failure to gain an adequate supply infuriated many in Congress. The country was left with less than a year's supply in the stockpile. As a result, a scrap rubber campaign was begun. The president went on national radio to kick off the campaign to gather as much rubber as possible. Gasoline stations were pressed into service to collect used rubber, paying 1 cent per pound. Calling for all citizens to turn in any nonessential rubber, FDR said unequivocally that "we are going to see to it that there is enough rubber to build the planes to bomb Tokyo and Berlin." Months later, a Senate

Rubber Problem Bouncing Around, by Berryman. *Washington Evening Star*, 1942

committee headed by Harry Truman began to inquire into the whole affair of war procurements. The *Washington Post* was especially critical of Jones as the inquiry proceeded. One evening, Jones found himself at the same reception in Washington as Eugene Meyer, the publisher of the newspaper and a former member of the RFC. After some harsh words, Jones shoved Meyer, breaking his eyeglasses. That caused the newspaperman to take a swing at Jones in retaliation (he missed). The *New York Times,* with understated tongue in cheek, reported the matter as "a fistic encounter at the annual dinner of the Alfalfa Club at the Hotel Willard." The rubber story had a happier ending when the United States began producing synthetic rubber in 1941 rather than rely solely upon the natural variety.

The Battle of Britain began in August 1940. The Germans bombed London extensively, for as much as eight hours at a time. Many Londoners took refuge in the Underground, which was set deep enough to provide safety. In retaliation, the British bombed Berlin and hit the Reichstag building, among other notable landmarks. The sorties so infuriated Berlin that the Reich stated it would continue the blitz until "the smoking ruins of industrial and military objectives, decimation of the British Air Force and shattered morale of the British people bring into power a government that will accept German terms."[6] The British need for war materiel was at the point where the backlog of orders placed in the United States almost outstripped their ability to pay. At one point England requested five thousand tanks, half of the stock of the American army at the time. But the administration felt that the RFC would be able to build new factories and produce the arms needed, and indeed Jesse Jones saw no reason why the enterprise could not be successfully undertaken. Toward this end, the Defense Plant Corporation (DPC) was created shortly after the Battle of Britain began. The DPC was a subsidiary of the Reconstruction Finance Corporation and was charged with building plants that would produce goods necessary to the war. Many times, the plants would be built and then leased for as little as $1 per year to a company that would operate it.

In order to ship the materials, Roosevelt began thinking about leasing American-built ships to London. That would satisfy critics who claimed that the British were receiving unfairly favorable treatment since the United States officially was not at war with the Germans. Despite the evident gravity of the situation abroad, some in the United States believed Britain was taking advantage of the United States to obtain soft terms for the assistance. Since the eighteenth century, the British had been the largest foreign investors in the United States, and suspicions were that they were hiding some of their assets rather than liquidate them to aid their own cause. Jones himself leaned toward this view at one point. But Roosevelt defused much of the talk about the value of the aid by couching the matter in terms of principle. He told Morgenthau, "I don't want to put the thing in terms of dollars or loans. . . . We will manufacture what we need . . . and then we will say to England, we will give you the guns and the ships that you need, provided that when the war is over you will return to us in kind the guns and the ships we have loaned to you."[7] That seemed an acceptable way to conduct the aid program. Jesse Jones agreed to buy some commodities from the United Kingdom so that it could be supplied with cash. But by late 1940 the British were running desperately short. In a message to Congress, the President stated that "the British commitments in this country for defense articles had reached the limit of their future dollar resources." As a result, the Lend-Lease program was conceived as a

Reviving Shipping from U Boat Attacks, Herblock in *Honolulu Star Bulletin*, 1942.

way to supply an old ally while at the same time maintaining the appearance of being a nonbelligerent. As it turned out, the timing was impeccable because the British were on the verge of bankruptcy.

Roosevelt described the plan in the simplest terms possible: "Suppose my neighbor's house catches fire, and I have a length of garden hose four or five hundred feet away. If he can take my garden hose and connect it with his hydrant, I may help him to put out the fire." The Lend-Lease Act was passed in March 1941. It provided for billions of dollars of aid in the form of weapons and food to the Allies, to be paid back in kind, in prop-

No Opportunism During the War, by Halladay. *Providence Journal*, 1942.
Reprinted with permission.

erty, or in any other form the president deemed appropriate payment at the time.

The program had clear benefits for the United States because it helped standardize arms, helping create a huge demand for American-produced goods from all of the Allies. Within the first several months, the program dispensed over 60 percent of the $7 billion Congress had allocated for it. The plan certainly had its detractors, however. The geographical split in the nation was visible again. Senator Burton Wheeler, a Democrat from Montana, fulminated about Roosevelt's assumption that the nation would back him in so openly aiding Britain. "Approval of this legislation means war, open and complete warfare. I therefore ask the American people before they supinely accept it—was the last World War worthwhile?" he stormed. Senator Robert A. Taft, a Republican from Ohio and son of the late president, rose in the Senate in 1941 and openly queried whether using American ships to supply the British, requiring an amendment to the

We Can't Equal Their Sacrifices, but We Might Try

Neutrality Act, would not involve the United States in the war in a de facto manner. "It is only because of the provisions of the Neutrality Act," he said, "which we are asked to repeal that we are not at war today." Other prominent Republicans also opposed it. Herbert Hoover and Alf Landon came out against it, as did Wendell Willkie, though by 1944 he had come to support it. In his unsuccessful quest for a second Republican nomination that year, Willkie then urged his fellow candidates to abandon the new isolationism advocated by the *Chicago Tribune*, among others, to ensure that the United States would remain involved in world affairs after the war ended. Organized labor was also split over the issue. Henry Morgenthau put the choices squarely when he said that "if Congress does not act on this bill, there is nothing left for Britain to do but stop fighting."

The program had its proponents and opponents in the academic world as well, and they too often split along geographic lines. James Conant, president of Harvard, said that "our only hope as a free people lies in a defeat of the Axis Powers," while Robert Maynard Hutchins, of the University of Chicago, fretted that "the American people are about to commit suicide." Yet Lend-Lease clearly was the best stimulus the economy had for years. Along with the official war effort, which began after Pearl Harbor was attacked, it created jobs and put millions back to work. The administration of the program was led by Stettinius, who was joined by several former members of the War Resources Board. Of the $12.9 billion dispensed by the lend-lease program, Stettinius later remarked, "We Americans are a hard headed people and the average American will naturally say to himself . . . have we got our money's worth? . . . I think that we have in more than a double measure. The total impact of Lend-Lease on our economy has been relatively small. The dividends it has paid have been enormous."[8] By "dividends" he was referring to the foreign policy coup that the United States had scored by facing the Axis powers, not the pure economic benefits. In reality, by the end of the war over eight million people were employed in the war effort, and the administration was very concerned about how much unemployment would be created once hostilities ceased. The administration did not wish to be remembered for going to war to stimulate the economy.

SPARE $150 BILLION?

Finding enough money to finance the war effort was a herculean task. In previous wars, Wall Street had given notable assistance by helping to sell Treasury bonds to investors. But in the atmosphere created by the New Deal, with its emphasis on state-directed capitalism, Wall Street's presence was not so clearly felt, even though the Treasury's appetite for cash dwarfed previous borrowings. The close connection between the Treasury's war efforts and its direct sales of bonds to the American public made the job easier. The financial community was not so enamored of the New Deal nor of taking a backseat in major bond financings, but the question became one of patriotism as well as practical politics. No financial institution could afford to be seen as reluctant to help the country raise funds.

Morgenthau devised a multiple-pronged campaign to raise as much from all quarters of society as possible. He had many precedents. The Treasury bond issues sold during the Civil War and World War I were the largest ever held at the time, and the selling methods of the past were well remembered. Banks, the wealthy, and the average citizen would again all be pressed into service to provide as much as they could afford to invest. Banks were sold Treasury bonds, and citizens, both wealthy and humble, were sold savings bonds that ranged from large denominations to small denominations represented by stamps that could be bought by schoolchildren for only a few cents per week. Cartoonists had good sport suggesting that Morgenthau shamelessly vied for children's ice cream money in order to sell more bonds. The program was determined to be as broad and equitable as possible; special marketing attention was paid to the workingman. Financing the war was to be something the average citizen could be proud of. Irving Berlin was commissioned to write a theme song for the effort. A weekly radio program, the *Treasury Hour,* was broadcast on CBS touting the program. Its first script was penned by an unknown writer named Herman Wouk, and it featured a wide array of stars enlisted to appeal to workers' patriotism. Many companies arranged for their employees to contribute to the program by deducting contributions from their wages. The list of participating companies read like a Who's Who of American business. Many of the companies mentioned in the TNEC findings were prominent on the list.

By Berryman. *Washington Evening Star*, 1944.

The Treasury mounted eight war loan drives that raised over $150 billion. It made strenuous attempts to limit the purchases made by banks so that they could not simply buy war bonds rather than make loans to individual and commercial customers, limiting their risks. That did occur, however, and the banks accumulated more treasury bonds on their books than they did loans to customers. So the Treasury took its borrowings directly to investors large and small to ensure that the banks did not acquire an advantage that could hurt the government after the war was finished. Politically, it did not want to be indebted to the banks after more than a decade of feuding. In that respect, the program was a success.

One other rarely mentioned aim of the program was to keep down

GUILTY
CONSCIENCE

By Webster. *New York Herald Tribune*, 1942. © 1941, *The Washington Post*.
Reprinted with permission.

inflation. Keenly aware of the price spiral that had broken loose after the
last war, Roosevelt's advisors were certain that the public investment in
bonds would keep demand for goods low, thereby keeping a lid on prices.
That, unfortunately, was not to be the case. The war was putting people
back to work, and the savings bond programs did not absorb all the extra
cash that their newfound employment was producing. *The Economist* reckoned that "slightly more than $1 billion a month is being mopped up in war
savings bonds, leaving the enormous amount of about $2 billion a

month . . . considerably more than the whole pre-war British national income—as a net addition to potential purchasing power."⁹ There were other domestic doubters as well. The chairman of the Federal Reserve, Marriner Eccles, wanted more authority for the Fed in borrowing programs. He suggested that the central bank be given more authority to fight inflation directly by increasing bank reserves. Eccles was a longtime critic of the Treasury who previously sponsored legislation enlarging the Fed's powers in the 1930s. The central bank was still fighting for respect almost thirty years after its founding and a dozen years after its less-than-sterling performance in the years leading up to the crash in 1929. But FDR would have none of it. In a statement that gave ample evidence of the Fed's overall influence at the time, Roosevelt told Morgenthau that "the Federal Reserve System is so unimportant, nobody believes anything that Mariner Eccles says or pays any attention to him. . . . The important thing is the war. England, that is the important thing."¹⁰

Fund-raising drives were also popular in the various war loan drives. Hundreds of volunteer bond salesmen were used nationwide to sell the various denominations. Boy Scouts donated their time and proved able salesmen, selling bonds door to door. In the summer of 1944 a three-way baseball game was held in New York featuring the Yankees, Giants, and Dodgers. A throng of fifty thousand saw the teams play each other on the same field for the first time. Bonds were sold in conjunction with the event. Scoring was so complicated that a Columbia University mathematician was employed to keep the tally. But the game was a great success for the Treasury, raising over $56 million, $50 million from the city itself and the rest from the public. As part of the larger nationwide drive, over $4.5 billion was raised. Many single investments of over $1 million were received. The Treasury symbolically sold a $100 bond to Winston Churchill, who was visiting the United States at the time. Even Joseph Stalin sent greetings, supporting the effort. One of the best places to sell bonds proved to be the floor of the New York Stock Exchange. At a drive in 1944, brokers subscribed more than $100 million in one day alone. Insurance companies were also heavy subscribers, using the bonds purchased to back their policies in force. But the enormous borrowings barely financed the war effort. When the conflict with Germany ended, even before Japan surrendered, Morgenthau put the estimated cost of victory at $275 billion. "Although

V-J Day may still be far off, every bond bought will bring the final victory nearer," he noted.

Despite all of the successes, the rates of return on patriotism were hardly generous. In 1940 the Treasury offered stamps that could be redeemed in ten years for a $25 bond at an interest rate of less than 3 percent. Inflation was already heating up and was at least twice that amount. The bond interest rate was also less than the rate the RFC was charging major corporations on its loans. Similar discrepancies existed throughout the war. Bernard Baruch took a dim view of what he considered the fleecing of the average citizen. He later wrote that "during World War Two, millions of families were persuaded to invest in U.S. savings bonds as the patriotic thing to do. These people have seen the value of their savings slashed by the lowered purchasing power of the dollar. . . . If any company listed on the Stock Exchange had engaged in equivalent financial practices, its directors would be facing prosecution by the SEC."[11] That was a bit of hyperbole, because not offering a decent rate of return was not illegal, just slightly mean-spirited. The war effort required the cheapest money available.

The amount of money borrowed by the Treasury was the largest in history. On the other side of the coin, business was expected to do its part. More important for business were the new taxes that took effect in 1940. One of the ideological centerpieces of the administration's war effort was an excess-profits tax. Roosevelt wanted to ensure that no business profited by the war effort. As a result, businesses that profited more after the war effort began than they had in the previous years would face an extraordinary high tax rate on those war-induced profits. But taxes of that sort were very difficult to enact. Although advocating them was politically correct, actually passing an equitable law was a different matter. The administration settled on a plan to tax a company involved in war production if its wartime profits exceeded those achieved in the 1930s. This astute political move ensured that large companies could join the war production effort without having to worry about paying much new tax. Newer companies would suffer if their profits increased, however. Although the excess-profits tax appeared on the surface to be a disincentive for business, more than one entrepreneur spotted a silver lining in the clouds and would soon be vigorously involved in the war effort.

"PRODIGIES OF PRODUCTION"

The war produced a new breed of industrialist. Both upstarts and seasoned veterans recognized opportunity when they saw it. The RFC was loaning money and leasing plants on terms that banks and Wall Street could not match. As a result, many schemes were hatched, some brilliant and visionary, others plain duds, that challenged the government administrators who oversaw the various bureaucratic programs to sort out the preposterous from the possible.

As part of his job as the czar of war production, Jesse Jones was brought into contact with many industrialists. He found himself in the position of having to negotiate prices with them for goods and materials, many of which he knew nothing about. That sort of one-to-one negotiating suited his personal style; he liked to take the measure of his opponent across the table and then sit down and negotiate down to the nitty-gritty. One vital material that required much negotiating was aluminum. America's production of aluminum was far behind that of Germany, the world's largest producer, and the War Production Board instructed Jones to see that several new aluminum plants were built. The industry was still dominated by the Aluminum Company of America (Alcoa), and in 1940 it was headed by septuagenarian Arthur V. Davis, who had worked for the company since its first days in Pittsburgh. Alcoa was the only logical choice, and Jones turned to Davis for assistance. But unknown to Jones at the time was the antitrust case the government had previously brought against Alcoa in 1937 and which was still outstanding (it would be decided by a federal court in 1945). Roosevelt certainly never forgot Alcoa, however, even during the war. Jones related that the president sent him a memo when it became clear that the RFC was financing twelve new plants. "What about this story about twelve new aluminum plants—all to be operated by Alcoa?" came the presidential query. "We find that they are all well organized and progressing on schedule," came Jones' reply. He also pointed out that Reynolds Metals Company was part of the project in order to keep up the appearances of competition, although Alcoa was the clear beneficiary.[12]

How much Alcoa benefited became clear as Jones continued his protracted negotiations with Davis. All during the time he was discussing terms with Alcoa, government orders for supplies were backing up badly.

His final deal promised to turn the plants over to the company when hostilities ceased, ensuring it a continued monopoly. The Truman committee, headed by Senator Harry Truman, investigating war contracts, was aghast at the prospect, and Jones himself became more truculent than ever when confronted with its dismay, refusing to answer the committee's questions when called before it. He called the committee's chief counsel and primary interrogator a "whippersnapper." When the major newspapers turned against him, he became increasingly hostile, since his political ambitions were now being openly questioned. Politics and deal making may have been his forte, but tact was not his strong suit.

Despite the foot-dragging and delays in the war production program, midway through the war it was clear the economic muscle of the United States had gained substantial strength. In a commentary that would have made Elbert Gary smile, *The Economist* noted that in Gary, Indiana, alone, "the 36,000 steel workers . . . are producing and partially or wholly processing more than 80 percent as much steel as the whole of Japan." But because the productive capacity of the country seemed to be creating excess even during wartime, many steel plants were actually scaling back production. Shipbuilding followed suit; it was able to supply more than enough ships regardless of the number lost at sea. One of the country's best-known shipbuilders was Henry J. Kaiser, who built hundreds of ships from his base on the West Coast. He was known as a daring entrepreneur who rarely said no to a new business deal. He ranked at the very top of the New Deal's list of favorite businessmen—and that accolade was very difficult to earn in FDR's administration.

Kaiser was much more than a shipbuilder. He was also one of the early New Deal's "earth movers" whose construction companies helped build the massive dams in the American West in the early 1930s. He was a direct beneficiary of David Lilienthal's efforts to ensure that the TVA occupied a central place in infrastructure investments for the power industry. Born in 1884 in upstate New York, Kaiser shared the entrepreneurial spirit and dogged determination of many industrialists of his era. He found his way to Washington in 1909, lured by the building potential of the Pacific Northwest. Recognizing the western mistrust of the East and Wall Street, Kaiser realized that the infrastructure needs of the West would create vast opportunities for wealth. When the New Deal arrived, the West also received sizeable government investment along the lines of the TVA. The final stages of Boulder Dam, on the Colorado River, and the Bonneville Dam, on the Columbia River, were two major projects funded by the government in attempts to bolster infrastructure and provide jobs at the same time. Kaiser's companies were integrally involved with both, and he became the darling of the administration because his jobs always came in on time and on (or under) budget. But wartime created new needs, and ships became of primary importance.

Answering the call, Kaiser managed to reduce the delivery time on a new freighter from over three months to just a week. He employed new steel fabricating techniques to drastically cut down production time. He also helped develop steel production on the West Coast, substantially reducing delivery times for California shipyards. Jesse Jones described him as someone "who was ready to try anything if the government would put up the money." The reputation was well earned. Shipbuilding led to magnesium production, another wartime necessity that Kaiser wanted to try, provided the RFC put up enough cash. Kaiser wanted to employ a Hungarian inventor to build and operate a plant that would extract magnesium based upon the inventor's proprietary method. As both secretary of commerce and head of the RFC, Jones knew that Kaiser was turning a profit of almost $100,000 per ship built. He agreed to build a $28 million plant to give the process a chance if Kaiser would put up $100,000 of his own money and turn over his shipbuilding profits as collateral. As Jones noted, "The whole set-up looked a little screwy to me, one that would be of doubtful outcome."

Jones was proven correct. The enterprise failed, and the Hungarian found himself in prison as an enemy alien. But the loss of the plant and his profits did not deter Kaiser, who subsequently offered to build a steel plant for the government, again using $100,000 of his own money. And again the RFC complied, loaning him a total of $100 million. This plant never returned its projected profits or even met its production standards during the war. But Kaiser's methods were becoming clearer as time went on. By using his shipbuilding profits as collateral, he was reinvesting them in other businesses free of the excess profits tax. If he had not done so, the tax would have taken a substantial part of his profits, leaving him with very little. But by plowing them into other businesses he was looking toward the day when the war would be finished and he would have useful production facilities, most likely built at government expense. This suggested that American industry was in better shape financially than many in government thought. The SEC lent some credence to this idea when it published a study in 1944 indicating that American companies were in as good a position as they had ever been financially. Their cash positions had increased substantially since the war began, increasing by over 70 percent.[13] That conclusion startled many government officials who thought the opposite.

One of Kaiser's better-known forays into the world of technology came when he proposed building the world's largest military cargo plane. Much skepticism surrounded the proposal until Kaiser persuaded Howard Hughes to join the project. Hughes at the time was the country's most prominent authority on airplanes and flight technology. With $18 million of the RFC's money, a plant was built to produce three of these monster cargo planes, each large enough to hold a company of soldiers. Unfortunately, because of a shortage of strategic metals, the plane prototype had to be built of wood. Hughes took over the project personally and never let Kaiser inside the plant after it was built. The plane became known as the "Spruce Goose." Kaiser eventually dropped out of the project, but Hughes continued development of the plane well after the war.

The war produced factories that matched the incredible production demands. In 1943 Chrysler Corporation opened in Chicago the world's largest aircraft-engine plant. Its chief products were two-thousand-horsepower engines designed for fighter-bombers. The plant covered five hundred acres and had a parking lot over a mile long to accommodate its workers, estimated to be over twenty-five thousand when the plant was in full operation. The plant was quickly dubbed "Hitler's headache" and outshone the previous record holder, Henry Ford's RFC-financed Willow Run facility outside Detroit, which covered over two square miles. The manager of the Chrysler plant bragged that he could take the whole Ford assembly plant at Willow Run and put it inside one of his buildings and still have plenty of space left for several baseball fields. Willow Run suffered its own production problems and was less efficient than General Motors in producing engines, but the public clearly wanted to see Henry Ford succeed despite his "bigness," his anti-Semitic remarks, and other eccentricities over the years. A reporter for the *Christian Science Monitor* blurted that "the Pyramid of Cheops or the hanging gardens of Babylon may have satisfied the ancients, but for me, I'll take a today's phenomenon to top my list of wonders," when discussing the mammoth facility. Equally, the *Detroit Free Press* gushed, "It will be written that the shadows cast by the flight of Willow Run's bombers in the spring of 1942 portended the coming doom of the enemies of humanity."[14]

Aside from bragging rights, it was clear that big business was aiding the war effort significantly and that the RFC was aiding big business. The average RFC loan charged around 4 percent interest, a rate better than many corporations could have found anywhere else. *The Economist* noted that over 70 percent of war supply contracts had gone to the top one hundred corporations between 1940 and 1942.[15] Industry was using the war to significantly increase its productive capacity. As the war was ending, the massive Willow Run facility became available because Ford no longer saw the need for it; by 1946 Ford Motor, now run by Henry Ford II, would fall to third place in auto manufacturing behind General Motors and Chrysler, and its future was no longer certain. Kaiser was quick to seize the opportunity and acquired the plant. While the war was in its final stages, he joined forces with Joseph W. Frazer, of the Graham-Paige Motor Company, with a plan to produce cars once the hostilities ended. The market seemed to be on his side, since for four years no domestic passenger cars had been produced while factories concentrated only on war production. By 1944 the price of used cars had been rising by about 1 percent per month since 1941, and Chester Bowles, head of the Office of Price Administration, announced a ceiling on used-car prices in that year. Kaiser had been lobbying for the conversion of war plants to peacetime use for some time. In 1944 he paid a visit to the White House to lay out a plan to FDR. His idea was to have companies take over plants on the verge of shutting down and then convert them to peacetime use. Characteristically, he added that he thought the president "believes that this pattern of aiding industry is an important step to assure now the transition to full employment in peacetime."[16] He knew that the prospect of full employment would be difficult to resist. As noted, the administration was very worried about the prospects for employment once the war ended. No one wanted a return to the 1930s.

In 1945 Kaiser and Frazer formed the Kaiser-Frazer Corporation and borrowed $44 million from the RFC to finance the venture. Immediately after peace was declared, they began production, making three cars named the Kaiser, Henry J., and Frazer. None was known for its design or reliability, but they represented the first new cars introduced in two decades. But within five years, production stopped. Kaiser eventually became Kaiser Industries, manufacturer of Willys jeeps. General Motors finally acquired Willow Run, and the Kaiser foray into automobile manufacturing came to an end.

Kaiser's failure to successfully penetrate the automobile market was something of a testimony to the oligopolistic structure of the industry. Even with significant government financing, something that he had relied upon since his earth-moving projects, Kaiser apparently did not possess the know-how or design capabilities to break the hold of the Big Three auto makers.[17] Smaller competitors such as Hudson did exist, but eventually they too left the industry. The public became accustomed to three auto manufacturers and their reliable products and ultimately did not purchase new products without a proven track record.

SPLITTING HAIRS?

Ever since the Justice Department filed suit against Alcoa in 1937, seeking its dissolution on the grounds that it was in violation of the Sherman Act, the case had been winding its way through the federal courts. Many of the over 130 charges made against Alcoa were historical in nature, dating back to the earlier part of the century. The fact that it was a Mellon company did not help its public image either, because Andrew Mellon, although secretary of the treasury under Coolidge, was not popular after the Depression began. Along with Charles Mitchell of National City Bank, Mellon, a rich man preaching frugality at a time when economic stimulus was needed to set the economy aright, was often portrayed as the embodiment of what was wrong with America in the early 1930s.

The first decision in the case came from Judge Francis Caffey in the Southern District of New York. In a decision that astonished almost everyone, he found Alcoa not guilty on all charges. It took him nine days to deliver his ruling, given the extent of the proceedings. In his conclusion the judge remarked that "the astonishing thing is the great number of witnesses who appeared on the stand, competitors as well as customers of Alcoa, who have completely exculpated Alcoa from blame . . . in great part a tribute to Mr. Arthur V. Davis." Davis himself was sartorially something of a throwback to the nineteenth century. He certainly never bowed to the power of public relations, and while the courts found him forthcoming, his public image was something of a modern-day robber baron.[18] Simply, the government had not proven its case, although it was clear that the company maintained a monopoly position in its industry. The government would not let the matter rest, however. It appealed to the Supreme Court.

But the high court could not muster a majority because several of its members had previously been involved in litigation against Alcoa in years past. Congress passed a law stating that when the Supreme Court could not muster a majority, the case was to be directed to the U.S. Circuit Court of Appeals. That brought the Alcoa matter under the jurisdiction of the famed judge Learned Hand. In his fifty-year career on the bench, Hand had declared only two laws unconstitutional and was known for practicing judicial restraint. He was one of the most famous federal judges never to reach the Supreme Court. A graduate of Harvard and its law school, he allied himself with liberal causes throughout much of his early life and gained a great deal of respect as a jurist. Appointed to the federal bench in 1909 by President Taft, Hand was a supporter of Teddy Roosevelt's Bull Moose Party in the 1912 election. That earned him the enmity of Taft when the former president became chief justice. Hand found himself on the outside looking in from that time and had to settle for the Court of Appeals for the Second Circuit until his retirement in 1951.

The decision issued by Hand and the two other judges of the court upheld the circuit court decision on all counts except one: It found that Alcoa had maintained a monopoly in the manufacture of aluminum ingots until 1940. In adroit language, Hand's decision pointed out that while Alcoa had not used its power to the detriment of customers, it had maintained a monopoly in aluminum ingots. The old idea about "good" and "bad" trusts was officially dead; a monopoly was a monopoly, and how it exercised its power made little difference in the eyes of the law. Concerning the dissolution requested by the Justice Department, Hand wrote, "It is idle for the plaintiff to assume that dissolution will be proper, as it is for Alcoa to assume that it will not be. . . . Dissolution is not a penalty, but a remedy; if the industry will not need it for its protection, it will be a disservice to break up an aggregation which has for so long demonstrated its efficiency."[19]

Alcoa petitioned for a judgment that it no longer had a monopoly in the ingot market. It cited World War II as an example, showing that it now had competition from Reynolds and Kaiser. The circuit court hearing the case decided in 1950 that competition now existed and there was no reason for Alcoa to divest itself of any assets. Size was evidence of monopoly, but it appeared that Alcoa had not exercised its dominant market position through prices. As a result, the final verdict favored Alcoa after thirteen years of litigation and delays. Both sides claimed victory. Learned Hand was remembered for his decision, perhaps the most significant antitrust decision made outside the Supreme Court. A year later, he handed down another notable decision that included a fair amount of economic reasoning in it and proved to be a precursor for the more rigorous economic analysis that antitrust law was to undergo thirty years later.[20]

The Alcoa case showed that history played an important role in judgments about monopoly power. It was a card the Justice Department played many times, not always successfully. Its use often begged a much larger issue: If companies had been exercising monopoly power for so long, why was it that the government waited so long to prosecute? The entire issue was very political and often depended upon the climate of the times before being filed.

In the 1940s two other well-known cases were decided in the government's favor. In 1946 the Supreme Court ruled against the American Tobacco Company for the second time in the century, upholding a lower court decision that the company, along with Liggett & Meyers and R. J. Reynolds, conspired to fix prices against other, minor competitors. The three all had raised prices in tandem and conspired to deprive competitors of a supply of cheap tobacco that could have been used to compete with them. Since the three held over 75 percent of the domestic market for cigarettes, they in effect had what was known as a shared monopoly between them. In the other case, the motion picture industry, one of the subjects of the TNEC investigation, found itself in the spotlight during the Depres-

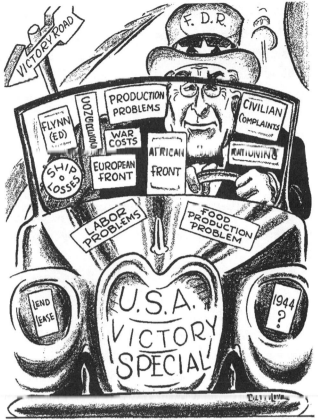

Sometimes it's hard to see the road ... By Betty Love

By Betty Love. *Springfield Leader & Press*, 1943.

sion. The industry had been consolidating since the First World War, and
the term "movie trust" was commonly used when describing the industry.
In the mid-1920s technology changed the industry when the first sound
tracks were added to film. *The Jazz Singer* in 1927 was the first "talkie" and
proved to be a great success. The major studios each had different methods
of producing sound, driving up the costs of production. The influx of customers wanting to see and hear the new technology helped accelerate a
trend already developing. If the studios could control distribution of their
films, they could also control the prices paid by the customers, avoiding
price competition. As a result, they began to assemble chains of movie theaters. The independent theaters complained, and a series of court actions
began in the 1920s to break the major studios' dominance.

The Justice Department maintained that one of the five major studios, Paramount, violated antitrust laws by controlling the market for theaters. Paramount was the largest operator of theater chains in the country, with about fifteen hundred under its banner and another five hundred affiliated with it. That represented about 11 percent of all movie theaters. Smaller and independent theaters complained that they were restricted in showing first-run movies and often had to show second-rate films instead, hurting their incomes. The chains also dictated the prices they could charge their customers, often stipulating charges for one of their films. Such studios were operating vertical monopolies by controlling the market for their films. Thurman Arnold filed suit against Paramount when he first arrived at the Justice Department, and similar suits were filed against the other major studios as well.

The movie industry was not wholly behind Paramount and the other major studios. Some saw the suit as long overdue and felt that the industry needed a shake-up. Samuel Goldwyn, as a member of the Society of Independent Motion Picture Producers, argued that the "divorcement of exhibition from production is essential to the health of our industry in order to break the strangle-hold held by a few companies on the exhibition market." The case went to trial in a lower court, where Paramount was found guilty of operating a monopoly. Appealing to the Supreme Court, the studio lost in 1944. After another trial on slightly different terms, Paramount was again found guilty of restraining trade, and once more appealed to the Supreme Court. The second time around the tension level in the industry was much higher, because the survival of the industry's distribution network was also at stake. Bosley Crowther, arts critic of the *New York Times,* noted before the start of the proceeding that "while the sixty to seventy million customers who go to the movies in this country every week may not be hanging breathlessly on it, an issue of momentous importance to the American motion picture industry will go before the Supreme Court."[21] In the second decision in 1948, the guilty verdict was upheld again. Part of the government's suit requested a severing of the theaters from the studios. This actually began after the decision when the major studios agreed to refrain from monopoly practices and set up independent film distributors. These new companies could not be owned by or share investors with the studios. Along with Paramount, the other studios affected were RKO, National, Stanley Warner, and Loews. The affair reminded many of the breakup of the banking industry fifteen years before through the Glass-Steagall Act; many commentators called it the greatest antitrust victory ever scored by the government in its battle against business. Paramount president Barney Balaban predicted that his company's profitability would suffer as a result: "I am certain that the decision in our case . . . will force transformations within the industry." He was right. In the years immediately following, the number of first-run movie houses increased—*Life* magazine estimated that there were fifteen hundred new first-run houses by 1951.[22] The public benefited as new first-run films were being shown to a wider audience than had been the case under the old vertical distribution system.

The commerce clause of the Constitution raised its head again in an antitrust case in *United States v. South-Eastern Underwriters.* Insurance was one of the original areas investigated by TNEC. For three-quarters of a century, insurance had been considered a state matter and was not subject to interstate commerce. The government charged that the association, representing over two hundred insurance companies in the South, colluded to fix premiums and monopolize insurance. But the Court, by a 4 to 3 margin (with two justices abstaining), agreed with the government that insurance was indeed a matter of interstate commerce and therefore subject to the Sherman Act. In a dissenting opinion, Justice Robert H. Jackson questioned whether it was the government's desire to nationalize insurance companies. "If it be desirable" to do this, he said, it should be done in an orderly manner, not by court decision."[23] The old pre–World War I argument about the proper role of the judiciary in framing economic and social policy had again raised its head.

LONG MEMORIES

President Roosevelt died on April 12, 1945. Harry Truman assumed the reins of power and was widely believed to be overwhelmed by the job he had assumed. But his image as a hard-line New Dealer remained. Truman had made some very strong statements about bankers and Wall Street financiers while he was a senator from Missouri, and now his administration was in a position to pursue some unfinished business with the Wall

Street crowd. In 1947 the Justice Department under Attorney General Tom Clark took action against another longtime nemesis of reform-minded Democrats—Wall Street investment bankers.

Despite all of the crises, new laws passed, and congressional hearings that had taken place since the turn of the century, Wall Street had never come under scrutiny for violations of the Sherman or Clayton Acts. Many techniques used by investment bankers certainly looked like fertile ground for modern trustbusters. So a suit was filed against seventeen Wall Street firms alleging monopoly practices in the investment banking business over the years. Trust busters again displayed a very long memory, perhaps too long. Clearly, a long history of violations seemed the best way to prove monopoly, as it had successfully in the Alcoa case.

United States v. Henry S. Morgan et al. struck at the heart of the securities business. Henry S. Morgan, Jack Morgan's son, was at the head of Morgan Stanley & Company, which had split off from J. P. Morgan & Company in 1934 after the Glass-Steagall Act mandated that commercial banks could no longer continue in the investment banking business and had to choose between the two sides of the business. Morgan chose to stay with commercial banking, spinning off Morgan Stanley to continue the lucrative investment banking business under the assumption that when FDR left office the securities business would be allowed to return to the commercial banks, where it had resided for over a hundred years. That miscalculation proved crucial to the development of Wall Street in the twentieth century.

Morgan Stanley remained the premier securities underwriter during the Depression and war years. As a sign of its closeness to J. P. Morgan & Company, its back-room operations were kept at the bank's offices. But the securities business had not made any friends during the 1930s. The most damning charge made against Wall Street concerned a "capital strike" during the years following the Glass-Steagall Act and the Securities Act of 1933. Most investment banks had resented the financial disclosures required by the Securities Act of 1933 when a company issued new stocks or bonds, considering a client company's finances sacred, not to be aired publicly, as required by the law. As a result, many investment bankers were slow to bring new stocks and bonds to market. The Depression did not help; many new financings were canceled or never made it to market because of the rapid deterioration of business conditions. What new bonds did come to market were sold privately by Wall Street, taking advantage of a loophole in the laws that allowed them to be sold without having to register with the SEC. Those maneuvers, along with the grumbling done in public by many Wall Street and business leaders about the New Deal, did not enhance the image of the securities business.

The suit brought against the Wall Street seventeen was the first brought against securities underwriters. The government claimed that there existed "an integrated, over-all conspiracy and combination formed in or about 1915 and in continuous operation thereafter, by which the defendants as a group developed a system to eliminate competition and monopolize the cream of the business of investment banking."[24] The date was significant, since the government maintained that the conspiracy began at the time of the Anglo-French loan of 1915, put together for those governments during the first war by Morgan. Over the years, the top Wall Street firms maintained a hold on their businesses through the use of syndicates, where only other banks invited could help underwrite a new securities issue. Proof that those syndicates had excluded smaller investment banks over the years while keeping the lion's share of the business for themselves was evidence of monopoly concentration, the Justice Department maintained.

While the terms of the suit were unusually broad, so too was the conceptual underpinning. Washington was putting history on trial and admitting that Wall Street had still been able to thumb its nose at the SEC after 1934 despite the new regulations put in place during the early days of the New Deal. The suit was another belated attempt by the government to pursue the industries investigated by the TNEC. In purely public relations terms, it seemed to have chosen the most vulnerable industry. Others were not as vulnerable because of their contribution to the war effort. Wall Street had less goodwill built up and was always a favorite whipping boy in any event. Fortunately for the Street, the federal judge presiding over the trial that followed was not an old Progressive like Learned Hand but the pragmatic Harold Medina.

Medina presided over the case for several years, although he admitted that at the beginning he knew little about the securities business. He set himself the task of learning as much about the business as possible with the help of friendly investment bankers not tied to Morgan or the other sixteen firms. He enlisted the help of investment banker Harold Stuart, the head of Halsey Stuart and Company. Stuart was something of a Wall Street outsider because he was on the record as favoring competitive bidding for new securities issues. Medina said that Stuart was a "man of complete integrity upon whose testimony I could rely with confidence." Asking anyone else to advise him would have been tantamount to Medina asking a fox to describe its poaching tactics to a henhouse full of chickens.

Medina's quick training course in securities underwriting, while admirable, only underlined the government's shortcomings when dealing with investment bankers. Not many in the Justice Department actually understood the methods employed from day to day by Wall Street when bringing new stocks and bonds to market, so testimony from the alleged collaborators was vital. Naturally, all seventeen firms maintained their innocence, denying that they ever colluded to price securities to the detriment of the smaller firms in their industry. The main thrust of the government's charge was that the syndicates underwriting securities had been remarkably similar since 1915. The securities houses responded that they maintained historic relationships with their clients that indeed stretched over decades; it was to be expected. Investment bankers sold services, not goods, and those sorts of relationships took long periods of time to develop. The reason many of the Morgan clients remained with the bank for years was because they received good service and advice, not because of collusion. Besides, was it not the government that had forced the issue by breaking up the industry in 1933, thus creating the present investment banking business?

The seventeen firms did enjoy a concentration of capital that did prove useful to oligopolies. Because of the capital-intensive nature of investment banking, not everyone could enter the business, not even the ambitious second- and third-tier securities houses that dreamed of joining the bigger firms on the Street. But again, proving a monopoly or oligopoly concentration based purely upon concentration of capital rather than tangible products was difficult, if not impossible.

After examining the evidence, which he found to be mostly circumstantial and cursory, Medina finally dismissed the case in 1953. He concluded, "I have come to the settled conviction and accordingly find that no such combination, conspiracy and agreement was ever made, entered into, conceived, constructed, continued or participated in by these defendants."[25] The decision evoked a collective sigh of relief from Wall Street—though it is an open question how seriously the seventeen firms named in the suit took it to begin with, since being one of the "seventeen" was a medal of honor on the Street, a sign of importance.

After the Korean War ended, the first chance for a peacetime recovery in over twenty years was imminent. How successful it would be depended upon the strengths of industry after the wars and the ability of consumers to reassume their once-prominent position by supplying over two-thirds of overall demand for goods and services. The Federal Reserve severed its direct hold on interest rates and allowed the market to take over their direction in the last symbolic gesture of wartime controls over the marketplace. Good times were about to intervene in business' favor. Years of pent-up demand for goods and services in short supply during the war created the greatest boom yet seen. Business was back in the government's good graces, at least for the time being. What that meant for the shape of American industry and how it was financed remained to be seen.

NEW FRONTIERS

Wall Street's strategy of advocating the greatest good for the greatest number of investors fell far short of the economic stimulus society needed during the Depression. The New Deal experiment with state sponsored enterprises filled some of this gap and continued well beyond the 1930s and the war years. The TVA model proved so successful that it began to be copied on many fronts. These mammoth agencies were able to provide financing at cheaper rates than Wall Street could, while fulfilling societal needs at the same time. The postwar period would carry forward the concept of state-sponsored capitalism even as business resurged. American politicians declared "war" on serious shortcomings in American life such as poverty, hunger, and political inequality. In each case, state-sponsored agencies were established that provided cheap money to favored sectors of society. These government-sponsored enterprises would prove to be vital to certain parts of the economy that Wall Street was not entrusted with. Within twenty-five years, government-sponsored enterprises, constructed like miniature TVAs, would be involved with home ownership, veterans' benefits, student loans, and loans to developing countries. Their names would become familiar household names—Fannie Mae, Ginnie Mae, Freddie Mac, Sallie Mae, and the World Bank—and their influence and reach would be stronger and deeper than anyone originally suspected or hoped. But as the Korean War ended, the business boom took precedence over all other developments as society went on a buying spree the likes of which had not been seen since the 1920s. New developments in monopolistic combinations would send the antitrust forces scurrying for new ways to prevent concentrations of economic power. But the blueprint of the depression years would linger. All of those government-sponsored agencies were actually state-sanctioned monopolies and would give rise to a new breed of enterprise. The once-familiar American business organization was about to enter a new era of uncharted territory.

6

DÉJÀ VU
(1954–1969)

Growth makes all kinds of wonderful things happen.
—Harold Geneen

A LONG-AWAITED EUPHORIA swept the country in the 1950s. The bad times of the Depression and the belt-tightening days of the war were gone, replaced by a pent-up consumer demand that made businessmen smile. Consumers bought cars, homes, and appliances, all of which had been in short supply during the war, at a tremendous rate, and industry prospered in the greatest boom of the century. With a Republican in the White House, the green light was given to proceed at full pace with an expansive economic recovery. The buoyant stock market and the surge in the bond market ensured that capital would again be available for new financing. With Wall Street providing the money and consumers providing the demand, the stage was set for a resumption of antitrust suits against a wide array of industries.

The 1960s were nicknamed the "go-go years," and with the growth came further consolidation in industry that attracted the attention of regulators. But a marked change in the structure of American business—the conglomerate craze of the 1950s and 1960s—in which both established companies and some new names, including W. R. Grace, Gulf + Western, Litton Industries, Occidental Petroleum, Teledyne, and TRW engaged in a vast array of enterprises so diverse it often seemed to make little sense—would change the ways in which the government pursued monopolies. RCA bought Hertz Car Rentals and Gibson Greeting Cards, among others. *Fortune* identified 46 companies that were classified as conglomerates in the mid-1960s. They helped contribute to the growth bandwagon that began almost as soon as the war ended and fitted perfectly in the mold of the concentrations formed in the 1920s after the First World War. It began a revolution that has lasted in one way or another throughout the twentieth century. In a sense, it was the natural outgrowth of the consolidation trend of the 1920s. Only the Depression and the war had managed to slow it down temporarily.

Perceptions about wealth also changed substantially. Individual and corporate wealth were no longer targets of criticism but something to be envied. Ferdinand Lundberg, whose book about America's sixty wealthiest families was seized upon by some New Dealers in the late 1930s, produced a new book entitled *The Rich and the Super Rich,* thirty years later. In it, he showed that America's financial elite was actually composed not of the heads of the new conglomerates, as might have been expected, but by the old guard, most of whom were older than sixty-five. While there was some new money, mostly that of oil men, the preponderance of wealth was held by families easily identified by the public, names like Getty, Kennedy, and du Pont, among others. But ten of the nouveau riche were still not listed in *Who's Who* despite their wealth.

Business began to assume its normal role in American life again. While in 1933 Hugh Johnson was named *Time* magazine's Man of the Year, underlining the importance of the NRA for the country, in 1955 Harlow Curtice of General Motors received the same honor. But the idea of a concentration of economic power was still a rallying point for trustbusters. If a company was suspected of a concentration of political or economic power, it was investigated, as in the past. But it was not the regulatory agencies that mounted many of the probes but Congress. The pervasive influence of big business became stronger than ever. Business and government became so closely intertwined that many critics suspected they were in bed together and would not separate unless forced to do so.

Populists remained the most vocal critics of alleged monopolies. In a description that easily could have been written at any time from the 1880s onward, Senator Estes Kefauver of Tennessee wrote, "In 1962 the 20 largest manufacturing corporations alone had $73.8 billion in assets, or about one-quarter of the total assets of United States manufacturing companies. In turn, the 50 largest companies held 36 percent; the 100 largest, 46 percent; the 200 largest, 56 percent."[1] The top 200 would prove to be a rallying point for antitrusters in the decade that followed. Coming from the southern Populist tradition, Kefauver would make the pursuit of monopolies a main item on his political agenda.

In the postwar period it was still clear that monopoly was a practice in search of a definition. Everyone knew that business was consolidating as much as ever and that the big-business vise was as tight as at any time in the past. The automobile industry was dominated by the Big Three, with American Motors running a distant fourth. The steel industry was in the throes of a consolidation that antitrusters claimed kept prices artificially high. The oil companies were consolidating faster than any other industry. But multinational business was also producing distinct benefits. The reputation of the United States abroad was growing, and the standard of living was rising at home. Some felt that prosecuting alleged monopolists was akin to killing the goose that laid the golden egg. Yet over a thousand cases were pursued each year, the vast majority of which were settled before trial rather than decided in the courts.

One factor that made prosecuting monopolists extremely difficult was that these new conglomerates defied traditional definitions under any of the existing antitrust legislation. Kefauver teamed with Rep. Emmanuel Celler of New York to sponsor the Celler-Kefauver Act of 1950, which amended the Clayton Act to remove a gaping loophole left by the assets clause (Section 7). Now, in addition to not being able to acquire the stock of another company, a buyer could not acquire the assets of another company if the two combined threatened to create a monopoly. This seemingly would put an end to a number of acquisitions that were being done despite their violation of the intent of the Clayton Act. It also provided more ammunition for the antitrusters in fighting the traditional horizontal and vertical mergers. But the amendment still needed court tests before it could be described as a success. And some of the court decisions that fol-

"Now How Do I Keep the Goose That Lays the Golden Egg from Killing Me?"

Big Business as Giant Goose, by Herblock. © *Washington Post*, 1975.

lowed convinced many that Mr. Bumble in Dickens' *Oliver Twist* may have been correct when he said that "the law is an ass."

Some Supreme Court decisions left conservatives hopping mad at what they thought to be absurd applications of existing law. In *Brown Shoe Company v. United States*, the Court under Earl Warren as chief justice ruled on Section 7 of the Clayton Act in 1962, in one of the early applications of the Celler-Kefauver amendment. Brown, a manufacturer, acquired G. R. Kinney and Co., a shoe retailer. Both companies held portions of their own market so small as not to be considered a threat to anyone—less than 1 and 2 percent, respectively. Yet the Court, in an attempt to apply the Section 7 amendment, ruled that the merger was illegal because of the vertical nature of the combination and noted that the trend in the industry toward alignments between manufacturers was a potential threat to com-

"They Act As If They've Been Doped"

Regulators Sleeping on the Job, by Herblock. © *Washington Post*, 1957.

petition. Critics of the liberal Warren court had a field day. Robert Bork, one of the Chicago School's most vociferous exponents, later opined, "It would be overhasty to say that the *Brown Shoe* opinion is the worst antitrust decision ever written. . . . Still, all things considered, [it] has considerable claim to the title." Even those more sympathetic wondered why giant combinations of all sorts were allowed to stand while the smaller fish were sanctioned. The response was that decisions were based upon principle, not size. The irony was that one of the fast-growing conglomerates could easily have swallowed Brown and Kinney and probably not have been brought to court because their other operations mitigated the purported effect of acquiring two companies in similar businesses.

The new conglomerate made nonsense of the existing antitrust laws because they appeared to be outside them. Conglomerate mergers certainly did not fill the idea of a traditional horizontal or vertical merger, since their only motive seemed to be growth rather than market domination. The FTC reported that in the 1960s almost 25 percent of the companies on the *Fortune* 500 list were bought by others and over 80 percent of the mergers were conglomerate mergers. Did the merger of two giant companies in different lines of business pose any less of a threat than a giant horizontal merger? But the term *monopoly* would have to become more comprehensive if it was to have any meaning in the new environment of the 1950s and especially the 1960s.

The conglomerate age produced more than just large corporations. It also produced a new breed of industrialist, the conglomerateur. These merger-driven chief executives were a curious combination of the nineteenth and twentieth centuries. Where the nineteenth century had its self-made men—the Carnegies, Goulds, and Rockefellers—the twentieth had its own version in the likes of James Ling, Charles Bluhdorn, and Tex Thornton. Like their predecessors in the 1920s, they were corporate men through and through but still had more than their fair share of swashbuckler characteristics. Ling reportedly thought about buying the Bank of England to add the LTV stable before being gently reminded that the British government probably would not look kindly upon someone trying to take over its central bank. Generally, most of this group were self-made men without the benefit of a first-class college background or business school training. Several were born outside the United States, and most came from relatively humble backgrounds. But their organizational abilities were clear. The head of the Rapid-American Corporation, Meshulam Riklis, a Russian Jew who immigrated to the United States via Israel, was a prime example of one who assembled a successful conglomerate but still marveled at the power of Wall Street, which he had to court in order to be successful.

Riklis and the other 1960s empire builders understood the logic of the conglomerate era from the very beginning. Royal Little, the head of Textron Corporation, founded a textile company in the early 1920s that became Textron thirty years later. He constantly acquired companies with good track records and sound management, a practice that would be followed by other conglomerateurs. Many tried to acquire well-known companies that were in oligopolist industries such as steel production or motion picture production but that had fallen on hard times or reported slow growth. While defying sound financial logic, it suited the buccaneer nature of many of the conglomerateurs. They were not successful in all cases because the more establishment corporate types who ran the companies and their Wall Street investment bankers often would have nothing to do with them, considering them interlopers on their own tightly guarded preserves. Some conglomerateurs did manage to become insiders, establishment men who kept a low profile but never lost their voracious appetite for power and corporate control. Harold Geneen, the architect of ITT, and his bankers at Lazard Frères are good examples, proving that this trend in corporate empire building depended upon the strong personalities of the people involved. Their activities sorely tested the influence of the SEC and accounting standards; idealists hoping for progress in the way business was conducted had little to smile about.

The 1950s and 1960s also produced a growing amount of literature on monopolies, more than at any time in the past. Economists were now taking a keen interest, and the evidence and analysis they could provide were needed if the government was to make any serious headway.

TOGA PARTY

The thirty years following the Second World War proved that the twentieth century was indeed the American century. American influence spread rapidly abroad, and the dollar became the world's premier currency. But it was not military might or banking influences that extended the country's reach; it was business. The multinational company was born during this period, and its industrial influence became the envy of the world. Envy did not always lead to admiration, however, as a chorus of international criticism arose to protest American domination. Was this a new form of gunboat diplomacy on a grand scale or the natural consequence of winning the war? Critics of the business and military establishments, together dubbed the "military-industrial complex" because of their extremely close economic relationship, claimed that it was an extension of American power and influence by indirect means; the new form of imperialism of the twentieth century. Essentially, what developed was an oligopoly of military suppliers that did the overwhelming bulk of the defense business with the government. Washington allowed this situation to develop and was unlikely to litigate against it, especially since national defense was involved. The cold war took precedence over other issues, just as the world war had a generation earlier.

The speed with which American companies spread throughout the world was a consequence of victory in the world war. The Americans were flush with cash and relatively unscathed by the war, and the Europeans especially needed the sorts of manufactured goods that U.S. companies could supply. Multinational companies were busy selling everything from telephones to heavy equipment and soft drinks. American products popped up on billboards from Paris to Rangoon, and their advertising slogans became universally recognized. In the 1960s American pop culture extended to Europe, Asia, and Latin America. It was not to everyone's taste, and it soon came under sharp criticism. Cries of "Coca-Cola imperialism" were leveled by the European left at what it considered unwanted American intrusions into European life and culture. The numbers, at least, bore them out. Americans poured six times as much investment into Europe as all foreigners combined invested in the United States. But it was not only the Europeans who had cause for complaint. The activities of multinational business also aroused concern in Asia and Latin America. Some countries believed that the powerful Americans and their multinational companies were capable of meddling with their domestic politics and even interfering with their economies when it suited them. In a larger context, however, what the multinationals created was the period of business internationalization. New markets could be found abroad, and strong arguments were made for expansion. Naturally, that expansion was best served by larger and larger companies, the sort that could establish branches in the countries where their goods were sold rather than just export from home. Multinational operations abroad often meant consolidation among businesses at home in order to meet the new challenge. When patriotism was added to the equation—the idea that overseas business was helping the balance of payments, creating jobs at home, and keeping the dollar strong—it was irresistible, especially to politicians.

The 1950s were the years during which the military-industrial complex first became a hot topic of conversation. Business and the military regularly exchanged officers and managers, each going to work for the other side. Hundreds of retired military men went to work for defense contractors, and scores of senior corporate executives went to work for government. The most well known was Robert McNamara of Ford, who became secretary of defense under John F. Kennedy and Lyndon Johnson. And it was not only the left that smelled conspiracy in the air between the military and big business. In his farewell speech before leaving the presidency, Dwight Eisenhower noted that "we must guard against the acquisition of unwarranted influence, whether sought or unsought, by the military-industrial complex." That single reference gave the term a permanent place in the American political lexicon.

Senator William Proxmire, who began investigating military waste in the 1960s, said that "the important names among the top military contractors in World War II were General Motors, Chrysler, Ford, U.S. Steel, General Electric and a few aircraft firms. . . . In the 1960s . . . firms like Lockheed, General Dynamics, McDonnell Douglas, Ling Temco Vaught, North American Rockwell, Grumman Aircraft, and Avco Corporation did over two thirds of their business with the Pentagon." The impression Proxmire gave was that many could not have stayed in business without the government's largesse. "The fact is that most of the big military contractors could not survive without weapons business. They have their noses and both feet in the Pentagon procurement trough."[2] Military expenditures by the Pentagon were reaching 25 percent of the federal budget, all in the name of fighting the cold war against the Russians. Cost overruns by the military were becoming legendary and the major suppliers of armaments benefited. The 1960s became known for the $50 ashtray and the $100 toilet seat, all in the name of national security. The business was so profitable that entire states devoted a large portion of their energy to attracting as many defense contracts as possible. Congressman Mendel Rivers of South Carolina, chairman of the House Armed Services Committee, dedicated his career to obtaining defense contracts for his state without the slightest trace of embarrassment; he became known as the greatest friend the military had in Congress, and members of the Senate occasionally felt his wrath when he pronounced them "soft" on national defense. The area around Charleston prospered because of his aggressive pursuit of contracts. He once told the press that his congressional record "exceeded even that of Julius Caesar." Given the power he accumulated in the House, he swore he would "never surrender my toga." The toga party with military contracts as the main course would last for years, since the Vietnam War would soon put new pressures on the military and its suppliers.

The rapidly changing world of growth-oriented companies meant that mergers in the 1950s and 1960s had other features that were distinctly different from combinations in the past. Many older firms were left languishing with low stock market values but decent assets. That meant they were relatively cheap for an acquisitions-minded buyer, who could then break up their assets and sell them to another company. Even if the acquired companies were not sold off, they would be expected to produce a specific return of income. Business schools preached return on assets and discounting of projected revenue streams, something relatively new to corporate finance. The stock market loved what it heard and bid the prices of the acquiring companies up in anticipation of even higher earnings. The acquiring companies were assumed to possess the expertise necessary to make the new "synergies" work. Synergy meant that a newly created company could reflect a value greater than the sum of its parts, a sort of mystical corporate theory that was purely growth-oriented. Bidding for other companies became the preoccupation of many postwar empire builders. The idea was a slightly more sophisticated variation of the principle that Insull and Morgan used in the 1920s when building their utility empires.

Even before the conglomerates appeared, business had taken huge strides in consolidating over the years, vertically as well as horizontally. Companies such as DuPont and General Motors forged dominant positions in their respective industries, often with each other's help. The investment made in General Motors by DuPont in the latter years of the First World War surfaced again in 1957, when the Supreme Court ruled that DuPont had violated Section 7 of the Clayton Act by acquiring the stock of GM because it also was purchasing itself a favorable position as a supplier of plastic products to GM in the process.[3] The doctrine established through this decision was that a merger could be undone by the courts regardless of when it had occurred, even a half century before. The market conditions at the time the suit was brought could be used as evidence. The doctrine resulted in a fair amount of criticism of the Supreme Court, which seemed to be bending over backward to assist trustbusters with a questionable historical argument. Previously, applications of the law were applied mostly to horizontal combinations. The ruling, along with the Celler-Kefauver amendment, did much to keep a lid on nonconglomerate mergers but was not to prove so effective against the newest form of corporate hydra. They continued to combine, this time in previously unheard-of organizations that seemed to defy logic.

A notable case of vertical combination made its way to the Supreme Court in 1967. In *United States v. Arnold, Schwinn & Co.* the Justice Department had sued the bicycle manufacturer with violation of the Sherman Act. Schwinn's market share had fallen during the 1960s and it was searching for ways to retain its market and its image. One of its major problems was discounters who often bought consignments of bicycles and sold them at less than the manufacturer's suggested retail price. Schwinn established relationships with its dealers that would purposely exclude the discounters and maintain its price through the dealer network. When confronted with the issue, the Court ruled that when Schwinn sold the bicycles to dealers, it effectively lost control of the dealers' actions. Justice Abe Fortas wrote, "Once the manufacturer has parted with title and risk, he has parted with dominion over the product and his effort to restrict territory or persons to whom the product may be transferred . . . is a per se violation of the Sherman Act."[4] Schwinn discovered that peddling its bicycles was something it did not have total control over in the political climate of the day. The decision would stand for a decade before a significant reversal in the late 1970s.

The major antagonist of monopolies and big-business combinations in the 1950s was a latter-day southern Populist who defied the tenor of the times and pursued business combinations at every opportunity. Estes Kefauver was born in Tennessee in 1903 to a family with roots in seventeenth-century Jamestown. He graduated from the University of Tennessee and the Yale Law School and then returned home to Chattanooga to practice law. He quickly became involved in local politics as a reformer and ran for the House of Representatives as a New Deal Democrat. Easily winning, he took his seat in 1939, beginning a long and distinguished congressional career. He successfully ran for the Senate despite the opposition of powerful conservative forces in Tennessee. Running as a potential Democratic presidential candidate in 1956 made him a household name throughout the country. Of his varied interests, antitrust was perhaps the most keen. He presided over the Senate Subcommittee on Antitrust and Monopoly between 1957 and 1963. The subcommittee's hearings and his own brand of consumerism reopened the old discussions about concentration of economic power that had not been heard since the 1930s. A new breed of antitruster was appearing under the guise of being a consumer advocate, attacking concentrations from a different angle. The United States was the largest consumer-oriented economy in the world, and this purchasing power would ensure that *consumerism* became a household term in the years ahead. Pressure on big business was building on more than one front and Kefauver was primarily responsible.

The *New Republic* said that "what George Norris was in the public power field, Estes Kefauver is in the field of antitrust legislation."[5] Similarities between him and notable predecessors were inevitable. His antimonopoly bent, especially for one who had practiced corporate law, was similar to that of William O. Douglas, another Yale law graduate. But unlike his predecessors, Kefauver did not have any monopolist "enemies" he could attack. The days of Jay Gould, J. P. Morgan, and Samuel Insull were gone. The new monopolies were professionally run modern corporations, dedicated to profits and shareholder wealth. Accumulating monopoly power by them was not so much an individual, ego-driven motive as simply one of good business in an increasingly prosperous and competitive world. In a sense, it was a wonder that Kefauver embarked upon the hearings at all, as his allies were few and far between. Yet he remarked in the Senate in 1961 that "with the emergence of big business, big labor, and big government as the central forces in our society, and with the pressures for greater secrecy and non-disclosure coming from everywhere, the need for the informing function today is far greater than in the simpler days of Woodrow Wilson." And that function is precisely what his committee set out to accomplish. His posthumous book *In a Few Hands* was much more than a series of committee findings. It delved into the world of steel, pharmaceuticals, automobiles, and a bevy of other monopoly industries. It also appeared to wander from its topic occasionally, discussing safety issues in those industries when appropriate. An antitrust lawyer would find it non-technical but the general reading public found in it issues otherwise not discussed in the 1950s and 1960s.

Kefauver did not shy from asking blunt questions of the corporate leaders of his era. Price leadership was clearly being practiced in many industries. Calling the chairman of U.S. Steel, Roger Blough, before his committee, Kefauver put to him the question of why steel prices had remained remarkably similar throughout the industry over the years. Blough replied, "My concept is that a price that matches another price is a competitive price. If you don't choose to accept it, then, of course, you don't accept it. In the steel industry we know it is so." To which Kefauver replied, "That's a new definition of competition that I never heard of." Kefauver then asked George Humphrey, chairman of National Steel and a former treasury secretary under Eisenhower, why his company did not lower its prices although it operated at only 80 percent capacity. "Mr. Humphrey," Kefauver said, " I have examined the prices submitted by your company . . . and can find no important instance where your price was lower than United States Steel." The reply was somewhat blunt. "Of course you cannot," replied the steel man, "because if we made a lower price, everybody would meet it. They will do the same as we do."[6] This response inadvertently embodied the kernel of the antimonopoly argument. Businessmen saw nothing wrong with holding prices steady. It was a way to avoid what they considered to be potentially disastrous price wars. Legislators, on the other hand, saw a conspiracy to control prices and, through them, production. It was a classic case of a practical business attitude clashing with what the corporate world considered regulators' paranoia.

Some cracks did occasionally appear in the corporate armor, however. In 1969, when the World Trade Center complex in New York was being constructed, the Port Authority of New York and New Jersey assumed only the largest producers could supply the massive amount of steel needed to complete the project and so asked U.S. Steel and Bethlehem Steel to submit bids. U.S. Steel bid $122 million, while Bethlehem bid $118 million. Considering both bids excessive, the authority then gave the contract to fifteen smaller firms, which supplied the steel at a total cost of $85 million. Bethlehem claimed that it was glad that it did not get the bid at the lower price, implying that it was uneconomical to cut prices so sharply. The smaller firms acknowledged that their profits were adequate, though not huge. But the deal had an ironic twist to it: As a result of the high, and similar, bids from the two largest producers, the Antitrust Division of the Justice Department began a probe into their pricing.

One other potential problem emerged that was certainly more modern than the classic arguments against big business combinations. This was the fear that steadfast pricing, especially when it was suspected that prices otherwise could be legitimately lowered, was inflationary. That did strike a responsive chord, because inflation was on the rise in the 1960s. Being able to attack big-business practices on monetary terms was an unusual twist in the history of antitrust. If prices were lowered, then inflation would not be a pressing issue. Ironically, during the heyday of the trusts before the turn of the century, deflation (the opposite of inflation) was often given as the reason why consolidation had to occur. Cutthroat competition in the face of deflation was ruinous in the eyes of the nineteenth-century industrialists. Now the opposite argument was taking shape: that price leadership and stamping out the competition brought with it inflation. Clearly, times had changed. In 1968 the Johnson administration imposed a 10 percent income tax surcharge on wage earners to try to dampen inflation. Unfortunately, it was unsuccessful. Inflation continued to rise and caused a crisis in August 1971, when Nixon introduced a series of wage and price controls. Wage gains and the pressure on prices caused by the Vietnam War suggested to some that the society was at the mercy of large pressure groups, each with its own economic agendas. Michigan State University president Walter Adams, an economist and an ally of Ralph Nader, said that union demands for higher wages and conglomerate control of many industries suggested that "government monetary and fiscal policy can be subverted by power groups immune from the discipline of the competitive market mechanism." Citing Nixon's plan to have government agencies oversee the different parts of his anti-inflation fight, Adams continued, "These agencies, not the impotent 'competitive' market in which he [Nixon] had formerly placed his trust, are to protect the public from the rapacious exploiters inhabiting the New Industrial State."[7] But as noted by John

Kenneth Galbraith, who coined that term a decade before, the new society was bound to be inhabited by rapacious corporate types because the antitrust laws did not work particularly well. Society was only getting what it deserved unless regulations were tightened effectively.

Attacking business on the grounds that it was violating policy that originated with the executive branch was a novel and ideologically charged approach but would not hold much water outside the fringe element among the antitrusters. One of the major problems encountered by trust-busters in the 1950s and 1960s was that society was becoming increasingly complex. As it did, so too did corporate strategies for producing goods and services. The exercise of monopoly power became more subtle as a result. Some thought, like Estes Kefauver, that excessive advertising was a sure sign of a monopoly because only a company already making vast amounts of money could afford to advertise its product on such a scale to ensure that it captured even more market share and make still more money. The idea was enticing and would be repeated many times over the next twenty years, but all a manufacturer had to do to counter it was to claim that it faced increasing competition and that without the advertising it would lose its competitive edge.

Detractors retorted that advertising often was nothing more than a charade designed to give the consumer the impression that price competition existed. For example, the car companies usually followed General Motors when increasing prices, proving that price leadership was still alive and well and being practiced more flagrantly than ever. Kefauver said this: "Even the gasoline stations selling under private brand names, with prices slightly lower in order to get customers, are careful to maintain the customary price differential and thus avoid shaking the sensitive price structure in the retailing of gasoline."[8] The essence of these arguments was that advertising was employed to create illusions rather than pass along useful information to the consumer. Even the advertisers could not actually disagree with that, although they would disagree about what constituted an informed consumer.

There were other ways to spot what were considered shoddy practices. One had to do with automobiles. By the mid-1950s it became evident that cars were not lasting as long as they had before the war, despite the new technologies used in design and production. When one became unusable, a customer would have to buy another to replace it. This was something of a new twist on the idea of growth. Rather than manufacturing cars that would last and seeking to expand markets, car companies seemed to plan for growth from the existing market by designing cars intended to fall apart within a predictable period of time. That also created serious safety problems that critics claimed were costing the country enormous sums annually for medical and related expenses. By the mid-1950s over one million people had died in auto-related accidents since the first auto-related casualty was recorded in 1899.

The idea of planned obsolescence was not new. In the 1920s manufacturers began to change their models every year, to give the impression that new cars were better than the older models. In most cases they were not; new ones were simply old models dressed up to look different. As consumer advocate Ralph Nader remarked years later in his book *Unsafe at Any Speed,* "Probably no other manufacturing industry in this country devotes so few of its resources to innovation of its basic product." Alfred Sloan, who ran General Motors in the 1920s, was one of the first vocal proponents of the idea. Henry Ford opposed it as nonsense; this was the man whose original marketing dictum was that a customer could have a Model T in any color he liked as long as it was black. But model changing was a way of enticing more customers to buy new cars. Another, less visible side of the annual model change affected smaller manufacturers, which had a difficult time keeping up with the Big Three. Changing models constantly required large capital investments for design and retooling, and the smaller manufacturers were often short of capital. Eventually the tactic forced many of them to the wall. But America's love affair with the automobile ensured that the process would continue—for a while, at least.

During the late 1950s new car registrations in the country declined for the first time since the Depression. Since there was also a recession, most commentators felt that it was the economic climate that was causing the downturn in sales. But at the same time, people were buying imports at a great pace, especially Volkswagens. The lesson for the auto industry was clear: American cars built in the mid- to late 1950s were falling apart at alarming rates as planned obsolescence took its toll. Kefauver spoke out against this, saying, "The dictates of styling engineers take precedence over everything else. Even safety of operation—not to speak of fuel economies and problems involved in parking—are subordinated to the whims of fashion experts."[9] Nader singled out a small, stylish car made by General Motors called the Chevrolet Corvair. It became the centerpiece of *Unsafe at Any Speed,* published in 1965, in which he unequivocally labeled the car a death trap, much to GM's chagrin. Foreign car companies, on the other hand, especially Volkswagen, earned a reputation for producing cars that were cheap to run and for being much slower to change models. That was not to say that foreign cars were any safer than their American counterparts; Nader later published another report entitled *Small—on Safety: The Designed-in Dangers of the Volkswagen.* But the perception had already been created that small foreign cars were better and cheaper. The prices of the imports remained relatively inexpensive when compared to their behemoth American counterparts. The decline in sales sent a message to U.S. manufacturers, who began to introduce compact models to compete with the foreign competition. But the effort was not entirely successful, inasmuch as the quality of the cars themselves was still very much in doubt, as Nader pointed out.

Nader's exposé revealed another negative aspect of big business. Within two months of the publication of *Unsafe at Any Speed,* General Motors began a secret investigation of him, ostensibly to discover whether he would receive any financial benefit from the numerous lawsuits filed against the company by angry customers. Because of the vindictive, clandestine nature of the investigation, the president of GM, James Roche, was summoned before Senator Abraham Ribicoff's Senate subcommittee to explain his company's actions. Roche publicly apologized to Nader, vindicating the crusading lawyer, whose reputation as a people's advocate was instantly made.

The scope of Kefauver's antitrust and monopoly committee was often wider than its name might have suggested. Pronouncing upon automobile safety issues and others was not necessarily what the committee had set out to do, but small details never stood in the senator's way if he felt that the digression was necessary to publicize the topic at hand. And it had another side to it: In addition to price fixing and price leadership, endangering the safety of consumers was quickly (if unofficially) becoming a cardinal sin for corporations. This would help consumer advocates such as Nader gain greater acceptance in the years immediately following.

Antitrust actions were not held in the highest esteem by many opinion makers of the day. Said John Kenneth Galbraith, "The conflict between the legal condemnation of monopoly and its *de facto* acceptance, in slightly imperfect form, as oligopoly, is stark."[10] Galbraith recognized the dichotomy between ideas about monopolies and their tactics and motives, on one hand, and the widespread acceptance of them, on the other. The 1960s experience with antitrust action bore him out. Regulators were pursuing some relatively minor cases of alleged monopoly while turning a blind eye to the most obvious combinations.

The automobile industry and the defense contractors were both good examples of oligopolies. Appearing before Kefauver's Senate subcommittee, George Romney, president of American Motors, admitted frankly, "I cannot ignore the prices of my competitors in setting the prices on my cars because I cannot sell my cars if my cars are not priced on the basis where they will sell in relationship to the price of the other fellow's product." Kefauver was more blunt about the situation. "There can be no doubt that the key role in pricing is played by GM," he concluded after hearing the testimony. "Its decisions establish the price level for the industry."[11]

Appearing before a congressional committee, the president of General Motors declared categorically that what was good for GM was good for the country. Equating the prosperity of his company with that of the country itself sounded a bit arrogant but was essentially true in the climate of the time. The company had come a long way since the days of Billy Durant. When Ford lost its status as the largest manufacturer of automobiles, GM took the lead and never relinquished it. Holding around 50 percent of the market, it was in a premier position to dictate prices and styles in the industry and was never afraid to exercise its power. Like DuPont, it was especially proud of its management structure, and its CEOs were among the most widely known in the country. Ever since Alfred Sloan had taken charge of the company's management in the 1920s, it had the reputation of being one of the best-run companies in the country. Critics faced an uphill battle fighting companies that produced the country's favorite consumer durables. The goose may have been large and domineering, but it still laid the golden egg. Antimonopolists would have to show that the egg was not always salubrious for the consumer.

EVERYONE INTO THE POOL

The secret that lay behind the success of the conglomerate was not good management or a brilliant corporate strategy. Rather, it was something as simple as an accounting technique. The conglomerateurs seized upon a device known as pool accounting to transform American industry. Wall Street was aware of the device but no one raised a dissenting voice; in the age of growth, anything that helped promote even more of it was intrinsically good, and those who preached moderation were not in step with the times.

Pool accounting is still the method of choice today in accounting for mergers and takeovers. In the 1950s it began to be used widely and helped account for the strong growth results reported by many conglomerates, especially after a good year of successful mergers. Pool accounting allowed the takeover company to incorporate the merged company's financial results into its own immediately. It did not require any write-offs. As a result, an aggressive conglomerate that chose its merger partners wisely could see its earnings rise every year as long as it bought successful companies. Most of the time, the purchases were made using the conglomerate's stock, not cash.

The lifestyles of the conglomerateurs matched their flamboyant acquisition skills. Both were accomplished on a grand scale. The most expensive new private home in the country was erected in Dallas by James Ling, the founder and chief executive officer of Ling-Temco Vaught, a Texas conglomerate. Valued at over $3 million, the home was stuffed with accessories fit for royalty of another age, including priceless works of art and an antiquarian's dream library. Star-studded dinner parties made Ling Texas' best-known dinner party host. All this opulence surrounded a self-made entrepreneur from rural Oklahoma who had started a small electrical supply company years before. Ling came to symbolize the best and worst of the conglomerate trend during the 1950s and 1960s.

After dropping out of high school, James Ling spent the remainder of his youth wandering the country as one of thousands of Depression-era transients. After a stint in the navy he became an electrical supplier in Dallas. He learned the art of self-promotion early. He sold shares in his modest company in 1955 to the public by going from door to door, and he raised more than enough money to purchase a similar but larger company in California. In fact, he raised so much money that he was overcapitalized for the size of the relatively small company he ran. That marked the beginning of his acquisition career, which finally ended in 1970 when Ling-Temco-Vaught ousted him and changed its name to the LTV Corporation.

Ling's contribution to the conglomerate trend is similar to Jay Gould's contribution to railroad consolidation in the nineteenth century. But Ling did not specialize in horizontal mergers. His companies were assembled for little apparent reason other than making the balance sheet look good. They seemed awful as organizations but reported good financial results— and that was the only fact Wall Street was interested in. In fact, the modest country boy hired some of Wall Street's best-known and oldest investment banks to work for him in his acquisitions spree. When his company took over another, Ling gave its management free rein to operate just as they did before. In fact, he often told its senior management not to bother him with details about their problems; they should just simply solve them on their own. But he did not give them such free rein when it came to financing. Often, he would sell off half of a newly acquired company, but retain majority control. The stock market, enamored of Ling's reputation, would bid up the price of the subsidiary to sometimes dizzying heights. Ling used the market to pay for his acquisitions. Bankers were also keen to lend him money when they saw how the market reacted, and consequently he acquired a massive amount of debt in a relatively short time. Ling became the 1960s' best example of how to do business using other people's money with a huge layer of borrowed cash on top of it.

Economists and academics argued that a conglomerate was in a good position to weather bad economic times because it was operationally diversified. If one company did poorly, another could be expected to perform better. If it was diversified internationally, all the better. The conglomerate was the new answer to downturns in the business cycle; in theory, it was a company that could not lose money. Unfortunately, that was not the case. Other factors interfered, and the growth age equation backfired on its proponents.

Ling-Temco-Vaught's reign on the corporate scene was relatively short but spectacular. At one time or other between 1961 and 1969 it owned dozens of companies, including Jones and Laughlin Steel, a company the young Harold Geneen once worked for. It was described by him as run by "macho types who lived and breathed steel and scorned the idea of moving into new areas." When Ling took over, it was considered one of the jewels in his corporate crown, an old-line established company that brought some respectability to Ling's operations. A steel manufacturer was a natural acquisition for a conglomerate. The entire steel industry was the focus of the Senate antitrust investigation in the late 1950s and early 1960s. Little had changed in the industry since the dismissal of the antitrust case against U.S. Steel at the end of the First World War. Citing a Justice Department study, Estes Kefauver stated simply that the major steel companies "that exist today have remained in their position of dominance for several decades . . . genuinely new entrants—such as Kaiser Steel Corporation—were usually the beneficiaries of sizeable financial aid from the U.S. Government. The new additions did not alter the basic structure and organization of the industry."[12] An established member of the oligarchy was a prize for the ambitious conglomerate.

The Justice Department challenged Ling-Temco-Vaught's acquisition of Jones and Laughlin. The merger became one of Richard McLaren's first targets when he was appointed to head the Antitrust Division after Nixon was elected. Ling-Temco-Vaught also owned Wilson Meat Packing, Braniff Airlines, Wilson Sporting Goods, National Car Rental, and the Okonite Cable Company, among others. The latter had an especially troubled history, having changed hands several times over within a relatively short period of time. Appearing before the House Antitrust Committee in 1970, Ling was questioned about Okonite by the committee chairman, Emmanuel Celler of New York. Allegations had been leveled that an Okonite employee passed inside information to LTV that allowed it to take over Okonite; the employee went on to become president of Okonite as an LTV subsidiary, with a substantial raise in salary and generous stock options. Celler castigated Ling by saying that he was "anxious to make a deal and you were going to take advantage of all available information. [The employee] had it and you availed yourself of it."[13] He asked Ling: "Suppose you were a shareholder of Okonite and it was purchased by Kennecott and then sold by Kennecott to LTV who subsequently sells it to somebody else. What would be your attitude as a shareholder?"

Celler failed to mention that Kennecott had been forced to divest itself of Okonite in 1965, the year Ling took over, after the Justice Department brought antitrust charges against it. Ling took almost no time in responding, replying, "My attitude would be, what price did they pay? They could not do all those things without buying up securities. If they offered enough money, I would be like the shareholders have been: I would probably sell it." Celler did not like the attitude, taking a more conservative, long-term view. He responded curtly, "If I were a shareholder, I would kick like hell."[14]

For Ling, making money was more important than how it was made. In one prime example of pool accounting, Ling purchased Wilson Meat Packing in 1967. The price was $225 million, of which only about $1 million was cash. The balance was borrowed, and preferred stock was also used to buy out Wilson shareholders. By adding Wilson's earnings to his own, Ling was able to raise the conglomerate's earnings per share by 31 percent.[15] He then added more debt for further acquisitions. Although the term "watered stock" was not used much anymore, that was essentially what happened here, as a huge amount of debt severely weakened LTV's equity. And for a time the strategy worked well. In the mid-1960s Ling-Temco-Vaught was in the middle of *Fortune*'s list of the largest American companies. Within five short years, acquisitions pushed it into the number fourteen spot. Its price-earnings ratio and share price soared, the latter rising to well over $100 per share. Ling's philosophy could be summarized in one short sentence: Buy them, incorporate their earnings, and then sell part of them off to a hungry investing public and use the proceeds to buy something else. John Kenneth Galbraith was an especially harsh critic of Ling, warning on more than one occasion that the party would soon be over for the conglomerateurs.

In strategy and personal style, Ling stood in stark contrast to the best-known conglomerateur of his time, Harold Geneen. Where Ling was somewhat folksy and exuded boyish exuberance, Geneen was the apotheosis of the corporate man. Although best remembered for his traditional business philosophy and being a stern taskmaster, Geneen's background was not as disciplined and business-school-oriented as it seemed. He spent his late teens as a runner on the New York Stock Exchange and experienced the crash in 1929 firsthand. Like many corporate empire builders before him, he knew the role that the stock exchange played in pricing new stock issues and assessing investor attitudes. He played to this with his corporate strategy, which was purely growth-oriented. Years later he recalled, "We built an organization around functions, not products. We formed a group of very savvy people to make acquisitions. At the peak of our expansion we were buying an average of a company a week. In all, we bought more than three hundred companies."[16]

Geneen built ITT into one of the country's best-known (if not respected) corporations. Originally organized by Sosthenes Benn in the 1920s to take over AT&T's overseas operations, ITT was effectively precluded from selling its products in the United States because of the AT&T monopoly. Its influence overseas was pervasive and its power envied and feared by some. It made its way back into the United States but still could not penetrate the phone market because of AT&T's dominance, so it took up diversification on a grand scale. The company's reach made it a household name. In 1972 *Time* commented on the company's influence in a statement eerily reminiscent of a comment made by Berle and Means forty years before. A consumer not happy with the company and who wanted to escape its grasp "could not rent an Avis car, buy a Levitt house, sleep in a Sheraton hotel, park in an APCOA garage, use Scott's fertilizer or seed, eat Wonder Bread or Morton's frozen foods . . . he could not have watched any televised reports of President Nixon's visit to China . . . he would have had to refuse listing in *Who's Who*; ITT owns that too."[17]

Geneen considered Ling-Temco-Vaught more of a holding company than a conglomerate. Geneen considered buying a company only if it made sense and if market share was at stake. He sought exclusively companies that were prominent in their industries. Pool accounting certainly served him well; in the mid- to late 1960s, that accounting method allowed ITT to overstate its earnings by 70 percent, according to the House Antitrust Subcommittee.[18] Geneen professed no desire to accumulate for its own sake, but that was exactly what he did.

Another major difference in style between LTV and ITT was that unlike Ling, and unlike many of the other conglomerateurs, Geneen was relatively low-paid. His salary was around $250,000 per year and his stock was worth around $5 million, making him one of the lesser-paid CEOs in the group. Ling's salary was about the same but his stock was worth over $45 million. Even that paled in comparison to the value of the stock owned by Armand Hammer of Occidental Petroleum, worth $135 million, or Tex Thornton of Litton, slightly over $100 million. Running a conglomerate was clearly profitable business for a CEO, but the stock market was vital. Without it, none of the CEOs would have been multimillionaires and their companies would not have been able to accumulate others at such a rapid rate.

The conglomcrateurs needed strong investment bankers if they were to succeed in their acquisitions strategies. Testifying before congressional hearings on conglomerates in 1969, Felix Rohatyn, a partner in Lazard Frères and a member of ITT's board, revealed the sorts of investment banker–client relationships that made many legislators uneasy. Rohatyn noted that of sixty-eight mergers arranged by his firm, twenty-seven of the companies had at least one Lazard partner on its board of directors. Arbitrageurs within the investment banking firms also could make fortunes by purchasing the stock of a takeover target, especially with the aim of selling it to the raider or to a second, higher bidder. One trader calculated that the Hartford Insurance–ITT merger orchestrated by Geneen was worth a 45 percent trading return after the merger was approved.

These new corporations certainly had the feel of monopolies in terms of power and bigness, but what exactly were the conglomerates monopolizing? The concentration of economic power raised its head again. The tactics used by large companies gave legislators an indication of how much economic or political muscle a corporation was capable of exercising. British writer Anthony Sampson produced one of the postwar period's most famous muckraking books with *The Sovereign State of ITT* in 1973. Other business writers and journalists also took up the gauntlet, but many wrote rather tame books that often ignored the larger context in which the conglomerates operated. Although the conglomerates and their CEOs produced much fodder for investigative journalism, criticism was tempered by the strong bull market on Wall Street and the pervasive influence of American corporate and political power.

One of ITT's corporate strategies in the 1960s was *reciprocity*, a practice clearly forbidden by the antitrust laws.[19] ITT subsidiaries and their employees were encouraged to do business with other ITT subsidiaries.

Since the conglomerate owned Avis, employees and even suppliers were "encouraged" to rent Avis cars when they were in a position to do so. Aetna, another subsidiary, could do a substantial business if ITT employees and their families bought insurance from it. The same scenario was replayed many times over. Even outside suppliers to the company were encouraged to do business with it by buying its products. Geneen saw this as a natural way to expand ITT's influence. Others saw it as outright bullying.

At one level, of course, this sort of encouragement is considered good business. But as practiced by many corporations, it turned into tyranny—"Do business with me or else or be prepared for the consequences." In a well-publicized incident in the 1970s, the head of a Madison Avenue ad agency that handled a soft drink account fired one of her staffers after the person was found drinking a rival's product in the office. Geneen advocated the same at the corporate level. The conglomerate in the hands of Geneen was a place where dissension was not well received. Using the competition's products was treason. Geneen naturally took exception to those sort of charges. "I have somehow gained a reputation as a harsh and impatient taskmaster. I was even accused in a best-selling book of having despotic tendencies," Geneen recalled, referring to the Sampson book, "but I believe that picture is undeserved."

Like LTV, ITT's growth was phenomenal. In 1960 it was already a large corporation, ranking thirty-fourth among American manufacturing companies. By the end of the decade it had vaulted to eighth place and was one of the largest employers in the country. ITT's dominance was challenged in antitrust hearings conducted by the House of Representatives in 1969, when Emmanuel Celler assembled his subcommittee and heard testimony from dozens of witnesses on the effects of conglomerates. Late that same year Harold Geneen made his appearance before the committee, flanked by a large coterie of lawyers. He was questioned about the viability of his vast organization and about reciprocity, which he denied ITT practiced. He claimed that the company would not knowingly violate the spirit of the antitrust laws, but Celler trumped him by producing internal company memorandums to the contrary. The committee's final report was highly critical of the conglomerates, especially ITT. But the matter did not end there. ITT was to become one of the chief targets of the surprisingly aggressive antitrust division of the Justice Department under Richard Nixon and his attorney general, John Mitchell.

The Justice Department had recently added Richard McLaren from Chicago as the head of its Antitrust Division. From the very beginning of his tenure, McLaren made it clear that he intended to focus on conglomerates, using all the tools the division had at its disposal. That won him few friends in the corporate world. Harold Geneen characterized him as a "rather pompous lawyer from Chicago whom nobody had ever heard of. And, suddenly, he was able to take center stage and get quoted in the *New York Times* and the *Wall Street Journal.*" The years under the Johnson administration had been surprisingly quiet on the antitrust front because the Democrats wanted Congress to pass new legislation specifically aimed at conglomerate mergers. Congress never obliged, and in the intervening years little progress was made against new combinations. McLaren was determined to be more forceful. He told the Senate Judiciary Committee at the time of his nomination for the job that he preferred to test Section 7 of the Clayton Act to see whether it would prove effective against conglomerates. A new interpretation of the section asserted that conglomerates should not be allowed to acquire other major companies because the enlarged company would then be an entrant into other industries, possibly creating barriers for others because of its size and muscle. Shortly after his confirmation, he elaborated on why he intended to pursue conglomerates. In a speech in New York, he said, "In my view many such mergers have a dangerous potential for substantially lessening competition. . . . We expect to move rather promptly in some such cases."

Ling's merger with Jones and Laughlin Steel came under fire from McLaren although the merger was eventually allowed to stand. It had the distinction of being the first salvo fired in the war with the conglomerates. When papers were filed against the Jones and Laughlin acquisition in March 1969 with the intent of forcing Ling-Temco-Vaught to divest itself of its interest in the steelmaker, the action apparently came as a surprise to the company. "There were no rumors beforehand, not a word," remarked the president of Jones and Laughlin. But McLaren's tactics of going public with his intentions were not appreciated by the conglomerates because they meant bad press, which could affect share prices. Ling-Temco-Vaught's president took exception to some of McLaren's remarks. He employed the traditional widows-and-orphans defense when he said that the company is "deeply resentful of the unwarranted public statements by officials of the government and of private agencies . . . whose statements have substantially deflated the investment value of millions of shareholders—big and small. This has resulted in the loss of hundreds of millions of dollars, including many life-time savings." The always sensitive stock market liked what it heard and pushed the price of the shares higher. Pulling few punches, he went on to say, "Ling Temco-Vaught has the somewhat dubious honor of being chosen by the head of the Justice Department's Antitrust Division to be a guinea pig, to test the applicability of existing antitrust laws to conglomerate acquisitions."[20]

McLaren opened several antitrust actions against ITT, the best-known being its proposed takeover of the Hartford Insurance Company. But in 1971 he suddenly made a 180-degree turn and proposed a settlement instead, in which several smaller ITT mergers would be negated (including that with Avis) but the merger with Hartford would be permitted. Additionally, ITT could not merge with any company valued at more than $100 million without approval. This resolution allowed both sides to claim victory.

The reason for McLaren's about face was revealed a few years later, when details of the Nixon administration's relationship with ITT were made public. Charges were made that in 1972 ITT had contributed $400,000 to the Republicans, specifically to influence the antitrust lawsuits brought against it. Although the definitive link in the payoff was never proved, documents did shed light on Nixon's views on the antitrust suits in progress at the time, brought by McLaren. A tape made at the White House in 1971 recorded Nixon as saying to Richard Kleindienst, who had been designated to succeed John Mitchell as attorney general, "I do not want McLaren to run around prosecuting people, raising hell about conglomerates, stirring things up at this point. Now you keep him the hell out of that . . . or either he resigns. I'd rather have him out anyway. I don't like the son of a bitch."[21] (McLaren left the Antitrust Division later in 1971 and took a job as a federal judge shortly thereafter.) ITT also appeared to have been caught in another loose interpretation of reciprocity, as it was reported in the press that ITT pledged to contribute money to the Republican Party if its 1972 convention was held in San Diego, where Sheraton

Hotels (an ITT subsidiary) just happened to be the largest innkeeper. The Republicans, clearly embarrassed, moved the convention to Miami after the revelations. At the annual Gridiron Club dinner, a singer impersonating Harold Geneen broke into song, to the tune of "Tea for Two":

> Antitrust is so unjust
> Let's you and me somehow agree
> There'd better be
> A nice consent decree
> Republicans can congregate
> And we'll keep our conglomerate
> And don't you see how happy we will be.[22]

Although the behemoth organizations were all lumped in the same category, they nevertheless had their own distinct personalities. While Ling-Temco-Vaught was aggressive and ITT establishment-oriented, Litton Industries was perhaps the slickest of all the conglomerates. Like LTV, it was assembled by one dominant individual. And it also owed much of its early success to the cold war, as many of the conglomerates did. By originally emphasizing avionics and defense technologies, Litton ensured orders at a time when the arms race was in full stride. The military-industrial complex dominated the corporate landscape, and Litton played a vital part in supplying the military with electronic defense systems. Its success in the 1950s was nothing short of phenomenal. Revenues increased thirty times over, and earnings per share, the most watched indicator of conglomerates at the time, grew almost tenfold. Litton subsequently acquired over a hundred companies before falling out of favor on Wall Street.

Litton was the brainchild of Charles "Tex" Thornton. Born in rural Texas, Thornton enrolled at Texas Tech but moved to Washington before completing his studies. He received a degree at night and then worked at a series of government jobs before moving to the private sector. Originally he was a statistician and data gatherer for several government agencies. Like Henry Kaiser, Thornton gained much valuable experience in World War II. While serving as an officer with the army, he headed its statistical division, and was credited with giving a young Harvard instructor named Robert McNamara his first job outside the academic world, in the division that was in charge of allocating resources and management talent for the service. When the war was over, McNamara joined a team of whiz kids led by Thornton who went to work for Henry Ford II as the scion of the automobile family tried to rebuild the auto manufacturer's sagging fortunes. During that time, Ford divested itself of Willow Run. Three years later, Thornton fell out with Ford and left to take a job as the chief executive of Hughes Aircraft. After successfully increasing the company's revenues several times over within a few years, he left to assume the reins at what would become Litton Industries in 1953. The stints at each company proved invaluable for the future of Litton.

Thornton seized upon the cold war in order to get contracts for his business. He hired a former assistant secretary of defense and made him a vice president. Litton's order book began to increase as a result, although all sides denied that there was any conflict of interest. By the late 1960s Litton was a major supplier of ships to the navy. This was not a business that Thornton knew well, but his approach was to consider ships, and especially submarines, as nothing more than a bundle of electronics. The navy began to account for almost one-third of Litton's revenues by the early 1970s, and one particular order for battleships in 1970 was reputed to be the largest in the history of naval procurement. But Litton's interest in the navy was prompted by relatively lax naval quality standards.[23] When compared to private industry, the navy was considered a cream puff of a customer, tolerating delays and cost overruns as no commercial customer did.

But Litton's laxness eventually caught up with it. Thornton purchased a sleepy shipbuilding company named Ingalls in 1961 in order to produce submarines at its Gulf Coast facility. In a highly publicized shipbuilding deal, Litton announced that it had invested more than $130 million in a venture to build ships for the navy in Mississippi. In reality, it put up $3 million of its own money while the state raised the balance through a municipal bond offering.[24] Pennsylvania helped fund the part of the project that fell within its borders by raising bonds as well. Litton accumulated a large number of orders as a result, but—in an outcome eerily similar to that experienced by Kaiser twenty years before, when he built plants in partnership with the RFC—the project failed as Litton fell desperately behind on its orders and eventually lost favor with the navy. As a result, its star as a valued military supplier began to wane.

Thornton's reach overextended his grasp on another occasion and his company began to attract attention as something of a lumbering giant, hardly as efficient as ballyhooed in its press releases. In the mid-1960s it became involved in social projects that had the strange ring of a brave new world about them. One involved building what Roy Ash, Litton's president, called "*de novo* cities." The best way to cure urban blight and solve the population problem at the same time, the company thought, was to build entirely new cities. In a classic overstatement, Ash confidently predicted that "by 1990, we will be designing cities for a million people with the prospect of growing to 5 million." He went on to note that the logistics would be more difficult than putting a man on the moon but still had great promise. But Litton's ambitions came crashing down when it attempted to put theory into practice, and city building never got off the ground. Another project proved an even greater embarrassment. Litton signed an agreement with the Greek government to provide infrastructure projects for the island of Crete, developing the island in a new type of business-government adventure that would encourage outside investment and tourism. But in so doing, Litton ventured into territory normally reserved for governments or organizations such as the World Bank. Success would have proved that multinational conglomerates did indeed have authority exceeding national boundaries (and Litton's fee for a successful outcome would be substantial). Unfortunately, almost no money was attracted from outside investors, and by 1968 Litton had quietly folded its tent and gone home, failing on yet another major project.

Charles Bluhdorn's Gulf + Western Corporation was not as ambitious on the international scene but was still one of the more aggressive conglomerates of the period. Founded relatively late, in 1958, G+W went on to acquire some of the more prestigious nameplates in the American corporate world. Like Ling before him, Bluhdorn started modestly, but friendly accounting techniques quickly helped him to assemble his impressive corporate stable.

Bluhdorn immigrated to the United States from Austria in his youth and studied for a degree at City College of New York at night. Eventually he was drawn to the action of the commodity futures markets. He was known for his mercurial personality from his first days in business. Some claimed that the same trait hindered him in later years, when his acquisitions binge was in full bloom, but it served him well early on. After the war he became a coffee trader, but found the business to be highly volatile and unpredictable. He began looking for a more stable way to make a living and he soon found a company to buy, an aging small manufacturer of auto parts in Michigan. Although the company's fortunes were declining, Bluhdorn realized that there might be some mileage in buying this sort of company at an extremely low price. He renamed it the Gulf + Western Corporation and began looking for other, similar sorts of companies. He bought many, most in the auto parts business. He paid for most of the acquisitions with stock of G+W. The stock moved from a listing on the American Stock Exchange to the New York Stock Exchange and quadrupled in price. By 1964 it reported net sales of over $100 million. He was clearly trading upon the growth achieved by merging and the expectations that surrounded it on the stock exchange. And reciprocity was one of his main tools for growth. Like Geneen, Bluhdorn preached free competition among his associated companies but was clearly practicing reciprocity. The associated companies were required to do business with each other, accounting for a fair amount of the income reported by G+W at the end of the year.

Despite all of the growth, in 1965 G+W was still mainly a somewhat uninspiring auto parts manufacturer when Bluhdorn caught the diversification bug. Then Chase Manhattan Bank loaned him over $80 million to finance a shopping spree. Eyebrows were raised at the loan because it was out of all proportion to G+W's financial strength at the time, but Chase went on to become the company's lead banker as a result. Bluhdorn bought the country's largest zinc producer. He then followed with acquisitions of a sugar company, the Consolidated Cigar Company, and Desilu Productions, among others. But the biggest plum was the acquisition of Paramount Pictures in 1966. He paid for the acquisition with securities worth $185 million when the company's book value was no more than $100 million. The price-to-earnings ratio for Paramount was sky-high, and everyone thought that Bluhdorn had overextended himself by paying too much. But the acquisition, made mostly with securities, proved successful in the short run. Although Bluhdorn admitted that he knew nothing about the film industry, the same general conglomerate philosophy prevailed: If the company could add to his earnings, that was all that was necessary. He moved to Hollywood and personally took charge of the ailing production company; critics contended that the glamor of the industry attracted him more than the company itself.

After the merger binge began, G+W began to record impressive growth. Between 1966 and 1969 its revenues shot up by 500 percent, while its gross earnings tripled. But its earnings per share never quite caught up. They increased only 50 percent, the result of issuing too much stock to pay for the acquisitions. But Wall Street was happy. Gulf + Western was now a full-fledged member of the conglomerate group. And Bluhdorn was considered a savvy corporate tactician, thanks to pool accounting, which allowed G+W to report an additional $20 million in earnings the year it merged with Paramount. Without the pooling, the increase would have been only around $3 million.[25]

Was it possible that the conglomerate stratagem could work over the long term? In Litton's case, the answer was an emphatic no. Litton's earnings began to decline in 1968. By 1970 Ling had been ousted from his position by the conglomerate's directors, and the company's stock started to fall. The honeymoon was over, not only for Litton and LTV but for many other conglomerates as well that had overpaid for their acquisitions. When the stock market began to fall in the early 1970s, their stock prices fell with it, proving that the diversification principle was not working as had been anticipated. The demise of the conglomerate trend was almost as dramatic as its beginnings. The market was invaluable to the conglomerateurs as long as prices were rising but proved to be their undoing when prices weakened. In their heyday, the conglomerates were thought to have revolutionized business, proving that modern management techniques could be applied to any sort of business and that the managers did not really have to understand the business as long as the techniques were assiduously applied. Technocracy ruled, and Wall Street and the banks helped substantially. As long as money could be found to finance the acquisitions from willing banks and profit-hungry investors, what these mammoth companies did was of little confidence. Everyone was interested only in the bottom line.

Despite the success and antitrust tribulations of the conglomerates, they were not the only companies under the regulator's spotlight. A merger between Atlantic Richfield and Sinclair, both oil companies, was originally opposed by the Justice Department, but the government eventually dropped its objections and the merger took place in 1969. In that same year, in its final act of antitrust bravado, the Johnson administration's Justice Department under Attorney General Ramsey Clark filed suit against one of the country's most traditionally run companies, IBM, charging it with monopolizing the market for computer systems. It claimed that IBM's hardware was not price-sensitive and that the company barred new competitors from entering the field by introducing models with very low profit margins that competitors could not match. Shades of the Robinson-Patman Act could be found in this charge. The case did not reach the courts for six years and took another six years to finish; by the time it did finish, only one of the original Antitrust Division lawyers was still left on the case. But the implications of the case were staggering because it was widely viewed as an attack against scientific and entrepreneurial spirit, something the country could ill afford. In the end, IBM was vindicated, but not without enormous legal costs.

One of the less endearing tactics that emerged during the 1960s was the hostile takeover. If a company proposed a merger with another but was rejected as a suitor by the target, it might well decide to simply seize control. Companies with dreams of becoming conglomerates, or just simply with dreams of expansion, often employed the tactic when all else failed. One of the earliest hostile takeover attempts occurred when Northwest Industries tried to seize control of the tire manufacturer B. F. Goodrich. Northwest was the brainchild of Ben Heineman, who changed it from the ailing Chicago and North Western Railroad into a conglomerate in a very short period of time. Like his other conglomerate counterparts, he was always actively seeking other acquisitions. Goodrich was a prize, ranking eighty-second on the *Fortune* list of top companies. Northwest was smaller, ranking sixty places below Goodrich. The proposed takeover, much to Goodrich's relief, was opposed by Richard McLaren's Justice Department under new merger guidelines announced by the Nixon administration in 1969. McLaren claimed that the proposed merger would be harmful because Northwest could use Goodrich in reciprocal dealings. But then the bottom fell out when the courts disagreed with the Antitrust Division and refused to grant an injunction. Goodrich was "in play."

Goodrich adopted defensive tactics that included the acquisition of a couple of companies of its own. It also adopted pool accounting, using the conglomerateurs' trick to save itself by instantly increasing its earnings and forcing up its stock price, both of which made the acquisition more costly. It also took out ads in newspapers to defend itself and relied upon every political friend it had at both the state and federal levels; the attorney general in Ohio issued an injunction blocking the merger in his state, evoking memories of another Ohio attorney general in the war with Standard Oil eighty years before. In the end, Northwest saw the fruitless nature of its bid and sought greener pastures elsewhere.

The longer-term implications of the conglomerate trend were staggering. Robert McNamara approached the Vietnam War in much the same way as a conglomerateur approached potential acquisitions: If the methods were correct and properly managed, then victory was assured. The assumption in both cases was that the war or merger could be won without primary regard for the nature of the enemy or the company being acquired. Ironically, the decline of the conglomerate and the end of the war occurred at about the same time, dealing a serious blow to the management technique as well as to investors' funds in the process. Although conglomerates faded slowly from the front pages, mergers would continue under different business philosophies, as growth for its own sake seemed as American as apple pie. But American confidence also suffered a blow during the 1960s as the country learned that not every business and social problem could be solved by trendy new techniques. The 1970s would be a more sober decade as a result.

TOONERVILLE TALES

The conglomerate fever infected not only manufacturing firms. Others, too, saw the trend as a way out of their miserable financial plights. One of the most unlikely conglomerates of the era was centered around the railroads, and the woes of the Penn Central became notorious. One of Cornelius Vanderbilt's basic maxims was that building a monopoly required the aspiring monopolist to extend his empire in areas he understood, not in those he did not. That sentiment was again clearly spelled out in the days of Louis Brandeis and Pierpont Morgan. In 1913 the ICC lamented that the "most prolific source of financial disaster and complication to railroads in the past has been the desire and ability of railroad managers to engage in enterprises outside the legitimate operation of their railroads." But this was considered ancient history in the 1960s, when rail lines came under pressure from long-distance trucking. Railroad revenues started to decline, and in this climate two old eastern lines, the New York Central and the Pennsylvania, decided in 1967 to merge. The ICC had no reason to object to the merger, especially because it would be a union between a freight carrier and a passenger line. They would also be able to use each other's rails interchangeably.

The story of the Penn Central began in the early 1960s, when Stuart Saunders, who had risen through the company ranks at the Pennsylvania, began an aggressive acquisitions campaign designed to shift the company's focus away from railroading. Saunders' background was in finance, and he saw himself as something of a latter-day Jay Gould. The Pennsylvania was well on its way to becoming a conglomerate by the time it merged with Vanderbilt's old, established line; acquiring the New York Central was simply a way to increase Saunders' borrowing power and gain additional notoriety. After the new company was formed, his vision of conglomerate glamor continued to dominate its corporate strategy. He singularly wanted to move the railroad away from its mundane business and give it the glamor of being a conglomerate.[26] He continued to acquire properties until his portfolio contained a stake in Madison Square Garden as well as the Waldorf-Astoria and the Six Flags Amusement Park. The First National City Bank of New York helped him finance many of his acquisitions. But because of its carelessness, it also contributed to what would become the largest bankruptcy in American history.

Saunders used creative accounting as adroitly as any of his fellow conglomerateurs. With First National City's aid, Penn Central acquired companies that reportedly never earned it a cent. But the public relations value of an acquisition and a rising stock market helped Penn Central's share price to rise, and its borrowing continued. Finally, when the interest owed could not be repaid, it became clear that the financial end was near. The company then played its trump card as a regulated industry, and it declared that the federal government should help bail it out under a federal program designed to keep afloat companies that contributed to the national defense. But then a figure from the past emerged. Rep. Wright Patman, still a member of the House, strenuously objected to any proposed bailout, regardless of reasons offered by the railroad. The handwriting was on the wall, and the company filed for bankruptcy in 1970. Despite opposition by Patman and others, however, the government finally had to intervene, as the failure was simply too large for the cleanup to be left to market forces. Conrail was the result—a publicly owned railroad company that began operating in 1976 with major portions of five other bankrupt railways in addition to the Penn Central. (Later its passenger traffic would be split off as Amtrak.) After the Penn Central fiasco, questions were immediately asked about the effectiveness of the ICC, Penn Central's supposed regulator. Particularly disturbing was the fact that one of the companies the railroad acquired was an airline called Executive Jet Aviation. A railroad's acquisition of an airline was a clear violation of federal law, although no one, including the ICC, seemed to have noticed at the time.

The conglomerate dreams that drove the combined company in its last years only hastened its doom. The diversification principle had again proven that it did not work as expected. When the company eventually went bankrupt, it was widely characterized as just another sorry chapter in the history of the railroads. But it was also another sorry chapter in the history of conglomerates, although it never received notoriety for that reason.

REPUBLICAN CHARGE

Not only large companies came under scrutiny by consumer advocates in the 1960s. Many federal agencies acquired the reputation of being fat and ineffective. The FTC in particular came under heavy criticism for its alleged phlegmatic approach to antitrust action during the conglomerate era. The agency, capable of initiating antitrust proceedings if formally applied to, was seen as merely a spectator to the events of the 1960s, more interested in preserving its bureaucratic domain and serving as a haven for political appointees without much legal or regulatory experience than in actively fighting the incursions of big business. Its reputation as something of a passive giant finally gained national attention in the late 1960s, prompted by a group of young law students working for Ralph Nader.

Nader sent his summer volunteers, appropriately nicknamed "Nader's Raiders," into the FTC to work as summer interns and study the agency's effectiveness. The group included mostly Ivy League graduates and law students; one was William Howard Taft IV, great-grandson of the former president and chief justice. The leader of the group, Edward F. Cox, who later married one of Richard Nixon's daughters, described the agency as a "self-parody of bureaucracy, fat with cronyism, torpid through an inbreeding unusual even for Washington, manipulated by the agents of commercial predators, impervious to governmental and citizen monitoring."[27] They reported that the agency was staffed with over five hundred lawyers for whom antitrust was a sideline at best, implying that most were looking for a sinecure rather than an active job as regulators. They also compared the background of the new lawyers hired by the agency in order to determine whether it was getting the best graduates for its money. They found that many had attended second-rate law schools rather than the top tier; in fact, gaining a job offer from the FTC was more difficult for a graduate of a top law school than for an applicant from a lesser-known one. The number of blacks in top management jobs also was negligible. The litany went on and on, but the picture painted was one of a bloated agency whose employees were more interested in their job perks than litigating against anyone.

Naturally, the head of the FTC took exception. The credentials of Nader's Raiders were called into question, since most had limited experience with the law and virtually none had worked in federal agencies. Also, the conclusions, while titillating, could be challenged because of their clearly inflammatory intent. Many considered those conclusions mean-spirited, embodying the anti-establishment trend of the decade despite the fact that the members of the raiders were all from the proper colleges and backgrounds. And there was a fair amount of evidence to counter their opinions. In 1969, the same year the report was published, the FTC took the unusual step of requiring companies with assets of $250 million or more to notify the agency sixty days before any proposed mergers. This was in keeping with the Nixon administration's newly adopted policy of closely monitoring the largest corporations. While the move was criticized from some quarters as possibly impeding the ability of large companies to merge, it did nevertheless show that the FTC was not entirely asleep, as the raiders suggested.

During this time many in the business world were surprised by the attacks from Republicans, who since the days of the McKinley administration had always been friendly to big business. After Richard Nixon beat

Hubert Humphrey for the presidency in 1968, there was every reason to expect that the same would be true again, especially since the new administration had very conservative cabinet members and supporters, including quite a number with Wall Street experience.

The Nixon presidency fooled everyone by becoming known for its avid trust-busting activities, although much of that could be traced to the Antitrust Division rather than to the White House. The year 1969 in particular was one of the busiest on the antitrust calendar for decades. Attorney General John Mitchell used terms not usually found in the Republican lexicon, like "concentration of economic power," when describing the successful conglomerates. Like the president, he had spent the years prior to assuming office practicing corporate law, not the usual breeding ground for trustbusters but not one that bred radicals, either. One explanation for the unusual antitrust activity was that mainstream big business was not particularly fond of the conglomerateurs and wanted them controlled for its own selfish motives. In 1969 three venerable companies, Chemical Bank, B. F. Goodrich, and Pan American Airways, were all targets of hostile suitors who wanted to devour them in the conglomerate craze, and in each case the Nixon administration was only too glad to help by becoming activist on their behalf, as McLaren's failed injunction against the proposed Goodrich takeover showed. Of course, the Nixon administration eventually became known both for pursuing monopolies and for being suspected of accepting kickbacks from corporate America.

John Mitchell's most significant contribution to antitrust history was the idea that the largest firms should not be allowed to merge for fear of the resulting economic power of the new conglomerate. Ironically, in the early days of the administration, a leak revealed the conclusions of a report written for the administration (but never officially released) by a group of University of Chicago academics led by George Stigler on the feasibility of attacking conglomerates using the existing antitrust laws. They concluded that "vigorous action on the basis of our present knowledge is not defensible."[28] Not enough was known about the economic effects of the conglomerates to pursue them avidly, they thought. The administration chose to ignore the report, however. A previous report commissioned by the Johnson administration (and never released by the Democrats) was cited by the Nixon administration as more to its liking. In it, Phil Neale and his associates, again of the University of Chicago, recommended that legislation be passed to break up oligopolistic industries where four or fewer companies account for more than 70 percent of sales. The Johnson administration never proposed such a bill to Congress, although it was widely supported in Democratic circles. The Nixon administration appeared to have no intent of introducing such a law either but liked the tone of the Neale report better than its own.

John Mitchell gave the new antitrust policy further definition in June 1969, when he announced that the administration would file suit to prevent any corporation in the top two hundred from merging with any other corporation in the same group, calling that a potential "superconcentration." "The danger that this superconcentration poses to our economic, political and social structure cannot be overestimated," he said. Sounding very much like Estes Kefauver, he went on to say that the nation's two hundred largest corporations accounted for 58 percent of total manufacturing assets, and the five hundred largest accounted for 75 percent of assets. Further combinations among them would be intolerable, he said, and he pledged to use the Justice Department actively. The department then drew up a list of the top two hundred to use as a guideline. But critics contended that the anticonglomerate stand taken by McLaren and Mitchell was largely on behalf of the more establishment corporations, which did not want to defend themselves against the nouveau riche conglomerateurs. Mitchell could do little to assuage his critics on that point.

The Nixon administration found a strange ally in the Warren Court, considering that the Court was actively supporting liberal causes although the same could not be said for the administration. In 1969 the Court ruled against a group of paper box manufacturers for swapping data on the prices paid by customers for their products. The companies routinely swapped data on customers and identified them by name. The majority opinion was written by former New Dealer William O. Douglas—no friend to Wall Street and big business in the 1930s, when he was one of the first members of the SEC. He held that the companies violated the Sherman Act by sharing the price information and naming the customers. Curiously, the nettlesome Robinson-Patman Act, the more obvious choice for claiming price violations, was not invoked.

The three-decade-old Robinson-Patman Act had been a source of irritation and confusion even to its advocates ever since its passage, and it came to be widely seen as anticompetitive in its own right, designed to protect small businessmen from the larger, more efficient ones. Emmanuel Celler of New York once said that the act "intended, under cover of devious but innocent appearing wording, to assure profitable business to a trade class regardless of the efficiency of service rendered the consumer. . . . The consumers owe no business a living." The sentiment became even stronger in the age of the consumer, when it could actually cost the customer more, not less. The *Wall Street Journal* wrote in an editorial that "even the most rational enforcement of Robinson-Patman, however, hardly justifies continued life for a law that was designed mainly to prevent competition, not to enhance it."[29] The newspaper clearly saw the law as a method of protecting small businessmen at all costs, including efficiency.

Big business was no longer considered the enemy, as many had seen it during the New Deal. Competition and fair prices for the consumer became the buzzwords of the 1960s and early 1970s, as they had in the past, but now they were being used in an environment that valued share prices and shareholder wealth as never before. Berle and Means would have appreciated the emphasis but probably also would have recognized that the concept of growth for its own sake was too inextricably tied up with the performance of the stock market to last forever. The merger trend continued as strongly as ever, and there were developing indications that it was slowly beginning to win its battle against the antimonopolists. The legal and ideological attack on alleged monopolies needed new energy. New ideas and new laws were in short supply on the antitrust front.

BACK TO SCHOOL

Part of the problem with prosecuting alleged monopolists was that the antitrust laws were very general. The language of the Sherman Act was so broad that it was becoming extremely difficult to prosecute all but the most egregious cases of horizontal monopolies with any success. If government watchdogs were to remain effective, they would need more ammunition in their arsenal to combat the ingenuity of big business. In addition, some of the other arguments used to criticize business were very theoretical, a little lame, or both. For example, Kefauver's assertion that excessive advertising was a sure sign of monopoly concentration did not square with business reality. In a rapidly growing country of vast proportions, advertising was nothing more than a way of reaching a far-flung consumer base. Fighting allegations based upon theory of that sort was expensive and time-consuming for companies, and while politicians may have profited personally by all of the press accompanying their monopoly inquiries, businessmen found themselves hampered by the notoriety and legal proceedings.

In order to bring a sounder method and more discipline to antitrust activity, economists began studying the effects of mergers, both actual and proposed, in greater detail. Many lawyers also attempted to use more economic analysis in their arguments, rather than relying strictly on the antitrust statutes and previous court decisions. The hope was that the result would be court decisions and regulatory action based more upon economics than politics. Economic analysis could help the antitrust cause immeasurably. It could also help business by separating fact from fiction in the minds of its potential enemies. The question was whether the new economic analysis could gain a foothold in antitrust work, leaving ideology and politics behind. The answer was obvious from the very beginning. Trying to separate economics from politics was not impossible; it was inconceivable.

In 1955 seven members of the Supreme Court owed their seats to appointments by Democrats Franklin Roosevelt or Harry Truman. Ten years later only three of them remained.[30] The four seats vacated were all filled by Eisenhower appointees, and since the days of McKinley, Republican philosophy held that business was best left to deal with market problems by itself. In the Supreme Court of 1965, that meant that the newer judges were apt to look cynically at some of the arguments used by the Justice Department or any litigant that invoked broad principles without showing some negative effect upon competition or prices. Although the number of antitrust cases in the 1960s doubled over the number brought in the prior decade, notable decisions were not in abundance.

Beginning in the 1950s, a group of scholars at the University of Chicago began to take a hard look at antitrust activity from historical, legal, and economic perspectives. Their common trait was that they were all advocates of as little government intervention in the marketplace as possible. The group became known as the Chicago School, and its influence spread quickly. Its writings and contributions to antitrust history and theory and to economics generally stood in direct opposition to the practices of the Roosevelt administration during the Second World War.

One of the early members of the Chicago School, John S. McGee, studied the practices of Standard Oil in the nineteenth century to determine whether the charges leveled against it in the original government suit were justified. McGee concluded that Standard Oil had not used predatory pricing in order to become a monopoly. His conclusion ran against the common assumption that Rockefeller cut prices drastically in order to force out his competitors.[31] But the case of George Rice years before proved McGee correct. Rice's problem was that his own undercutting was not well received by Standard Oil's traditional customers, who turned down his lower prices and remained loyal (for whatever reason) to Rockefeller's company. The fact that Rockefeller's customers feared his wrath if they did business with someone else was central to the entire issue, but the net effect was that predatory pricing was not involved. This was especially important because predatory pricing had been a fundamental assumption of antitrust until that time. If a company was a monopoly, then it must practice predatory pricing. How else could it have accumulated dominant market power? Obviously, Rockefeller was able to accomplish it in other ways—for example, making shipping more of a problem for his competitors through arrangements he made with the railroads themselves. Carnegie used the tactic early in his own career as well.

McGee's study did not disprove the conclusion that Standard Oil maintained a monopoly but did challenge the assumptions that had been made about monopolies in general. The Chicago School's interpretation of the effects of monopoly power would become valuable to antitrusters because they wanted to be seen using the most recent research that economics could provide rather than simply being slaves to the language of the antitrust laws. Taken collectively, this research would have a profound impact upon the way legislators and regulators viewed the industrial concentrations of the 1970s and 1980s. They provided an intellectual counterforce to the more traditional Harvard School, which took its inspiration from Louis Brandeis and viewed antitrust work, as a broad body of laws, court decisions, and political influences that, taken together, determined whether monopoly was present in business structures. How business conducted itself in the market was an important element in determining concentrations of power. In the simplest sense, everyone knew John D. Rockefeller was a monopolist because Standard Oil behaved like one. Perhaps, countered the Chicago School, but predatory pricing was not one of its sins. In other words, one could not simply assume that because certain practices created monopolies, therefore all monopolists practiced them.

The Chicago School's approach coincided closely with traditional Republican thought on antitrust action and was espoused by Republican administrations in later years, especially those of Ronald Reagan and George Bush. Perhaps one of its greatest achievements was to reduce the pressure that had begun to be applied to conglomerate mergers during the late 1960s. The same was true of vertical mergers, though this new view did not much benefit the organization that grew by swallowing smaller fish through horizontal mergers; this type of business was still the object of antitrust action. The Chicago School's disproving of predatory pricing as a general characteristic of all monopolies had a great deal to do with the movement away from seeing conglomerates as a menace to society. In order for a company's actions to be truly predatory, prices would have to be raised back to previous levels after the competition had been forced out by the aggressive, dominant company. Once it became clear that driving competitors out of business by cutthroat price slashing was not always in a company's best interest, one of the main charges leveled at many businesses in the past became less significant. What had happened was that antitrust theory was attempting to become more complex in response to the increasingly sophisticated operating methods used by business over the years.

Capital barriers to new business expansion were not much of a problem during the 1950s and 1960s because of the overall boom in the stock market and in the economy in general. But smaller businesses could only provide so much competition for the conglomerates and multinationals, and like the developers of the Nickel Plate Railroad a century before, many smaller outfits could not wait to sell out to a conglomerateur. Realizing that their prospects were limited, they took the money and went their separate ways. Others set themselves up in business in order to be bought out, realizing that conglomerates paid top dollar for companies they coveted. The great irony was that within ten years, big was no longer in vogue and many of the conglomerates began to divest themselves of their disparate holdings. Wall Street made money on the divestiture trend as well. But all of the apparent business activity did not alter the fact that the conglomerates were not good deals for their investors in the long run, nor were they good for the economy as a whole. Arthur Burns, chairman of the Federal Reserve in the 1970s, noted, "Being preoccupied with corporate acquisitions and their conglomerate image, many businessmen lost sight of the traditional business objective. . . . The productivity of their businesses suffered, and so too did the nation's productivity."[32]

After over a hundred years of monopoly formation and antimonopoly sentiment, it was clear that many of the practices of monopolies and the antimonopolists had not changed substantially over the years. A more in-depth analysis of how monopolies operated was being developed, however, in a sweeping attempt to understand more about the nature of big business and how it reacted to competition. In the 1950s and 1960s business discovered international markets, and the American century hit its highest point in terms of trade and business. Internationalization became cited as another reason why businesses should continue to consolidate—they needed size to reach foreign markets properly. Republicans provided some surprises for their traditional allies in business: Eisenhower enunciated the idea of the military-industrial complex, which was to be used countless times against Republicans for years afterward, and Richard Nixon, surrounded by cabinet members and advisors from Wall Street and corporate law, presided over some of the most rigorous antitrust prosecutions since the days of Franklin Roosevelt—though most of the cases were won by the companies. And in a challenge to baseball's fifty-year-old antitrust exemption, a player for the Philadelphia Phillies, Curt Flood, sued the baseball commissioner, Bowie Kuhn, to become a free agent, using language that clearly implied that he was being treated like a slave. He wanted to play for whomever he chose, something that baseball had not permitted since the 1922 ruling. Kuhn refused, and the case made its way to the Supreme Court, which again ruled in baseball's favor. The Court acknowledged that times had changed, but since Congress had never acted against professional baseball to change its antitrust exemption, it would not do so. There was something ironic in the fact that the game that billed itself as America's pastime was a protected monopoly. The history of monopolies certainly was providing some dramatic and contradictory moments.

7

BEARING
DOWN
(1970–1982)

*Unique among the nations of the world, this country
has entrusted the development and operation of its
communications resources to private enterprise.*
—JOHN DEBUTTS, CHAIRMAN OF AT&T

THE HAPPY DAYS of the 1950s and early 1960s began to wane by 1965.
Inflationary pressures caused by the Vietnam War and international trade
problems began to destabilize the American economy, and the country
entered its grimmest economic stage since the Depression. The dollar
began to experience problems in the foreign exchange market. As a result,
the stock market weakened significantly toward the end of the decade,
causing problems for the conglomerates and their numerous investors. As
the 1960s came to a close, the economic situation appeared weak but it was
destined to deteriorate even more. Twenty years of growth in the postwar
period were ending in a collision of inflation, reaction to government
authority, and general skepticism. The worst days since the Depression
were yet to come.

The general questioning of authority and confrontational politics of the
New Left could clearly be seen on the corporate front as well. A small
telecommunications upstart company under an opportunist Harvard
M.B.A. would tackle the authority of AT&T, run by a chief executive who

represented the entrenched old school of corporate managers. Indeed, the entire question of whether the government should sustain the unique monopoly held by AT&T would be brought into question. The question had been asked many times before, but the moment was right to ask it again, this time more forcefully. The largest company on earth was in the nascent stage of its decline. Ten years before, Ralph Nader had effectively tackled General Motors over the quality and safety of its products. But that victory would be minuscule in comparison to the eventual outcome of an unknown company challenging AT&T.

As the 1970s unfolded, markets and institutions all across the globe developed links to each other that would grow stronger over the years. The world's economy was beginning to show the early signs of what would be known as "internationalization." Newly independent, developing countries meant new markets for the developed exporting countries but presented previously unseen sorts of risks as well.

By 1971 the stock market's problems had been exacerbated by an international currency crisis and continued inflation at home. The United States was suffering trade imbalances, and the dollar was under pressure on the foreign exchange markets as a result. Several years before, Prime Minister Harold Wilson of Britain had devalued the pound sterling under similar conditions. As he did so, Wilson blamed the pound's travails in no small part upon international currency speculators, whom the British press dubbed the "gnomes of Zurich." According to the popular myth circulating at the time, little faceless money changers in Switzerland and other exotic financial centers were speculating with currencies with scant regard for the impact they might have on the world economy. This marked the beginning of a trend of blaming speculators for domestic problems that would last for decades. It was convenient and helped deflect attention from economic problems and mismanagement at home. In 1971 the idea made its American debut. After months of speculation and uncertainty, President Nixon announced an economic package in August designed to curtail American inflation through a series of wage and price controls aimed at both labor and manufacturers. Intended to put a stop to inflation, it was the most dramatic set of economic proposals made since the Second World War. In a nationally televised speech, he outlined his program, then turned to what would become the longest-lasting impact of his administration other than the Watergate legacy: He announced the severance of the link between the dollar and gold. That relationship had been the cornerstone of the international economic system since the late 1940s. Citing currency crises in the foreign exchange market, Nixon asked, "Now who gains from these crises? Not the working man, not the investor, not the real producers of wealth. The gainers are the international money speculators: because they thrive on crisis, they help to create them."[1] With this move to delink the weak dollar from gold, he put the first nail in the coffin of what was known as the Bretton Woods system of fixed foreign exchange rates. In effect, the devaluation amounted to about 10 percent of the dollar's value against the other major currencies. Within a year, the entire fixed rate exchange system, administered by the International Monetary Fund, would be dead, supplanted with what became known as floating exchange rates. A week after the measures were announced, *Life* claimed that "the President was somewhat demagogic, in the manner of Britain's Harold Wilson, in blaming unnamed international money speculators for the dollar's troubles abroad which are in fact the result of inflationary forces in the U.S." Part of the problem would be to recognize the economic problems as internal rather than rely upon the old Republican chestnut of blaming them on outside interference. But during the 1970s events abroad were a convenient scapegoat for domestic economic problems. Though the decade became one of internationalism, it was not always understood in a positive sense.

Despite Nixon's assertion, speculators did not cause the most serious economic crisis of the postwar period. American trade problems soon would be multiplied by events that were set loose by the devaluation of the dollar. In the winter of 1973 the price of oil was officially doubled by the Organization of Petroleum Exporting Countries (OPEC). This marked the beginning of several more oil price rises over the next several years that resulted in the price of a barrel exceeding $30 by the end of the decade. In 1971, the price had been slightly under $3. The oil producers raised the price in part to protect their own purchasing power, which had been severely diminished by the depreciation of the dollar. The chain of events that led to the severe recession of the 1970s had begun, and the mantra of growth that had been recited many times in the previous years was replaced by a fear that assets would be eaten away by inflation.

Industry was quick to seize upon the oil crisis as an argument for the relaxation of the antitrust laws. The idea was to allow oil companies and other energy companies to join to achieve economies of scale in the face of rising prices. But the Antitrust Division would have none of it. Thomas Kauper, its chief in 1974, rejected the idea flatly, saying that "such a move would not put oil in the ground." He was aware that some might use the crisis for their own benefit, adding, "It's also true that monopolistic and conspiratorial behavior can enhance price and further reduce output, and history tells us that restraints and relationships born out of crisis tend to endure long after the crisis ends."[2] Indeed, rumors abounded for a few years that the oil companies were benefiting from the oil price rises by enjoying higher profit margins and conspiring to keep supplies low, further raising prices.

The events of the 1970s spurred the beginning of a trend toward deregulation in many areas. Exchange rates were no longer regulated by the IMF, although it would take another several years before that became painfully obvious to a world accustomed to thinking of currencies as relatively stable. Gold was freed from its constraints, and it appreciated every year as inflation increased. AT&T's monopoly was in the early stages of being challenged, and many observers were amazed at how quickly the giant monopoly acquiesced to demands from competitors that it open its markets. After almost forty years, the vestiges of regulation inherited from the New Deal and war years were beginning to recede. But the New Deal legacy, while fading, was not entirely dead. It would remain effective long enough to score the biggest victory in antitrust history. There were still many judges and lawmakers who adhered to the idea that business needed to be curbed to protect society. But prosperity and a rapidly changing world were pushing for deregulation in many areas that once had been considered sacrosanct by Congress and the courts. And no one imagined that the events of the early 1970s were only a prelude of things to come.

The number of antitrust actions usually dropped in bad economic times. Just the opposite occurred in the 1970s, although the intensity of the antitrust fervor began to wane. Big business was again being blamed for the country's economic woes; the Justice Department pursued some of the country's largest companies, and antitrusters in Congress continued to hold hearings on concentrations of power. The editor of an influential antitrust journal said with a fair degree of understatement, "There are probably no more than 100 industries in the whole United States economy that are worth suing by the FTC and its budget of $30 million couldn't sustain more than a dozen such price lowering lawsuits in any given year." Editorials clamored for increased examination of monopolies, and one even suggested a new TNEC to deal with the resurgence of the concentration of economic power. Despite the calls, little was ever done to satisfy those who thought that big oil, steel, and other industries were profiting again while the economy continued to slide, though the Justice Department continued the pressure on what it considered the most egregious violations. Nevertheless, the *Wall Street Journal* took strong exception to some of the antitrust tactics practiced by the Justice Department in the late 1960s and 1970s: "According to a theory held by the Brains Trust of the Antitrust Division of the Justice Department, a merger shouldn't be allowed because it eliminates 'potential' competition," the paper commented sarcastically. Noting that the Supreme Court thought little of the concept as well, the paper added, "This is a most welcome development. There is still a minority on the high court that would frown on the takeover of Mom's Café by Pop's Diner if the Antitrust Division gave the cue. But for the first time in more than two decades there is a majority on the Supreme Court willing to try to distinguish between economic efficiency and anti-competitiveness. If the process can be encouraged and continued, there will be one genuine sign that someday the nation might be able to slow down its construction of law schools."[3] The comment was in part a not-so-subtle reference to the old New Dealers still sitting on the Court.

The case against the Court was a bit overstated. In a notable ruling in 1975, the Court ruled that the Clayton Act could be applied only to interstate mergers, not those occurring between two service companies located within the same state. But it still carried the baggage of the New Deal, which was becoming increasingly heavy. And others enthusiastically embraced the notion of forestalling potential competition—including Richard McLaren of the Antitrust Division. His archrival Harold Geneen recalled that "McLaren was really stretching things in the 1960s and 1970s. At one point [during the proposed Hartford-ITT merger] he tried to establish a nefarious link between Hartford Insurance and a company we owned that made sprinkler systems for office buildings. He argued that

Hartford could undercut its competitors in buildings that had ITT sprinklers. He produced no evidence for such a conspiracy, for the good reason that none existed. Even so, Mr. McLaren insisted on addressing the 'potential' as though that proved his point of improper action."[4] Worrying about the potential threat to society through mergers was nonsense to Geneen, but to the antimonopolists, these sorts of combinations could and should be nipped in the bud.

The *Wall Street Journal* editorial also was referring to the fact that antitrust fervor was at least in part kept alive in a few elite law schools that had been training lawyers in antitrust work since the days of Louis Brandeis. Using the courts to sue was a budding American cottage industry that required a constant flow of lawyers, but not everyone was well versed in antitrust. These elite law schools were the repositories of almost a century's worth of antitrust law and theory. Many of the notable antitrusters, both in Congress and in the federal agencies, had graduated from these schools. Most of Nader's disciples came from the same institutions— hence, perhaps, part of their criticism of the FTC's lawyers, who had gone to other schools. Where did the graduates of state universities and diploma-mill law schools ever learn about antitrust? Certainly not in the classroom. How, then, could they be expected to carry the torch at federal agencies? While New Deal reforms were waning in some areas of public policy, these law schools carried them forward. Without that influence, concepts such as predatory pricing and bottleneck monopolies (used in the AT&T case) would never have maintained their popularity in the 1970s.

The shaky logic of the antitrusters came under further attack when Robert Bork's *The Antitrust Paradox* was published in 1978. This was perhaps the most comprehensive account (and most acerbic critique) of antitrust legislation and court decisions yet written. Bork, who had been solicitor general, federal judge, and law professor at Yale, was a scathing critic of "antitrust policy," a combination of law, court decisions, and government policies toward monopolies over the years, not just during one administration. Looking back at the history of antitrust activity since the Sherman Act, Bork stated unequivocally, "Antitrust is a subcategory of ideology," and he argued that its application depended entirely upon politics. But by beginning his discussion with the Sherman Act, Bork left out a significant piece of antimonopoly history. By not discussing the anti-bigness trend in American thought or the fundamental clash between Hamiltonian and Jeffersonian ideals that antitrust represented, he could deal only with the apparent inconsistencies revealed by comparing one case to another. Taken in that manner, antitrust indeed looked silly. But even before the first federal antitrust law was passed, indeed even before the great industrial monopolies appeared, opposition to monopolies—and, simultaneously, the recognition that monopolies existed—had already become part of the American civil religion.

With that said, Bork was especially critical of attempts to curb the conglomerates using antitrust. Conglomerates were not horizontal or vertical combinations, and as such there was "no threat to competition in any conglomerate merger." In fact, it was possible that the discouragement of some conglomerate mergers actually did more harm than good. Bork also excoriated Ralph Nader's approach; commenting on one of Nader's periodic book-length reports on the structure of business and antitrust, Bork claimed that *The Closed Enterprise System* "shed the complexities of antitrust so completely that the reader is given no hint at their existence." Quoting a colleague, he concluded that "if we would only stop thinking so much about the problem and throw the book at the bastards our monopoly problem would be solved."[5] That criticism ignored the fact that while Nader's book was a curious mix of the history of antitrust law and diatribes against monopoly concentrations, it was also the contemporary version of muckraking. What it could not accomplish by sound argument it was able to accomplish by sensationalism.

As mentioned, however, despite conservative complaints, the number of antitrust suits filed rose during this period. In a case harking back to the days of the sugar trust, the Justice Department filed suit in 1974 against six major sugar refiners. Sugar prices had soared since 1970, along with inflation, and the companies allegedly conspired to control the prices charged consumers. Almost immediately after the suit was announced, several refiners not charged in the indictment declared extraordinary dividends on their common stock, seeking to be shown sharing the wealth created by the higher prices with their shareholders. While the sugar industry was highly visible, challenging it at a time when oil prices and other more vital commodity prices were rising seemed to be a frivolous use of the Justice Department's resources.

On the surface, it appeared that any company preying on another in the latter 1970s especially could have had a charge of monopoly laid at its door. The stock market was not strong, and while that provided some good bargains for those companies in a position to take over others, it also raised the question of how such companies could maintain their financial strength when inflation was rising and the Dow Jones average was falling. During the 1930s that would have raised questions among antitrusters. In the 1970s other affairs vied for attention—productivity and technological innovation seemed to be declining, imports were on the rise, and with the decline of the Bretton Woods system it seemed that the much-ballyhooed American century was about to end prematurely—and so such matters were viewed less passionately. For example, Senator Philip Hart of Michigan was a dedicated trustbuster in the New Deal mold who held subcommittee hearings in the Senate beginning in 1973 that occasionally became quite heated. The Senate subcommittee did not have much influence, however, due to a generally friendly attitude toward business in Congress. Hart was popularly known as "the conscience of the Senate." In 1973, he introduced a bill in Congress entitled the Industrial Reorganization Act. This avowedly antitrust bill would have classified as monopolies industries in which four or fewer companies together held more than 50 percent of the market. Though it was similar to proposals made in the past, especially those made by John Mitchell during the late 1960s, the act failed to garner support in the Senate and frightened many industrialists and trade groups. A more long-lasting development began in 1973, when an economic analysis unit was established within the Antitrust Division. Though it would take some time to establish the success of economic analysis in studying alleged monopolies, the approach become nothing short of a revolution in antitrust within ten years.

SATURDAY NIGHT FEVER

Stock markets around the world suffered badly from rising inflation and falling productivity. The Nixon administration was powerless to intervene, being preoccupied with the Watergate affair. The Dow Jones average lost almost 40 percent of its value, and new investment plunged. The market staged a rally in 1975 and 1976 but then quickly gave up the gains. By 1977 the price of a seat on the New York Stock Exchange had declined to $45,000, less than the price of a New York City taxi medallion. Under similar circumstances in the past, antimonopolists would have been quick to blame industrial concentrations for the country's economic ills. The ingredients all seemed to be in place. Charges of price rigging in commodities and conspiratorial talk about the nefarious OPEC cartel. Would the same pattern be repeated again?

The deteriorating economic conditions, the weak stock market, and rapidly rising inflation actually posed an opportunity to engender economic activity—and produce wealth—without creating new value. This opportunity was based upon mergers, but the motive for these mergers had changed since the 1960s, when it had been all about the desire to become larger. Now, however, inflation created a curious situation. Many companies' assets had been acquired before inflation set in, so they were relatively cheap in comparison to the prices for new, similar assets in the 1970s. A company that bought another with a relatively low book value would certainly enjoy an advantage. For those who could afford to go shopping, prices were right. But those who found themselves on the bargain shelves often had other ideas. In the parlance of the 1970s, the bridegrooms were willing but the brides were often adamantly opposed. Thus developed the setting for the hostile takeover.

Originally, a hostile takeover was a quick cash offer to buy the outstanding shares of the target's stock. The acquirer made its offer but gave shareholders very little time to consider it. These sorts of deals became known as "Saturday Night Specials," named after a cheap handgun that was used for a "quick job." As described earlier, mergers and acquisitions reached new heights of hostility with the failed bid for B. F. Goodrich by Northwest Industries in 1969. Goodrich fought off its unwanted suitor with ads placed in national newspapers, used pool accounting, and merged with other companies in order to fend off Northwest. Its tactics were remembered and would be adopted several times in notable cases where the bride wanted to remained single. What this case made clear was that mergers and acquisitions were no longer just a way for big companies to swallow up smaller ones but a strategy that any company could practice, for a price. Sometimes smaller companies even made an attempt to acquire larger ones. The old conglomerate philosophy had lingered after the conglomerates themselves had declined in popularity: The best way to expand was not to start an enterprise from the ground up but to buy someone else's company. The idea of synergy, first launched in the 1960s, began to become better defined. Many new industries depended upon start-up companies for innovation and fresh ideas. Older, more established industries were poised to enter a new stage of takeover. Like many new trends, it would begin on an unfriendly basis rather than smoothly.

The merger and acquisition scene also gave rise to arbitrageurs on Wall Street, those speculators who bought and sold the shares of takeover targets and their pursuers, hoping to profit once the merger took place. Of course, arbitrageurs stood to lose huge sums if the deal was blocked for antitrust reasons. Even on Wall Street, their activities were on a different plane from those of the average stock trader. As one put it, "I think of them as vague shadows with European backgrounds. I don't even know who they are." But as the business became more profitable, many would soon know who they were and how they earned a living. The arbs, as they are called, added a new dimension of risk to potential mergers that had been unknown in the past. They would bet on the probability of success of a merger or, conversely, on its chances of failure.

One of the great ironies of the decade was that for all of the mergers and acquisitions that occurred there were also a greater number of divestitures. Many of the conglomerates began to shed companies they had acquired in the past, either because they could no longer afford to keep them or were forced to divest because of previous antitrust arrangements with the Justice Department. ITT began to sell off some of its most prominent acquisitions as part of the 1971 deal with the Antitrust Division that allowed Geneen's company to keep the Hartford Insurance Company. Many of the charges leveled at ITT by its critics assumed that the contributions it made to the Republicans in past elections were designed to ensure that it would not lose money as it was forced to sell off some prize holdings. The *Wall Street Journal* commented in 1974 that "during the past two years, antitrust troubles and a reputation for domestic and international politicking have made International Telephone & Telegraph Corp. perhaps the most controversial U.S. corporation since John D. Rockefeller's old Standard Oil Co." Some of the moves certainly enhanced ITT's reputation as a wheeler-dealer. The Avis divestiture earned it $55 million, and the sale of the Canteen Corporation, a vending company, earned it $7 million. But some of the companies were losing money at the time they were sold, catching ITT in the reverse of what it had tried to accomplish by buying them in the first place, and causing the corporation to suffer losses itself. Wall Street benefited regardless of the conglomerates' problems, because it really made little difference to financiers if a company was acquiring or divesting—the fees were about the same either way.

Conglomerates' reputation as companies that could not lose money had been badly tarnished by the mid-1970s, but they were still a potent force to be reckoned with. In addition, liberals in Congress did not abandon attempts to control conglomerates' acquisition of other companies even though the legal basis for doing so was still shaky. In 1979 the Justice Department announced that it was planning inquiries into conglomerate mergers. The head of the Antitrust Division, John Shenefield, said, "The time has come to face up to the long-term social, political, and economic problems" that the mergers presented. The Justice Department proposed a ban on large mergers that would create a combined company with $2 billion or more in sales. Originally, the government wanted to ban all sizeable mergers unless the companies involved could show positive effects upon competition. At the same time, Senator Edward Kennedy of Massachusetts proposed his own bill on conglomerate mergers that would have required a large company that acquired another to divest itself of an equal amount of existing assets. This was essentially the concept that had been forced upon ITT ten years earlier.

Both proposals clearly adhered to the idea that big is bad. Kennedy's proposal was cloaked under the guise of protecting small businesses from big ones, in a resurrection of the Robinson-Patman principle. The outcry from business and its supporters was quick in coming. Even Jimmy Carter, a Democrat and no special friend of big business, declared that he wanted to study Kennedy's proposal before endorsing it. The *Wall Street Journal* tersely remarked, "Chairman Edward M. Kennedy of the Senate Judiciary Committee has now kicked off the hearings on his new anti-conglomerate merger bill, which in a burst of Orwellian fancy he has dubbed the Small and Independent Business Protection Act." The paper excoriated Kennedy for proposing such a measure, which was bound to be popular, without having any viable economic basis for it. In fact, more thoughtful analyses of the proposal saw elements of the proposed legislation that could open the door for problems in the future. Kenneth W. Dam of the University of Chicago testified before the Senate Judiciary Committee that if domestic mergers were blocked by such proposals, then the incentive for American firms to move overseas would be increased substantially, because the trade rules favored foreign investment over domestic. He concluded by saying that "the conglomerate merger bill thus could result in exactly what the critics of multinationals deplore—the exporting of jobs."[6] Critics saw Kennedy's bill as nothing more than another politician's opportunistic stab at big business for the sake of publicity.

At the same time a number of shifts were beginning to take place in trade and industry. The decline of the dollar did not actually spur exports as much as had been hoped, and the dollar began to rise again, anyway. Industrialized countries started selling more cars, steel, and other goods to Americans, American-made goods began developing a reputation for shoddiness, and the country's dependence on imported oil became more and more noticeable. Much political and business hand-wringing began, trying to explain the apparent decline in American quality and production. American energy companies especially began looking around the globe for potential merger partners or takeover candidates. Exxon made overtures to Rio-Tinto Zinc of Britain in an unsuccessful attempt to link with another commodity-based business; the discovery of oil in the North Sea had catapulted Great Britain into the front ranks of oil-producing nations. Since the United States had the world's largest appetite for imported oil, despite being a major producer in its own right, rising OPEC prices played havoc with the dollar and interest rates. The high interest rates made raising fresh capital difficult and expensive, and industry quickly began to show signs of strain. It became clear that the problem was inflation: If it could be tackled, then industry would recover and become internationally competitive again. But business could not wait for a change in the economic cycle. Many large companies looked to mergers as a way of diversifying their bases and maintaining their markets in the face of rising costs. The activity quickly swamped the Antitrust Division and the FTC, with the result that only the biggest cases with the most potential impact were pursued.

In 1975 antitrust's long arm tried to extend to the oil companies and OPEC, who were widely thought to be rigging the price of oil in the name of greater profits. The rise in petroleum prices had quadrupled the price of a gallon of gasoline, seriously damaging the automobile industry, still primarily known for producing large, gas-hungry automobiles. Calls for the breakup of the big oil companies began to be heard before the elections of 1976. One of the more intriguing ideas to emerge was that of suing OPEC itself for violations of the Sherman Antitrust Act, assuming with a rather large stretch of logic that a sovereign group of countries could be treated like a domestic company in the eyes of the law. The idea was nothing more than wishful thinking, although it began to take on sinister tones later in the decade as talk intensified about using military force against certain Arab oil producers if prices did not fall; suing the countries involved would not have evoked a response from them, but the idea that all legal avenues had been explored and found closed could then have been used to justify military force. Neither the suit nor the military action ever materialized, but the mere idea of suing showed how far the Justice Department was willing to extend domestic antitrust principles.

MA BELL'S DIVORCE

The American Telephone and Telegraph Company (AT&T) occupied a unique place in American business and, indeed, among American social institutions. The giant company was one of the few state-recognized monopolies allowed to exist other than the electric utilities. And unlike the other giant monopolies of the past, from early in its history it was dominated not by its founder but by a class of professional managers. Ever since Alexander Graham Bell relinquished control of the company toward the end of the previous century, AT&T had grown as one of the first truly modern corporations, squarely in the hands of its managers and shareholders. The managers often discussed the share value of the company and its impact, realizing early that AT&T was one of the first widely held corporations in American history. Whatever Berle and Means may have thought about the diminution of wealth through share ownership and a weak stock market in the late 1920s and early 1930s, AT&T had grown to be the exception. It was the most widely held stock in the country and the symbol of American ingenuity and efficiency.

AT&T's development, especially in the early years, was a testament to George Stephenson's century-old admonition about size, capital, and monopoly (originally made about the railroads). Alexander Graham Bell was initially forced to license his technical expertise to outside operating companies because he lacked the capital necessary to keep the operations under one roof. After his original patents ran out in the mid-1880s, other, smaller phone companies sprang up to challenge him, mostly on a local level. AT&T became the network manager for its affiliated companies, providing technical support and innovation while the local companies financed themselves. AT&T's fortunes changed considerably after banking interests led by J. P. Morgan acquired an interest in the company in 1907. Morgan and George Baker of the First National Bank of New York began supplying it with capital, replacing Kidder Peabody & Co. of Boston as its major banker. AT&T's board became filled with Morgan and Baker allies as a result. One of them was its best-known chief executive, Theodore Vail. Vail himself was plain-spoken about competition; he once commented that competition "means strife, industrial warfare . . . resorting to any means that the conscience of the contestants will permit." In his view, its absence spelled greater room for growth. When he took over the reins of AT&T, he was convinced that competition was detrimental to providing universal telephone service. He began consolidating immediately. By 1912 he had doubled AT&T's capacity by adding previously independent companies to the AT&T structure. Before the First World War, over 65 percent of the independent companies were already allied with Bell. While he was consolidating, the financiers continued with their traditional behind-the-scenes maneuvering. The closely allied syndicate of bankers began by underwriting an issue of AT&T common stock and followed it with a large bond underwriting. The banks acquired enough common stock from the offering and held enough bonds to ensure effective control over the company for themselves. Telephone services fell under the temporary aegis of the postmaster general during the First World War, but otherwise the system enjoyed comparative freedom over the years. The bankers shrewdly took over the company before its government-granted monopoly was officially sanctioned in the 1920s, and so AT&T joined U.S. Steel, International Harvester, and the giant utilities in the Morgan stable of companies.

With the advent of the Depression and the New Deal, AT&T's monopoly naturally came under scrutiny. All Morgan-controlled industries, from banking to public utilities, came under close examination, and AT&T was certainly no exception. Congress added to AT&T's anxiety by passing the Communications Act of 1934, which founded the Federal Communications Commission (FCC). The law required the FCC to promote an efficient nationwide communications service that provided service at reasonable prices, an especially sensitive issue during the early years of the Depression. Its mission was to respond to the interests of all parties involved in communications, users as well as providers. When a service was not being provided for a distinct need, the FCC could act to ensure that necessary steps would be taken to rectify the problem. AT&T, as a giant monopoly, was especially vulnerable to the changing times and the economic philosophy of the New Deal. Shrewdly, it responded to the passing of the law by lowering telephone rates nationwide twice during the 1930s. It also added better dialing services to its phones in the 1930s, so that it was seen to be both moving ahead and charging less for its services during a time of national economic crisis.

In the late 1930s, a highly contentious FCC paper known as the Walker Report concluded that the Morgan-Baker domination of AT&T brought about "an abrupt change in the Bell System policy from one of meeting competition through rapid expansion to one of financial competition through absorption and purchase of independents."[7] This was a time-proven method of criticizing Morgan-related industries. According to this view, AT&T succumbed to the ever-increasing need for capital to meet its rapidly increasing market and lost its financial innocence when the bankers took over. But the term "telephone trust" was not used in the nineteenth or twentieth centuries. Unlike the other trusts, the telephone consolidation took place in a high-tech industry, not in a commodity-based industry such as sugar or oil, and the strategic and business importance of the technology served to insulate it to an extent from criticism over the years.

Despite the anti-big-business slant of the Walker Report, the FCC's report did not call for the breakup of AT&T or suggest that it be restructured to be more publicly responsive, an acknowledgment that the company was aware of its public responsibilities as a natural monopoly. As early as 1913, AT&T had shown its willingness to be constrained through the Kingsbury commitment made with the Department of Justice during the progressive era. Among other things, that commitment required AT&T to provide services to any independent companies requiring connection. But the war intervened and then its monopoly was made complete by Congress. In 1927, during the heyday of utility consolidation and the stock market boom, the president of the company, Walter Gifford, had gone on record as saying that "It would be contrary to sound policy for the management to earn speculative or large profits for distribution as . . . extra dividends. Earnings must be sufficient to assure the best possible telephone service at all times and to assure the continued financial integrity of the business."[8] Besides being good public relations, the statement was essentially correct. AT&T was not an Insull-like organization. The corporate organizational structure, set by its chairman Theodore Vail after the Morgan takeover, had survived intact for over twenty years and would continue for another fifty before being altered in response to the changes that took place in the industry in the 1970s. In the 1960s and early 1970s, AT&T's finances were sound, and there was no speculation using high degrees of borrowed money. While seeming lackluster to securities analysts, it still commanded respect as the largest company on earth. Its sheer size and technological innovativeness made it seem impregnable.

Unlike many other early New Deal laws, the Communications Act of 1934 went largely unnoticed. It was not as controversial or potentially radical as the banking and securities laws or the NRA. But it did serve as the basis for the eventual breakup of the Bell System by opening the door to complaints from small, potential competitors that claimed that Bell was not providing enough innovative new services in accord with its original mandates. By law, the FCC was obliged to entertain complaints from AT&T's competitors, and when it did in the 1960s the arguments proved compelling enough to begin the long, arduous process that led to the government's suit against the phone company in 1974.

The Bell System had been challenged before the landmark lawsuit of 1974. In 1949, the Truman Justice Department filed suit against Western Electric in one of the postwar legal battles that also resulted in the suit filed against the securities industry, among others. The idea that monopolies had actually prevented an economic recovery during the 1930s had not died. The spirit of the *Walker Report* was still alive and found its way into the 1949 suit brought by Attorney General Tom Clark's Justice Department. But the government was facing a difficult test in making its case for the separation of Western Electric from AT&T. The companies' joint record in advancing technology was significant. Its laboratories, later to be cited as part of its monopoly, had won several Nobel Prizes in science and were developing the transistor; area code dialing, which would link the country's phones without the need for a long-distance operator; and computers, along with a host of other innovations. And its wartime record was also excellent, especially aiding in military communications. The government's case was based on the notion that the close relationship between the two companies led to an overstatement of the assets of the local Bells, allowing them to charge higher rates than would have been the case if Western Electric was divorced from AT&T. If Western Electric were forced to become independent and compete with others for Bell business, prices would necessarily fall. In short, the country was paying excessive rates for phone service. AT&T was profiting excessively from its ownership of Western Electric. This was not the sort of argument that had been made previously against huge companies. It was sophisticated and relied heavily upon the vertical structure of AT&T itself, an issue that would also arise in years to follow.

Wall Street and the securities analysts begged to differ over the profitability issue. AT&T was not a Street favorite at the time. Its payrolls were rising as its revenues were slowly falling. Its stock price lagged the Dow Jones average and it was not considered one of the top manufacturing companies in terms of return.[9] But it remained the favorite stock in the country among investors; it was the most widely held common stock of all time, with the widest investor base. Attacking it was not an easy task. The Justice Department mounted an attack that included AT&T's long history as well as its alleged violations. It asked for the separation of Western Electric from its parent company and also required AT&T to acquire its equipment in the future by competitive bidding. This was a tactic widely used during the Depression, which required companies to request bids for certain kinds of services. The investment banking industry and public utilities both had the idea imposed upon them by Congress during the New Deal.[10] Competitive bidding was a natural concept to be applied to AT&T since the phone company was the world's largest utility. Unlike the other two industries that followed the practice, however, it did overlook the fact that high technology may not have been subject to the same quest for lower prices as securities issues and utilities rates without sacrificing quality or efficiency.

AT&T agreed to a consent decree with the Justice Department in 1956 in which it agreed to concern itself only with communications and technologies related to it, including defense technologies. The company dodged the bullet for the last time in its corporate history. The suit and the eventual consent decree were not successful in the eyes of the old New Dealers in the Justice Department. The New Deal connection was alive but its influence was slowly beginning to fade. Rep. Emmanuel Celler of New York, one of Congress' long-standing Roosevelt allies, was one of many in Congress who objected to the consent decree. According to the settlement, AT&T's bigness, achieved in telephony over the years, was not to be extended into other areas. The old bugaboo about the concentration of economic power was still a powerful message. Western Electric remained an integral part of the company, but in the future it had to share its patents with competitors, not only its subsidiaries and others to which it licensed. The consent decree was a victory for AT&T which was able to successfully deflect the last vestiges of the New Deal qualms about bigness that still lingered in some quarters of the Justice Department and the Truman administration. But the same technological skills that saved it from the first suit would work against it in the second, still almost two decades away.

In the 1960s, the Bell System looked much as it had in the past. AT&T ran nationwide long-distance services while the regional Bell companies provided local phone services. Western Electric manufactured the equipment needed for the system and its laboratories were still regarded as world-class facilities in their own right, holding literally thousands of patents attributed to them. Financially, the result of this concentration of telephone services was a very low cost of capital. AT&T and the local Bells could raise money very cheaply when needed. Investors flocked to their bond and stock offerings because the companies were highly rated. Their government-granted monopoly ensured them the highest credit ratings obtainable from the credit rating agencies. When money was needed for expansion or development, it could be raised on the best terms available. Few companies could ask for more. As a result, AT&T was the largest company in the world, whose assets far outstripped those of its nearest rival. In 1970, it had almost three times the assets of its nearest American rival, Standard Oil, and eight times as many employees.

The first challenge to AT&T's dominance came in the 1960s from small competitors who provided alternate single-line service to the telephone giant's comprehensive services. Small companies were providing internal telephone communications to large companies that wanted their own private services so that they could communicate with other parts of the company without switching into AT&T's network. In 1968, the FCC ruled against AT&T in the Carterfone decision, ruling that the previous prohibitions against using non-AT&T equipment were unreasonable. Thomas Carter operated a parallel relay system to AT&T and sold the service to clients. AT&T refused to let him connect to its local phone network, and the company filed an antitrust suit against AT&T. The suit was referred to the FCC, which proved to be a more sympathetic place for Carterfone to get a hearing. The agency approved Carter's plan and AT&T suddenly found itself with competition, however insignificant it may have seemed at the time. This opened the door for suppliers other than Western Electric to begin building all sorts of equipment, from switchboards to phones, that could be attached to AT&T's lines. The decades-old monopoly enjoyed by AT&T over telephone services was about to end in a dispute over who could provide equipment to be attached to AT&T services. The FCC's ruling was the first chapter in the eventual dismantling of the AT&T monopoly. As Ralph Nader put it, the Carterfone case "amounted to a preliminary birth certificate for companies looking to manufacture telephone equipment to complete or supplement equipment produced by Western Electric."[11]

The Communications Act of 1934 sanctioned this sort of competition and there was little that AT&T could do about the growth of the small but profitable industry. Then in the 1960s it responded to the competition by offering its own version of private lines for large companies with a package of services called TELPAK. Little did it know that it was signing its own death warrant by attempting to be competitive. The TELPAK prices were substantially cheaper than those of any of AT&T's small competitors, opening it to the charge of predatory pricing. It appeared to pitch its new package so low that competitors would be forced from the field or would not bother entering it at all because they would stand to lose money from the outset. If AT&T had been a newcomer to the field, the prices would have been considered competitive. Since it held the monopoly, its motives were suspect from the start.[12] The lessons of TELPAK would not be forgotten in the corporate world.

AT&T's TELPAK prices did not square with the consent decree it signed concerning Western Electric. The door was now ajar for competitors to gain a toehold, if not a foothold, in new businesses that were once the telephone company's preserve. In 1963, a small company named MCI Communications applied to the FCC for a license to build a microwave communications line that it intended to sell to others for their private use. This was slightly outside the established guidelines since previously private lines were built by companies for their own use; the services were not being provided by a small contractor as a user but simply as a provider. MCI was a novice in the business but attracted the attention of financier William McGowan. When he took control of the company shortly thereafter, AT&T's fate would change substantially. McGowan realized that the only way to penetrate AT&T's market was to remain constantly aggressive. The practical result was that the aggressiveness would shorten the time it would take to get AT&T's attention. Regulators needed to be constantly barraged with complaints and requests; otherwise, AT&T could ignore McGowan for long periods of time, during which he could easily become insolvent.

McGowan, described by Ralph Nader as a "trustbuster," achieved that status by recognizing the weaknesses of AT&T and quickly parlaying them into his own small company's strengths. He found a sympathetic ear among some of the FCC commissioners who were still avowed New Dealers. One, Bernard Strassburg, cast himself in the mold of Thurman Arnold.[13] He had joined the FDR administration as a junior lawyer in the early 1940s and had served at the FCC since the early 1960s. The connection served McGowan well. He proposed that MCI would build parallel service on microwave lines and then sell it to other large companies. By not actually using the lines itself, MCI would be in direct competition with AT&T. Then McGowan proposed that his customers should be connected to the AT&T network system. The FCC allowed him to go ahead with his plan and he became a direct competitor with the monopoly, using its own network and lines in the process.

In themselves the Carterfone and MCI cases did little to affect

AT&T's business. But they were still seen by the company as dents in its armor, challenging its monopoly in principle if not in reality. And the phone company had other problems potentially more serious than its two small competitors. Its management structure was becoming increasing phlegmatic, and its services were beginning to erode. Poor phone service and outages were becoming common in the Northeast. As part of a management shakeup, it named John deButts chairman in 1972. A lifelong AT&T employee, he was charged with breathing new life into the company, and as he embarked on his new task, it became clear that his style would not be materially different from that of his predecessors. AT&T would retain its monopolist attitude toward the outside world. It would quietly continue to do what it did best—dominate the market. If MCI or anyone else presented itself as an obstacle, it would incur AT&T's wrath. DeButts was the most aggressive chief executive AT&T had since Theodore Vail.

Many of AT&T's problems had to do with its lackluster stock market performance, which was beginning to have an impact upon its cost of funds. The company traditionally relied upon its new stock offerings to provide it with expansion capital. If the existing stock did not perform well, investors would not buy new issues, driving its financing costs higher. The same would occur with its bonds. If its credit ratings slipped, new bonds would become more expensive to issue, again driving up its costs. That would make financing new capital ventures more expensive. Since the rates AT&T charged, as well as its expansionary plans, were based upon its costs of raising money in the markets, the impact could be significant. Higher costs would mean higher rates charged to customers.

Shortly after deButts took his new position, he had a meeting with William McGowan at AT&T's corporate headquarters in New York at 165 Broadway. The MCI chairman took notes at the meeting; deButts apparently did not. In it, the AT&T executive admitted to his competitor that "a problem for us is the reaction of the investment community. We have tried to convince them that the company deserves better treatment but they react emotionally. . . . If we hold next year's annual meeting as planned, we will have ten thousand stockholders there and I must say to them that we will compete vigorously." McGowan responded by saying, "I don't understand why you need to be that aggressive. Why don't you tell them the facts—that is, there is no way [MCI] will have the majority of any future business," reiterating a fact that everyone in the telephone business already knew. But deButts would have none of it. He fired back, "We tried to do that in the Carterfone case. After that decision we announced that it would be good for us, but the investors did not believe it and we can't do that with you. . . . I have many friends and contacts on Wall Street and I have asked them, 'Why does our stock sell so low and why does the public refuse to support us in the market?' They most frequently mention you as the reason."[14] Either deButts was overstating the case or had been badly informed; assuming that MCI was a genuine threat to the Bell system at that point was as absurd as believing that North Vietnam was a threat to American national security in the early 1970s. The claim was out of proportion with the facts but Wall Street had been known to overreact to simple facts before.

Capital was again a problem for AT&T, as it had been when Bell eventually relinquished his company to Morgan interests seventy years before. How well AT&T responded to this new challenge would help decide its fate as the world's largest company. Unfortunately, deButts maintained his position and continued to identify MCI as the nemesis that was impeding his capital funding. The two companies found themselves in a minor rate war a year later, when AT&T lowered its rates for TELPAK services and MCI followed by correspondingly lowering its own rates. Ordinarily, the rate war should have been nothing more than a sideshow for AT&T. DeButts was attempting to tackle its management problems and boost sales, issues clearly more important than MCI, which itself was running short of capital. But McGowan sensed that AT&T was vulnerable. MCI requested permission for access to the AT&T system at special rates that had been afforded Western Union three years before by the Justice Department. AT&T reluctantly agreed under the provisions of the Communications Act, but deButts then inauspiciously cut off MCI's access. The FCC disagreed with AT&T's actions in quite strong language and the matter eventually found its way to an appeals court. While the case was being considered, MCI further upset AT&T by filing an antitrust case against it.

There was a general consensus among politicians and regulators that AT&T, and particularly deButts, had grown too arrogant when discussing the company's virtues. In 1973 he delivered a speech to an association of regulators in Seattle. Besides representatives from state and federal agencies, the room was full of securities analysts anxious to hear about his plans for the future. His speech did not disappoint the analysts but did infuriate more than one regulator in the audience. Referring to the debate about the nature of AT&T's monopoly, a subject discussed in congressional committees, deButts said that as far as he was concerned, "the time has come, then, for a moratorium on further experiments in economics, a moratorium sufficient to permit a systematic evaluation not merely of whether competition might be feasible . . . but of the more basic question of the long-term impact on the public." At a time when faith in the American political process was at a low point and a general distrust of bigness in government prevailed, he chose to defend AT&T at all costs against opportunistic competitors (such as MCI) and regulators who discussed too much economic theory. The speech would come back to haunt him within a year.

In the audience listening to deButts defend the traditional monopoly was Bernard Strassburg, from the FCC. As one of the FCC staffers who avidly believed in competition, and the author of the FCC ruling allowing MCI and others to offer parallel services to AT&T, he was disappointed by deButts' position and surprised by his rigidity, since it was clear that AT&T still faced no serious competition in telephone services. Shortly before his retirement from the FCC, Strassburg got the FCC commissioners to sign a letter allowing MCI to offer other parallel services to AT&T that had been in contention for over a year. The signed letter had the effect of law, and MCI was delighted. However, AT&T was not informed of the FCC's position and only discovered what had happened when informed of it by MCI.[15] The case proceeded quickly to a federal district court, where it was ruled that AT&T had no choice but to reconnect MCI's access. DeButts acquiesced, and the rivalry that he had tried desperately to prevent began to gain momentum.

AT&T became the subject of discussion in Senator Hart's hearings. The tactics of the FCC and the Senate Antitrust Subcommittee were not warmly received in all quarters. Many AT&T supporters fired back criticisms of the agency and the subcommittee on more than one occasion. At one of these hearings AT&T took the opportunity to defend its position, arguing against Hart's bill proposing a breakup of industrial concentrations considered too large. Testifying on behalf of the telephone company was

Eugene Rostow of the Yale Law School, who defended AT&T against both the FCC, which he claimed "practiced protection while preaching competition," and the subcommittee, which he said "would put the industrial heart of our economy under bitter and unremitting siege," referring to Hart's Industrial Reorganization Act.[16] His defense proved to be too little, too late. Hart later announced he would not seek reelection, depriving Congress of another active self-styled New Dealer but providing some relief for industry. Before he stepped down, however, he cosponsored another bill that would help regulators maintain a grip on corporate mergers.

In 1976 Congress passed the Hart-Scott-Rodino Act, which requires companies desiring to merge to file notification so that the FTC and the Justice Department have time to review the consequences of the proposed corporate marriage. The amendment was similar to the original securities law written in 1933 that required all companies wanting to issue new securities to register them before bringing them to market. The new act would become part of the standard operating procedure in the next decade, especially when the merger craze began.

The particular interpretation of monopoly used by the Justice Department against AT&T was vital in pursuing the case. The economists working on the suit framed a charge of "bottleneck" monopoly, contending that AT&T charged high prices for essential services that in turn prevented others from competing or gaining access to the market.[17] Since all telecommunications services ultimately had to pass through AT&T, unreasonable prices for this group of services could drive competitors out or, more contentiously, provide a barrier to entry for potential competitors. Since AT&T had received its monopoly from the government in the first place, a simple argument against its size alone would have been ineffectual. The government had to show that the company was abusing its privileged position and that the public ultimately suffered as a result. The notion of bottlenecks also touched other sensitive areas. Capital access was one. AT&T's traditionally low cost of capital was preventing meaningful competition. MCI's flirtation with insolvency on several occasions was evidence of that, although proving capital barriers was very difficult for the Justice Department.

The ultimate insult in AT&T's eyes came during the Ford administration. Attorney General William Saxbe filed an antitrust suit against the company in November 1974. The government contended that the company monopolized the telecommunications market. Its proposed remedy was shocking. It sought to have Western Electric separated from the parent company. And it also sought to have the long-distance carrier and the local Bell operating companies separated as well. DeButts' response at a news conference following the filing of the suit would be echoed across the country many times before the case was finally settled. "I cannot understand why the Justice Department would want to get rid of something that is working efficiently," he stated. He was genuinely puzzled, as were many others who felt that AT&T, despite its problems, provided the best telephone service in the world.

The AT&T case, like many other antitrust cases in the Nixon and Ford administrations, appeared to occur independent of the president himself. Nixon's earlier remarks about Richard McLaren suggested that the Antitrust Division, run by assistant attorneys general, often decided on cases without presidential assent. By telling his attorney general to have McLaren stand back from further antitrust action, Nixon helped disarm critics who thought that he personally was behind some of the late-1960s actions against the conglomerates. When Saxbe filed his case against AT&T he claimed that he had the consent of President Gerald Ford, but later statements by the president suggested that Saxbe acted on his own. Ford was generally supportive of antitrust measures but appears not to have been informed about the suit immediately. While it could easily be said that presidents were far removed from trust-busting ideologies, the attorneys general and their staff were still imbued with ideological fervor, much of it inherited from their law school days when New Deal ideas still abounded.

Like many major antitrust cases before it, the AT&T case would take years to be settled. The Justice Department began adding new staff to its ranks just to deal with the case, its biggest in years. Additional finances for the move were pushed in the Senate by Philip Hart before his retirement. MCI's previous complaints and actions against AT&T were also an integral part of the case for the Justice Department. Essentially, the company was charged with being a vertical monopoly, with Western Electric and Bell Labs helping the parent company create a monopoly by exclusively researching and manufacturing equipment that had to be used with the Bell System to the exclusion of others. The *Wall Street Journal* did not agree with the suit, arguing that vertical integration at the phone company was not the same thing as a vertical monopoly.[18] "What the Justice Department attacks," the paper stated, "is not monopoly but vertical integration. . . . Where is the problem that justifies risking possible damage to the efficiency of a vital part of the U.S. infrastructure?"[19] AT&T's defense seemed logical as well. The company had received its monopoly from Congress to begin with and its businesses had grown over the years under the watchful eyes of the FCC. Its technologies were top-notch and its rates reasonable. The suit did not seem to have much merit with one exception: The age-old debate about bigness and competition had taken a distinct turn against bigness. In the wake of the Vietnam War and the Watergate scandal, the idea of a bumbling government protecting a large company would not sit well with the public once the charge of monopoly had been leveled.

At the time the suit was filed, one of deButts' fears was realized. AT&T had been planning a huge bond issue, the largest in American history to date. The bonds were intended to raise $600 million for capital investment purposes but had to be canceled because of the suit. Investors would have been furious to hear of the legal action after they had purchased bonds and certainly would not buy them with AT&T under a legal cloud from the outset, so its investment bankers decided simply to forgo the matter. The failed deal was an embarrassment for the company and Wall Street— AT&T's main investment banker at the time was Morgan Stanley & Co., the post-1933 successor to J. P. Morgan & Company. The Justice Department apparently filed the suit knowing that the bonds were in the process of being underwritten. Although it will probably never be known if the investment bankers also came under the Justice Department's unofficial gaze, attacking a vertical structure meant that close relationships with investment bankers would also suffer.

The antitrust case was originally presided over by Judge Joseph Waddy in federal court. He had little experience in antitrust matters but, like many before him, was determined to learn all he could about the issues involved. AT&T's claim that it provided excellent service was not the issue; no one argued that AT&T's service was not the best. The government centered its case around MCI and competition, and at issue was the fact that it allegedly tried to stifle competition, not providing the best possible service for its customers. Ironically, MCI and Carterfone were both customers as well as competitors. AT&T tried arguing that because it was a monopoly and regulated, it was no longer subject to the antitrust laws, but to no avail. Yet it apparently had an ally in Judge Waddy. The judge was skeptical of the Justice Department's case and remarked to its lawyers that he "was having trouble finding out exactly what you're complaining about."[20] But before he could rule on the case, he died. In many respects, AT&T's case died with him, for the tables turned against the phone company after that.

Waddy was succeeded by Judge Harold F. Greene, another newcomer to antitrust cases on the federal bench. Greene proceeded with the case, already four years old, by organizing it without a jury. The case had already heard from hundreds of witnesses and required hundreds of thousands of pages of testimony. In fact, some cynical critics of the Justice Department claimed that the case could not be considered because of the costs of copying the materials alone. And Greene's attitude toward AT&T was somewhat different from his predecessor. He later stated, "It is antithetical to our political and economic system for this key industry to be within the control of one company."[21] This comment, made in 1983, neatly summarized the attitude of those wanting to break up AT&T. The company, despite its government granted monopoly, just was not in tune with the business climate in the country; it was an anomaly in the minds of many.

John deButts retired from AT&T in 1979, leaving the rest of the battle to his successor, Charles L. Brown. Discussions continued among all parties about a settlement, but the issues were immensely complicated. Essentially, the central issue was that AT&T should not remain in both the long-distance and local phone businesses. They would have to be separated. The other issue concerned Western Electric and Bell Labs. Where would they ultimately reside—with AT&T or the local phone companies, or would they become independent? AT&T's fear was that the labs and Western Electric would be severed from the parent company—being "gutted," in Brown's words. But the settlement discussions were further complicated by the appointment of William Baxter as the Reagan administration's new head of the Antitrust Division. He insisted that AT&T divest itself of all unregulated businesses before any settlement could be discussed. His presence proved to be pivotal to the case and the settlement that AT&T and the government finally settled upon.

The direction of the case suggested that AT&T would have to settle and give up part of its empire. Finally in January 1982 it agreed with the Justice Department to divest itself of the local phone companies while keeping long distance. Bell Labs and Western Electric remained with it as well. The case had already been in the courts for seven years and the likely outcome was becoming evident, so AT&T had little choice but to comply with the Justice Department's wishes and come to some sort of accommodation. Brown decided that pursuing the case in court hoping for an acquittal was not in AT&T's best interests, but critics contended that they gave up the fight too early. As of January 1, 1984, the twenty-two operating companies would become seven separate operating entities, nicknamed the "Baby Bells." They would retain their right to produce the individual Yellow Pages for which they had become famous. AT&T also agreed not to acquire the stock of any of the operating companies, closing the back door to a reintegration of the vertical monopoly the Justice Department had claimed it had been for decades.

Much discussion followed the breakup of AT&T for years after the fateful settlement changed the face of American telecommunications. Ten years later, Baxter still maintained that "there's no question about whether it was a good thing and a dramatic thing." Supporters of the original move attributed all of the telecommunications breakthroughs in the 1990s, such as improved international dialing, quality of calls, and fast Internet connections, to the breakup of AT&T. But the costs were enormous. The seven new Baby Bells all became self-supporting as a result of the breakup and had to individually raise money in the marketplace rather than rely on "Ma Bell."

United States v. AT&T proved to be the greatest victory for the Antitrust Division of the Justice Department since the Standard Oil and American Tobacco cases seventy years before. Ironically, since Standard Oil was still the second-largest company in the country, it could still be legitimately questioned whether that 1911 breakup had any lasting effect. Would the same thing be said of AT&T in the years to come?

The government's other major case of this period, against IBM, lingered until 1982, when the computer company was exonerated of the antitrust charges brought against it in 1969. The Justice Department under Ronald Reagan decided to drop the suit after thirteen years, almost immediately after settling its case with AT&T. Antitrust chief William Baxter said that the IBM suit was "without merit" and that the government's claims were flimsy at best. Unlike AT&T, IBM fought the Justice Department to the end, preferring a long court battle to a settlement that would have cost it its competitive position in the marketplace. During the record-setting trial, IBM's monopoly in the computer business was proven to be a myth, as dozens of smaller competitors entered the market for the new personal computers. Some of that increased competition was new, however. Over the years, IBM began to unbundle its software from the inclusive packages that it previously had made customers purchase. By doing so, it could claim that competition had increased and therefore it was not a monopoly after all. Dozens of smaller competitors entered the market as a result, selling software previously dominated by IBM. One of them was the company that would become the industry's dominant force in another decade, Microsoft. And IBM's strategy would be remembered in the late 1990s when Microsoft itself was sued for acting in monopolistic fashion. One dubious distinction IBM could now claim was that it had been the target of what turned out to be the longest and costliest case in history. The company spent millions on its defense, and the court documents totaled over sixty million pages. The only consolation for IBM, as its defense attorney acknowledged, was that all of those costs were tax-deductible.

BANKING ON IT

Ever since the 1930s, banks had been severely limited in the sorts of services they could offer to the public. Less visible was the fact that they had a great deal of governmental protection through those same regulations. The original 1933 banking legislation created the modern commercial banking and investment banking industries, separating them so that they would not encroach upon each other's most important functions: taking deposits and making loans, for commercial banks, and underwriting long-term securities, for the investment banks. But as the economy grew, the legislation began to show signs of strain. The growth of business during the postwar period also led the banks to expand to keep pace with their customers' changing financial needs. As one of the country's most regulated industries, commercial banking was even under more constraints than the average corporation when it came to expansion and merger. Ever since the Glass-Steagall Act, banks had been severely limited in their activities. Unlike many other laws, the Glass-Steagall Act actually defined banking and clearly stated what it was not allowed to do. One main benefits to the commercial banks was a provision in the banking law that enabled the Fed to dictate the maximum amount of interest banks paid on savings accounts. Over the years this figure had been kept relatively low, allowing the banks decent profit margins. But banks' desire to expand presented both antitrust and bank regulators with one of their greatest challenges: how to keep to the letter of the law without causing credit problems for businesses that wanted to grow.

The task was not easy. Banks were not allowed to branch across state lines nor engage in the securities business, and they were subject to a host of federal and state rules.[22] Over the years, the banking laws had proved to be remarkably resilient—many attempts to roll back the Glass-Steagall Act had failed, and others were doomed to fail in the years ahead—yet the banks managed to break out of their regulatory shells and still manage to find ways to expand. For example, Congress passed the Bank Merger Act in 1960, requiring several layers of federal regulatory approval if two banks wanted to merge. The law directed the regulators to consider the effect on competition that a proposed bank merger might have had on the local banking market. Banks evaded this requirement by acquiring large amounts of stock in banks in other states through a loophole in the holding company laws that had applied to banks since 1957. About ten years later Congress closed the loophole to ensure that banks did not escape the regulators' watchful eye. In amendments made to the Bank Holding Company Act, bank holding companies were not allowed to own more than one banking company. This was a variant on the death sentence provision in the Public Utility Holding Company Act, passed in 1935, which proved so controversial at the time. One of the advocates of stricter laws regulating bank expansion was Rep. Emmanuel Celler of Brooklyn, still one of Congress' most ardent New Dealers.

In the 1970s inflation began to create some serious problems for the banks. The most serious challenge to their traditional business eventually came from Wall Street. In the early 1970s brokers began developing the money market mutual fund, which allowed investors to obtain market interest rates, which were much higher than the traditional bank savings account interest rate, which was still dictated by the Federal Reserve. The Fed had been protecting the banks for years by keeping that rate relatively low. But in the 1970s, when it lagged behind the money market rate substantially, investors began withdrawing their money to obtain the higher yields. This was the largest financial problem since the great money hoard of the early 1930s, all because of what superficially appeared to be a simple new investment vehicle. The Fed had no regulatory authority over these Wall Street products, and the repercussions were widespread. All of the problems that arose could be traced directly to the strict banking legislation passed forty years before, designed to break the grip of the money trust. Much of the legislation passed since that time was designed to ensure that the trust did not raise its head again through oversights in the original Glass-Steagall Act.

Banks reacted by creating new products, many of them not officially sanctioned. One was the NOW account, a checking account that paid a low rate of interest. They also desperately searched for any new products or lines of business to enter so that they would not become dinosaurs, much like the American automobile industry was becoming at the time. Then they hit upon the concept of buying other banks that were floundering financially. In normal times these mergers would have been frowned upon by the Fed, but in times of financial distress the idea meant that a strong, solvent institution could take over a failing one, saving the public an enormous bailout cost. It was not used frequently, but the failing-bank ploy did allow banks to expand, albeit not without great expense and risk to themselves. The idea was not new, having been used for years to justify mergers. Usually the acquiring firm was buying a failing one with no dowry, so regulators could not plausibly object. But when applied to mergers between institutions that otherwise would have been prohibited, the failing-concern doctrine provided a way around tight regulations.

The banking problems of the 1970s set the stage for even more profound problems in the 1980s. The situation was exacerbated by the fact that most of the banking legislation that had existed since 1933 was at heart a matter of antitrust more than it was banking, being a narrow set of rules about what banks could and could not do. As a result, anytime the economy changed, the rules quickly became out of date. And the banking laws were difficult to apply as well, like their models, the Sherman and Clayton Acts. The old bugaboo about bankers and their invisible powers had not yet been dispelled, and until it was, the banking system was destined to be looked at suspiciously by Congress and regulators.

The greatest mistake made by bankers during this period was extending loans to Third World countries. In order to circumvent their highly restricted markets and earn fat profit margins, the banks began making loans to foreign countries, including developing economies in Latin America and Asia, in an attempt to diversify. By the early 1980s the wild lending spree, unregulated by domestic banking supervisors, had exceeded $250 billion. While taking some of their business abroad may have seemed clever at the time, the banks soon discovered that many of the loans made to developing countries would be in serious trouble in the 1980s as worldwide oil prices began to tumble. But the banks never came under serious reproach from their regulators or Congress because it was recognized that many of their problems were government-inspired in the first place. It would take another twenty years before they would be free of the New Deal restraints.

CEREAL KILLERS

The 1970s were a period of intense antitrust activity. Over three thousand cases a year were being pursued in the courts, tripling the rate from the 1950s and 1960s. In addition to the cases brought by the Justice Department and the federal government agencies, there were thousands also brought privately, by one company against another. Almost every industry, major and minor, had at least one notable antitrust case. Antitrust activity hit its stride during Jimmy Carter's presidency, although activity did not necessarily mean success in fighting combinations. In the 1970s antitrust regulators applied an old concept under a new name. It began charging companies with what it called "shared monopolies," another (more politically correct) term for an oligopoly. One of their most visible targets of this approach was a group of major cereal makers. The government charged that their shared monopoly and its price fixing had cost consumers hundreds of millions of dollars over a fifteen-year period.

The FTC had been pursuing an investigation against the top three cereal producers—General Mills, Kellogg, and General Foods—since 1972. In voluminous documents, it contended that the three, which held over 80 percent of the market between them, arrived at a tacit understanding to fix the price of cereals. The FTC estimated that the companies charged about 15 percent more than justified through their arrangement. This was the embodiment of the argument of shared monopoly. The industry relied upon Kellogg as its price leader, and the other two then followed suit when prices were raised. The Justice Department suggested that Kellogg be fragmented into three companies in order to reduce its market share. The cereal companies vowed to fight, maintaining that the FTC was fabricating most of its argument. Not helping the companies' cause was the fact that Ralph Nader's study group had already pronounced on the complaint when it was first issued by stating blankly that "three giant firms . . . control 82 percent of the market and their high advertising expenditures (some 20 percent of sales) intimidate potential competitors."[23] Conservatives had grounds for complaint but the sensational value of that and other FTC complaints helped keep the antitrust banner flying.

Not all antitrust was aimed at large, market-dominating companies. In a period dominated by high-profile cases against huge companies, the Justice Department began a drive to involve small businessmen and even individual citizens who thought they had spotted price fixing arrangements or other antitrust violations. The idea originated with Ralph Nader, and the Justice Department produced a booklet laying out for citizens the most common signs of violation of antitrust laws. Price fixing topped the list, and the rhetoric was aimed directly at consumers' pocketbooks. "Such laws, when effectively enforced," said the pamphlet, "can save consumers millions and perhaps billions of dollars a year in illegal overcharges." The Justice Department actually established citizens' hotlines at its regional offices so that irate citizens could call to report suspected antitrust activities. The first one was established in Pittsburgh; not coincidentally, the steel industry, which called that city home, was again under the microscope for alleged pricing practices that violated the antitrust laws. The Justice Department soon discovered that many people called to vent anger at a manufacturer or service provider without providing any good leads on antitrust matters. Shortly thereafter it announced another program that encouraged companies to reveal their part in price-fixing conspiracies, a sort of whistle-blowing program aimed at companies rather than individuals. It was dubbed "Operation Rat." What actually took place at the grassroots level gave the impression that antitrust was becoming more of a public relations exercise than substance, but the *Wall Street Journal* gave the programs the benefit of the doubt—though the newspaper got in a whack at one of its favorite subjects: "Once consumers become educated to price fixing illegalities," an editorial stated, "they may also become less tolerant of government price fixing of oil prices, airline fares, and what have you."[24] This presaged the age of deregulation, during which many areas that had been sheltered in the past under the umbrella of antitrust exemption would soon be under pressure to dismantle the protections they had enjoyed and compete in the marketplace. Like AT&T, government-tolerated monopolies were about to tumble and enter the competitive marketplace.

The consumer movement picked up a great deal of momentum with these measures, designed to show industry that monopolistic activities had direct consequences among consumers that would not be tolerated. One of the most important consequences of this trend during the 1970s was the deregulation of many traditional professions and trades that, like major league baseball, had enjoyed antitrust exemptions for years. Many of these professions were nicknamed the "Untouchables" because their professional activities had been considered sacrosanct, immune to price fixing and price leadership arrangements. The name also recalled the name of a popular television series about the fight against organized crime in Chicago, indirectly raising the specter of organized crime when discussing antitrust that had proven successful in the past. The group included a wide array of occupations, from medicine and law to undertaking and pharmacy. Often the professional associations that governed the occupations set prices for their members. These price structures came under attack from state antitrust departments as well as the FTC on the federal level. Prices quickly began to vary from area to area, and members, traditionally not allowed to advertise, began to do so in an attempt to win over new, competitive business from the public. Antitrust Division head Kauper even indicated his intention to pursue organized labor, exempt from the antitrust laws since the passage of the Clayton Act. Also of interest were professional baseball and the farm cooperatives, along with insurance companies and export companies. But securing congressional blessing for such moves was far from certain. "What's the task force [studying the matter] going to do—let the Antitrust Division break up the auto workers' union?" asked a senior Justice Department official. But the drive to examine the exemptions had already begun rolling. "We've concluded that it's about time some of the sacred cows were slaughtered," an Antitrust Division lawyer said.

Despite the public relations gimmicks and the victory over AT&T, antitrust was not in good shape as the Reagan administration took office in 1981. IBM won its case by outlasting the Justice Department, and many other investigations and cases did not pan out. Senator Kennedy's anticonglomerate bill stalled, and the oil companies, suspected and investigated for price rigging for much of the 1970s, remained outside the reach of regulators. Older ideas about antitrust seemed to be losing their grip and appeal in the economy of the post–Bretton Woods years. Kennedy's attack on bigness, apparently influenced by Ralph Nader, turned out not to have the same appeal it would have had in the 1930s. While the 1970s were indeed considered the worst economic period since the Depression, the old remedies of the New Deal were no longer in vogue.

8

GOOD-BYE
ANTITRUST
(1983–1999)

*Are these guys really Robin Hood and his Merry Men and
their camp followers, as they claim to be? Or are they Genghis
Khan and the Mongol hordes?*

—LEE IACOCCA

AFTER A HUNDRED YEARS of attempting to come to grips with
alleged monopolies, no one expected the 1980s and 1990s to become a revolution in industrial organization and a boom for Wall Street's mergers-
and-acquisitions specialists. Yet American industry was on the verge of its
greatest change since the days of Gould and Vanderbilt. To add some
humor and sarcasm to the financial trendiness of the 1980s, an off-Broad-
way play with a distinctly Brandeisian tone went on nationwide tour. *Other
People's Money* was a satire of all of the favorite corporate raider devices of
the decade, including poison pills, shark repellents, and greenmail.

Based upon past experience, the slowdown in economic growth and the
ebbing of the conglomerate trend suggested that large corporations were
poised to take a breather in their quest to merge and consolidate. In fact,
some of the largest and traditionally most vulnerable industries, such as
steel and oil, were making plans to merge. Apparently corporate America
and its investment bankers were correctly gauging the waning influence of
the Antitrust Division even before it became readily apparent to legislators

and the public. Since so many former FTC and Antitrust Division attorneys regularly shifted to the other side of the fence and began practicing corporate law privately, they were in an ideal position to advise companies on potential plans to merge. The speed with which mergers reappeared surprised not just many pundits and legislators but investment bankers as well. "The vitality of the merger mania that began by the end of 1983 was unexpected and unprecedented," commented arbitrager Ivan Boesky, himself involved in some of the most notable deals of the decade.

The most recent developments in the merger movement would aid consolidation from within. The rules of the game were not being changed but reinterpreted, in this case to favor big business in its hundred-year-old battle with antitrusters. It became clear in the latter 1970s and early 1980s that not even a weak economy beset with inflation could slow down the merger trend. By the mid-1980s an inescapable fact had emerged: Consolidation and mergers were not trends within business but an ineluctable force that could be stymied occasionally but never successfully defeated. The Sherman and Clayton Acts were still as vibrant as ever but now were being applied along with concepts like shared monopoly, bottleneck monopolies, and "sum of the squares" statistical methods. Those involved in the more recent battle with slow economic growth proclaimed that existing antitrust laws were actually noncompetitive and were standing in the way of prosperity. Critics of the laws, many of whom were in Ronald Reagan's cabinet and among his close advisors, seized the opportunity to pronounce that the antitrust laws should actually be abolished once and for all.

After the antitrust battles of the 1970s, the country remained in the economic mire caused by inflation, high interest rates, and unemployment. Jimmy Carter lost the 1980 presidential election to Ronald Reagan amid the greatest economic crisis since the Depression. Interest rates were at historic highs, unemployment was high, and the term "stagflation" became widely used to describe the country's economic plight. Against this depressing background, even the symbols of economic might seemed to be crumbling. AT&T was officially dismembered in 1984. The "smokestack" industries such as auto manufacturing and steel producing were losing market share to foreign imports, and American-made goods were gaining a reputation for shoddy quality. It would not be long before someone equated the decline with rigorous enforcement of the antitrust laws. The "enemy within" was no longer big business but now suspiciously looked like the antitrust laws themselves.

Although it superficially appeared that the antitrust battle was being carried on as usual, a distinct ideological shift was in the air. The press would dub the period the "decade of greed," although the lust for bigger and bigger deals with lucrative fees attached would not have been possible without a lax antitrust environment. Now, bigness would be balanced with the economic benefits that size could bring. Even more important, the economic environment in which companies operated would now be examined more closely for actual evidence of whether monopolies were present, impinging on competition and controlling prices. Pursuit of monopolies was not quite dead by 1985 but certainly was in a deep state of hibernation.

The Reagan administration left the inflation fight to the Federal Reserve, led since 1979 by Paul Volcker. A veteran of the negotiations that led to the Bretton Woods agreement after World War II, the veteran civil servant attacked inflation by concentrating on bank reserves, under the assumption that smaller reserves meant fewer loans and less money growth. The process began in 1979, shortly after his appointment as chairman, and it took until 1984 before substantial results began to be seen. Interest rates were extremely volatile during that time, dropping several times only to be followed by new highs. Bond yields were also at historic highs, and stock prices were depressed. Finding capital for new business investment was difficult, and many companies put their expansion plans on hold until Volcker's policy showed some signs of success.

The early years of the Reagan administrations were dominated by what was known as "supply-side economics." This was the most recent version of the "trickle-down," or percolator, theory of the 1920s, which caused severe political and economic problems for the Hoover administration. Supply-side theorists claimed that if incentives were provided in the form of tax cuts, then the economy would be stimulated by an increase in demand for goods and services of all kinds. Like its earlier version, this approach purposely stimulated business and those in the higher individual income tax brackets in order to achieve its goal. The administration was a passionate advocate of the theory, claiming that it would provide the necessary stimulus to pull the economy out of recession. Although the notion was dubious, it quickly caught on among a public tired of almost a decade of inflation and growing unemployment, and became the buzzword of the early 1980s. It was, however, diametrically opposed to Volcker's policies at the Fed. Volcker was pleading for monetary restraint, while the supply-siders wanted to stimulate the economy by increasing money for investment. White House counselor (and later attorney general) Edwin Meese defended the position by claiming that "restarting the economic engines and getting greater production can also contribute to price restraint."[1] The conflict did not augur well for a coordinated White House effort at industrial expansion. If monetary policy and the Fed were considered as out of date as the antitrust laws, then the immediate expansionary program did make sense. Unfortunately for antitrusters, Meese said nothing about pursuing big business, only encouraging it. Ignoring antitrust actions became a cornerstone of the Reagan administrations.

Putting the popular supply-side ideas into practice, the administration proposed a bill to stimulate the economy called the Economic Recovery Tax Act, enacted in 1981. Its two main provisions were a cut in the long-term capital gains tax and a change in depreciation rules, allowing companies to accelerate write-offs for spending on big-ticket items such as new plants and equipment. Investors now were taxed at only 20 percent on gains incurred after an asset was sold for a profit after one year. The combination of the two provisions provided a powerful stimulant for the weak economy. The Dow Jones Industrial Average, at the same time hovering around 1,000, began a long-awaited move upward after years of treading water at the same level. Capital spending by companies also increased, and the last great bull market of the century began. Wall Street merger-and-acquisition specialists were overjoyed. Deals began to spring up everywhere as companies sought merger partners. In the same spirit of providing a stimulus to the economy, the administration also proposed a new banking law called the Depository Institutions Act of 1982. Aimed primarily at savings and loan associations, the law had one fatal flaw: It allowed the thrifts to purchase corporate bonds for their own investments. At the time, the idea seemed logical enough, but no one paid much attention to the fact that the S&Ls began making large purchases of junk bonds.

Late in 1984 Volcker's interest rate policy finally had an effect and interest rates began to fall from their historic highs, although detractors claimed that this was accomplished at the expense of increased unemployment, declining productivity, and a postwar historic high exchange rate for the dollar. The fall in interest rates was another of the factors creating a situation that was very conducive to mergers and acquisitions. Many companies' stock was selling cheaply, as the companies themselves were still ailing from the previous seven years. As a result, their asset values were low and provided enviable targets for acquisition-minded companies. When the stock market began to rally after the Reagan tax package was announced, it became clear that the bargains were not going to last for long. Society appeared to be ripe for a consolidation movement, and the mergers and acquisitions specialists on Wall Street sprang into action. Arbitrageurs had their hands full keeping up with the pace of new deals being announced. Antitrusters were horrified to find that both horizontal and vertical mergers were being approved; ten or twenty years before, they would have been scrutinized in much greater detail. The Antitrust Division provided an economic and legal justification for such deals that was well suited to the administration's ideological bent.

That policy was the idea of William F. Baxter, who became the first head of the Antitrust Division under Reagan. He was a former professor of law and economics at Stanford who opposed antitrust actions unless they could be justified on economic grounds. His philosophy rested on economics more than that of any of his predecessors, most of whom were preoccupied with the potential size of a company formed after a merger. He was best known for his dogged pursuit of AT&T while settling the long-standing suit against IBM at the same time. Traditional antitrust ideology would no longer work as long as he ran the Antitrust Division. The new standard was now "economic rationality," under which regulators considered each proposed merger on its own merits, looking at the potential for economic growth before deciding whether a merger would be blocked or allowed to proceed. Arrangements between manufacturers and suppliers, such as that cited in the *Schwinn* case, would be tolerated as long as no price collusion existed between them. Clearly, the rules of the merger game had been liberalized considerably, and antitrust was now to be considered a form of economic regulation to be used only when competition alone would not force prices to remain at reasonable levels above a producer's cost of supplying a product. Antitrust Division chief Douglas

Ginsburg stated uncategorically in 1986 that "change became inevitable when economic analysis was incorporated into the Antitrust Division's operating procedures." The new position was distinctly in the consumer's corner. The change in emphasis showed how far consumerism had progressed at the expense of the traditional historical, institutional method of evaluating potential antitrust problems. It certainly fell on the same side as Ralph Nader's approach but was distinctly more analytic than Nader's, which remained firmly in the tradition of the Harvard School of antitrust economics.

Although Baxter's tenure in the job was not particularly long, it was controversial. Ever since Thurman Arnold took the reins of the Antitrust Division before World War II, prosecuting alleged monopolies had been an almost sacrosanct tradition at the Justice Department. But now the new ideas introduced had the net effect of reducing the number of prosecutions substantially. The *Wall Street Journal,* never a fan of avidly pursuing alleged monopolies, stated that "if Mr. Arnold was a great antitrust leader because he redirected antitrust to its historical purpose of checking economic power, then Mr. Baxter must be judged for what he has done in restoring its focus on preserving consumer welfare."[2] In other words, by allowing companies to compete with each other, the consumer would receive a better price than if a merger was forbidden simply because the new company that would be formed appeared to be too large. The Chicago School held that the old antitrust approach was nonsensical because it was in many cases actually preventing competition rather than fostering it. Between the two positions, however, was a gap that critics maintained was too large.

There was little joy to cheer antitrusters, even on the lighter side. In the 1970s Ralph Anspach created a new board game called Antimonopoly to compete in the same market as Parker Brothers' famous Monopoly game. In his game, the winner breaks up monopolies rather than assemble them. Anspach, a professor of economics, was quickly sued by General Foods, the owners of Parker Brothers, for trademark infringement. In 1976 a California court upheld Parker Brothers, but the decision was overturned on appeal and sent back to the district court. At one point thousands of copies of his game were confiscated and dumped in a landfill. The Supreme Court finally heard the case, and Anspach won in 1984. Then, in a twist of events worthy of fiction, Parker Brothers was purchased by Hasbro, Inc., the country's largest toy maker, which as a result of the purchase found itself with a large share of the board game market. Anspach claimed that Hasbro then entered into agreements with two large distributors of board games, Toys "R" Us and Kmart, to exclude his product from their stores, causing it to rapidly lose market share. The case presented an intriguing question for the courts to ponder. Was "monopoly" a term that could be copyrighted? Supporters of Anspach asked whether Parker Brothers originally had the monopoly on the name even though copyrights and patents allow the creator of an idea protection from competition for a specified amount of time.

BY THE NUMBERS

The field of antitrust economics, which had begun with the 1958 study of predatory pricing concerning Standard Oil, was growing, and the increase in analyses coincided with the reduction in the number of antitrust cases being brought by the Justice Department and the FTC beginning in the late 1970s. The question raised was simple: Did economic analysis of antitrust prove that most cases had little merit, or could the lack of cases being brought coincide with the election of conservative Ronald Reagan in 1980?

Another factor that had to be considered was the end of the New Dealers' period of dominance. In previous decades, the continuity of antitrust fervor in Congress was attributable to the New Dealers who had survived the 1930s and 1940s and continued to carry the torch for their cause. With the retirement of Senator Philip Hart, that tradition was almost defunct. Armed with economic theories, the conservatives began to assert themselves and dismiss much antitrust principle as unfounded economically and unjustified politically. Tools of economic analysis were replacing vague notions of concentrations and predatory pricing or were proving their applications incorrect. Antitrust entered the same stage that corporations had decades before. Rather than rely upon strong individuals to carry the torch, it now had to rely upon interpretations of the law and professional monopoly hunters, much as industry relied upon professional mangers and its legions of corporate lawyers.

Those detecting more than just a subtle shift away from antitrust sentiment pointed to a law and economics program conducted by Miami and Emory Universities that provided economics briefings and education for federal judges. By 1985 almost half of the country's federal judges had been through the program, which was generally conceded to have a distinctly antitrust bias. Many of those who attended were introduced to Learned Hand's formula for liability damages as an introduction to incorporating more economics into their rulings, presenting an unusual opportunity to enlist Hand on the Chicago side of the antitrust argument. When combined with the profound impact the Reagan administration would have on appointments to the federal bench, it was easy to see how antitrust was in serious trouble.

In the early 1980s the Justice Department adopted the Herfindahl-Hirschman Index, or HHI, an economic tool that was applied to mergers and acquisitions in order to determine whether market concentration would be affected if a proposed merger went through as anticipated.[3] It attempted to show the effect of a proposed merger on an industry in numbers rather than just in the minds of the antitrusters. As it turned out, the HHI proved to be quite conservative, and the number of cases brought before the courts dwindled to a trickle. And those that did often did not produce any victories for the antitrusters. Politically, the courts were in no mood to uphold cases that did not merit action either economically or politically. When combined with the Hart Scott Rodino measures adopted in 1976, the Justice Department was now armed with significant new tools in the antitrust battle. Equally, the Wall Street merger boom was about to begin in earnest.

In a notable case, reminiscent of the *Schwinn* decision in 1967, the Supreme Court again had the opportunity to rule on a case involving distribution of a manufacturer's goods. In *Continental TV Inc. v. GTE Sylvania*, Continental, the distributor, accused the manufacturer, GTE, of restricting its ability to sell its goods where it chose. GTE required its franchisees to sell its products from approved locations. In this instance, the Court sided with the manufacturer. Justice Lewis Powell wrote that the Court would revert instead to "the standard articulated in Northern Pacific Railway Co. . . . for determining whether vertical restrictions must be conclusively presumed to be unreasonable and therefore illegal. . . .

There is substantial scholarly and judicial authority supporting their economic utility."[4] Relying upon both the old rule of reason and contemporary economic analysis, the Court found in favor of the company, reversing
Schwinn and causing serious distress to antitrusters.

The composition of the Supreme Court had also changed. Now several
conservatives were prominent on the court. Justice Powell was one, Justice
William Rehnquist another. Warren Burger was chief justice until 1986
and was accompanied in the liberal camp by Justices Marshall and Bren-
nan. But the New Dealers were gone, and vertical mergers and combinations were no longer viewed with suspicion. As in the past, bad economic
times tended to deflect criticism from business because no one wanted to
be seen slaying the goose that laid the golden egg. But the economy was
clearly in a transitional stage, as the government's response to several
merger deals would shortly reflect.

In the recovering economy, new merger deals began to spring up, and
the Antitrust Division's new philosophy was quickly put to the test. Baxter's more liberal methods of dealing with potential prosecutions were
aimed primarily at vertical mergers. Horizontal mergers would be more
difficult to tolerate because they were almost always considered to be
monopolistic unless the proposed merger partners could prove that they
were not seeking to dominate a market and control prices to the detriment of the consumer. And the new wave of deals would see the old-line
banking houses getting involved in ways they had previously eschewed.
This trend actually began in 1974, when a large merger deal was
announced in which the International Nickel Company launched an
unfriendly bid for ESB, a maker of batteries. Morgan Stanley advised
International Nickel in the deal, breaking a tradition in which traditional
investment bankers usually remained above the fray of hostile takeovers.
As a result of its involvement, the door opened for other investment
banks to participate in the sort of activities that many of them previously
frowned upon.[5] The consolidation phase of the 1980s itself started almost
as soon as the decade began. And the deals themselves were large, even by
contemporary standards.

The 1980s began with several notable deals. In the fall of 1981 Mobil
made a complicated, two-way offer for Marathon Oil. Marathon balked,
however, and actively sought a white knight to fend off Mobil. U.S. Steel

stepped into the breach and made an offer that Marathon accepted amid a political fury in Congress. The steel industry, like oil, was still suspected of price fixing and was constantly seeking government protection from imports. Many congressmen wondered why they should favor industries that both flirted with monopolistic behavior and sought protection from foreign competition at the same time. Other bidders appeared, but finally U.S. Steel prevailed, with Marathon agreeing to sell part of its operations to ward off the antitrust issues that the deal raised. The deal was the second largest in history at the time. Arbitrageurs had their hands full with the stock of both companies. Ivan Boesky pointed out that money was made in all the markets that touched upon the issue, even the more exotic derivatives of the day.[6] There were ways of making money that the uninitiated had never thought of before. Arbitrageurs were important to proposed merger deals, as they affected the price of proposed takeover stocks, and many dealmakers shrewdly knew how to appeal to their instincts for profit.

Within months of the Reagan administration taking office, another familiar corporate name proposed a huge merger. DuPont announced that it was seeking a merger with Conoco, an energy company involved in oil and gas exploration. The chemical company proposed a cash-and-stock deal originally valued at $7.25 billion, the largest merger deal of its kind to date. The result would be the seventh-largest industrial company in the country. *Business Week* quipped that "there appear to be no antitrust roadblocks [left] to this type of vertical merger." Conoco had other suitors, among them Mobil, which was involved in the Marathon deal as well and would have raised problems with the Antitrust Division because it would have been horizontal, not vertical, as in the plans with DuPont. The chemical company was aided by the First Boston Corporation, a New York investment bank that astutely arranged the terms of the deal and the financing. Mobil was defeated in its bid, and DuPont emerged victorious. One of the dealmakers here was investment banker Bruce Wasserstein, who would help lead the merger mania of the latter part of the decade and the 1990s as well. Strangely enough, he had been on the opposite side of the fence several years before, when he was one of the coauthors of Nader's book *The Closed Enterprise System*, which had been roundly criticized by Robert Bork and other conservatives.

The new antitrust policy was called "an evolutionary change, not a revolutionary change" by Attorney General William French Smith. After setting the guidelines for the administration's antitrust policy, Baxter left the job to return to teaching and consulting with a major law firm. He was succeeded at the Antitrust Division by J. Paul McGrath in late 1983. There was some indication that McGrath would not blindly follow his predecessor's policies. Theory and policy were quickly put to the test when the LTV Corporation, formerly Ling-Temco-Vaught, made a bid to acquire the Republic Steel Corporation in the fall of 1984. LTV was now operating without James Ling as its chief executive, having forced him out when the conglomerate's financial fortunes began to fade. Suffering from cancer, Ling contented himself with other ventures but nothing as grand as building up LTV from a small electrical company. Such an obvious horizontal merger required extensive justification if it hoped to clear regulators. LTV provided it by invoking an international argument. It claimed that the threat of imports from foreign steel producers posed a threat to prices that only strong domestic companies could counterbalance. The proposed merger with Republic thus was in the best interests of the consumer. Patriotic overtones resonated in the background as well. The international argument was one to be heard many times again in the future, especially as American industry suffered from low growth rates and high interest rates.

Since domestically produced steel was already protected by import quotas and the industry was asking for even more, the Justice Department was reluctant to accept the argument. The affair sounded like a replay of the circumstances surrounding the creation of trusts in the 1880s, when protective tariffs shielded the newly formed combined companies from foreign competition. There was also difficulty in determining the market for HHI purposes. Should it be restricted to just the domestic firms, or should it include the international companies selling in the U.S. market as well? Some steel companies backed the merger as a means of self-preservation from foreign competition, while others opposed it. Ultimately, the world market argument would win the day. Even Baxter concluded that anyone who opposed it would "take an awful lot of grief." Antitrust and big business in general were suddenly being thrown onto the international stage.

The Antitrust Division under McGrath claimed that the combination of the two companies would result in a high concentration of steel products being manufactured by the same company. But LTV did not take no for an answer, announcing that it would press the Justice Department for a solution to the problem. It had some ammunition on its side. The FTC had been giving its own blessing to other, smaller horizontal mergers, casting vast confusion over what exactly antitrust policy was at the time. McGrath apparently had departed from the policies of Baxter within a very short time. A former staff member of the Antitrust Division remarked that Baxter "really thought like an economist, and if he didn't think the law was right, he didn't apply it," while McGrath was "using traditional case law, what the Supreme Court has ruled." The issue was far from resolved. The battle was not so much between the Harvard and Chicago Schools as it was between the adherents of case law versus more skeptical economists. The economic climate of the day helped swing the decision in favor of merger.

Finally the world market argument won the day and the Justice Department and LTV settled. LTV was allowed to merge with Republic as long as it divested itself of two domestic steel plants. The decision proved to be a precedent for many more proposed mergers in the future. In 1985 Attorney General Edwin Meese claimed, "We now have to look at our antitrust laws and competition in light of a global economy." Critics contended that was a justification for a purposely lax antitrust policy, and this argument would continue throughout much of the 1980s.

The past also came under review at the Antitrust Division under McGrath. In 1981 the department began studying the consent decrees that Paramount and other movie studios had signed forty years before. Three years later McGrath stated that the Antitrust Division was "very close to final action" on once more allowing the studios to own chains of theaters. Faced with a changing movie industry and demands for deregulation, the Antitrust Division favored abolishing the restraints. The theater owners were less than thrilled, but over the course of the decade, the restrictions on studios owning theater chains slowly began to loosen. One sagacious distributor of movies claimed that if that trend were allowed to develop it would eventually lead to the $7.50 movie ticket in the large cities. It was not clear how the de facto deregulation actually helped the consumer, but cinema chains moved closer to the studios once again.

JUNK MEN

The merger mania of the decade would not have been possible without the development of the junk bond market. Developed by Michael Milken at Drexel Burnham Lambert, the market was an adjunct of the traditional corporate bond market for investment-quality borrowers. It allowed companies of less than investment grade to issue bonds, something from which they were previously excluded.[7] Milken began experimenting with junk bonds in the 1970s after leaving the Wharton School and taking a job on Wall Street. After spending several years with Drexel Burnham in New York, he moved his increasingly successful operation to Los Angeles, where the movement blossomed into a major source of business for the firm and Wall Street in general. The trend was enticing for investment bankers. Junk bonds commanded twice the underwriting fees of a traditional investment-grade issue. By the end of the 1980s, over $250 billion in bonds had been issued. At underwriting fees of up to 4 percent of that amount, it is easy to understand the allure for the underwriters. The junk bond business helped propel Drexel Burnham into the top league of Wall Street underwriters by the end of the 1980s, a coveted position in the investment banking fraternity. But not all Wall Street firms joined the junk underwriting groups. Many considered junk a passing phenomenon that would dissipate with the bull market.

Junk bonds enabled many corporate raiders to mount hostile bids for companies that wanted to remain independent. Unfriendly takeovers had become more frequent and sophisticated since the days of James Ling, and now they often captured the financial headlines. They also captured the attention of influential lawmakers as well as the Fed. Peter Rodino, a congressman from New Jersey and chairman of the House Judiciary Committee, pointed out that hostile raids were "focusing management's attention on short-term survival, not on the productive, long-term planning and development that is vital to economic growth."[8] But he and other lawmakers realized that they were fighting a losing battle. The merger fever was growing stronger each year, and antitrust action was not proving to be an effective weapon against it.

Junk bonds were only the financing tools in a larger game of leveraged buyouts. Acquisition-minded companies would borrow enormous amounts of money and use it to buy the stock of another company. In some cases, the management of a company itself would offer to buy its own company, taking it private, with large amounts of borrowed cash. But when the junk bond market could not supply the funds, "junk bank loans" were arranged that carried a higher interest rate than a normal loan to a highly creditworthy customer. The technique was not new for the banks; they had been practicing it since the days of the conglomerateurs, many of whom got their start in the acquisitions business with the assistance of banks.

In response to the hostile takeover bid, companies developed defense strategies that they hoped would ensure their independence. Despite the SEC's plan to modify its cooling-off period after a buyer's notification of acquiring a 5 percent stake in a company, hostile bids could still be launched with astonishing speed. Companies needed to react defensively in similar fashion. Otherwise, they could lose their independence in a very short period of time. One of the more popular methods that was devised included using debt or preferred stock to ward off an unwanted suitor. These "poison pill" defenses allowed a target company to quickly issue new preferred stock or bonds when someone announced, following the 5 percent rule, that they were interested in acquiring it. The pill was one of several types of "shark repellents" used by companies to ward off other, unfriendly companies attempting to swallow them. The potential acquirer would then have to service the additional interest or dividends—not a pleasant prospect.

Issuing new securities quickly could not have been accomplished under the SEC's old registration requirements. That required companies to file a new issue and then wait twenty days for a cooling-off period, during which the securities could not be sold. But in 1983 the SEC obliged by establishing Rule 415, or the shelf registration rule. A company that had previously filed a preliminary registration statement could issue new securities without waiting if all of its paperwork was in order. This helped speed up the new issue process considerably and helped pave the way for poison pill filings. By passing Rule 415, the SEC also helped bring the investment banking industry quickly into the new merger era as well. Technically, the rule meant that since new securities could be brought to market at very short notice, many investment banks did not have much time to assemble an underwriting syndicate in the normal, gentlemanly fashion. Now a bank would have to vouch for the entire deal itself and then find syndicate members willing to enter the deal after the fact. That required increased capital on the part of the investment banks themselves, and many had to add capital by going public or by finding merger partners themselves. What the investment bankers had been helping their clients do for so long was finally happening to them.

As an alternative to poison pills, some companies favored seeking a white knight. Another company would offer to take over the target, promising to make no changes to its corporate philosophy or management style. So great was the fear of hostile takeovers that companies often went to extremes to ensure their independence. The hostile takeover had come of age. As in the 1960s, the hostile takeover extended to large companies as well as the small and medium-size. No firm was too big not to fear a hostile bid from an aggressive dealmaker. Some of these bids came not from other companies but from private investors or small, boutiquelike firms set up in the late 1960s to engage in the buying and selling of companies, relying heavily on borrowed money.

Perhaps the greatest hostile takeover of the 1980s was the bid made for RJR/Nabisco by the investment house of Kohlberg Kravis Roberts (KKR). The sheer size of the eventual takeover and the way it was financed made it perhaps the most noteworthy acquisition of the decade. KKR was set up in the mid-1970s and became well known, and extremely wealthy, using leveraged buyouts to take control of several noteworthy companies, including Houdaille, Inc., Fred Meyer, Inc., Norris Industries, Beatrice Foods, Duracell, and parts of Owens Illinois and FMC Corporation, among others. It borrowed vast amounts of money from banks, pension funds, and insurance companies to buy the stock of the companies it was interested in. With only a small staff and headquarters, it was able to exercise the sort of financial power in the marketplace not seen since the heyday of the Morgans. But it was the acquisition of RJR/Nabisco that was the crowning moment and subsequently became the subject of a book and a TV movie.

RJR/Nabisco was a huge tobacco and food company headed by F. Ross Johnson. Intrigued by the deals of the decade, Johnson proposed a management buyout of the company by himself and colleagues in 1988 for $75 per share. Some members of the company's board were not informed of the proposed deal until the last moment and subsequently made the details public. From that point, it became apparent that the company was vulnerable to an outside bid. Kohlberg Kravis Roberts responded with an offer of $90 per share, and the bidding war began. Other bidders emerged but quickly dropped out of the picture, finally leaving the path clear for the KKR bid to succeed. The total cost was slightly less than $25 billion, making the deal the largest ever consummated. Two years later, however, the deal almost backfired on KKR when RJR faced a bond default on some of its existing obligations and KKR had to increase its equity in the company in order to avert disaster. The most significant aspect of the entire affair was that it was ever financed and consummated at all. The performance of the company afterward was almost anticlimactic.

The Reagan administration's neglect of antitrust received a vote of support from the SEC. After contemplating legislation designed to prevent corporate takeovers, the SEC decided against proposing it in the spring of 1985. The SEC also thought of forbidding "golden parachutes"—the practice of an acquired company's giving its executives a hefty compensation package for leaving the company once a merger had been sealed—but it decided against it. It also declined to regulate greenmail, probably the best-known takeover topic of the early 1980s. In greenmail, a potential acquirer bought more than 5 percent of the outstanding stock in a target company and then filed the SEC-required statement disclosing the stake within ten days. The goal was to make the management of the target nervous enough to contemplate buying back the stock at a premium.[9] Long-term investment or adding value to the company was not the intent of greenmailers; the only thing that interested them was profiting from the transaction. Greenmailers always claimed that they were operating in the best interests of stockholders, who would benefit from the pressure they put on corporate management. They usually stated their cases in terms of corporate control and accountability: Management had to show they were operating in the best interests of the shareholders or it would be ousted if their bid was successful. Lee Iacocca, the chairman of Chrysler, took a dim view of greenmailers and arbitrageurs. Noting that they were not in sight when Chrysler was in bankruptcy in 1980 and could have used some financial support, he asserted, "When the raiders and the arbs get involved . . . you've got even bigger problems. You're forced to do things that make no business sense at all just to stay alive," echoing a lament heard in many corporate suites.[10]

The greenmailers adopted a technique that had not been seen on Wall Street since the days of the robber barons. Using the stock market as a place to actually raise capital for takeover purposes by exacting cash from companies not wanting to be taken over was a modern version of the market corner so successfully used by Jay Gould and others in the immediate post–Civil War period. But even Gould would have been impressed by the amounts his modern counterparts were able to extort from companies. The most profitable was T. Boone Pickens, who cashed in for almost $900 million between 1982 and 1984 alone. Pickens was in his mid-fifties, a native of Oklahoma with a degree in geology. He went to work for Phillips Petroleum in his native Oklahoma before striking out on his own as a wildcat oil driller. Accumulating enormous debts, he decided that playing the stock market might be the solution to his problems. Having accumulated a war chest, he decided to threaten to take over oil companies so that they would buy back stock he had accumulated in them. Unlike many other raiders, Pickens tended to concentrate on industries he knew and understood. The first company he and Mesa Petroleum, the company he founded to pursue his activities in the takeover market, set their sights on was Cities Service, an old, established company. The events that followed were the archetype of an early 1980s takeover play.

Cities Service was typical of a company run by stodgy management whose fortunes were lifted by the rise in oil prices more than by its innovative approach to the energy crisis. Pickens, using Mesa's resources, acquired slightly more than the obligatory 5 percent in the company, putting it into "play." Then Pickens slowly put together a package of junk bank financing aimed at acquiring 20 percent of Cities Service's outstanding stock. Next he quickly approached Cities with an offer to buy it outright. Initially it was not clear how he would raise the money to finance the purchase, because its value clearly exceeded his resources; banks were playing a major part in assembling financing for Mesa, but it soon became clear that Pickens could not succeed in his quest. Cities Service finally bought out Mesa's share for $32 million. While Pickens prospered, Cities was not left in good financial shape. Shortly thereafter, it accepted an offer from Armand Hammer's Occidental Petroleum.

Other notable financiers of the period included the Bass brothers of Texas, Carl Icahn, and William Simon. All had very different methods of making money. Simon, who was treasury secretary under Richard Nixon and a former Salomon Brothers bond trader, used high degrees of leverage, enabling his Wesray Capital to buy Gibson Greeting Cards and resell it for a profit of over $70 million. Carl Icahn, a Princeton graduate from New York City, bought a seat on the NYSE while in his early thirties and, like Pickens, used it to accumulate enormous trading profits. He then used that cash to begin buying stakes in other companies. Bruce Wasserstein described the tactic that Icahn and Pickens employed as "the bear hug." After accumulating a stake in a company, the investor embraces its board of directors, who must naturally make the offer known to investors because of their fiduciary responsibility to ensure that investors are apprised of all deals that may increase their share price. Then the stock would be put into "play" and hopefully a white knight or other investor would come to the rescue with a higher bid price. In the late 1970s Icahn greenmailed several companies, including Saxon Industries and the Tappan Company, for profits of over $6 million. But it was in the 1980s that he made his mark, greenmailing the old-line Chicago department store Marshall Field for a profit of over $40 million. The company was so distressed by the prospect of Icahn's assuming control that it successfully sought a white knight to take control and buy out his interest. Similar tactics with the American Can Company and Hammermill produced similar results.

A battle with Texaco in 1988 won Icahn few friends. Having accumulated about 15 percent of the company's stock, he then made an offer for the balance of the outstanding shares at $60. Skepticism began to grow when he gave the company only forty-eight hours to respond to his offer. Texaco was sure that he could not raise the financing needed, almost $20 billion, and also pointed to his ties with convicted arbitrageur Ivan Boesky to prove that he was unsuitable. After a particular nasty battle, Icahn sold his stake in Texaco for $2 billion. That gave him a large war chest with which to pursue other acquisitions, and Wall Street was abuzz with rumors about which company might be next on his list. But the largest prize in Icahn's early career was his acquisition of TWA. Critics would always use the episode as evidence that raiders did not necessarily evolve into good corporate executives. TWA, besides being an airline, was the apotheosis of a lumbering postconglomerate company. Once owned by Howard Hughes, the airline had acquired several former ITT companies such as Hilton Hotels and Canteen Corporation in the 1960s in an attempt to diversify. Taking control of the airline in 1986, Icahn was faced with several obstacles, the greatest of which was a strike by its flight attendants. Icahn broke their union, but the publicity surrounding the affair was particularly unpleasant. Eventually, TWA filed for bankruptcy and Icahn retired from the company for other pursuits. Not everyone thought of Icahn as an unscrupulous raider, however. Harold Geneen remembered him fondly as "one of America's savviest investors."

The Bass brothers of Texas were the best-known financial family involved in the merger antics of the 1980s. Inheriting over $1 billion in family money, they played a major role in the merger of Marathon Oil with U.S. Steel by accumulating 5 percent of Marathon's stock cheaply before being bought out. Their profits totaled more than $150 million. They also made substantial gains in other deals involving Suburban Propane, Blue Bell, Sperry & Hutchinson, and Walt Disney. The $1 billion was estimated to have multiplied to around $5 billion within a decade. Although the four brothers officially separated their investment activities after 1985, they were still considered a major force in deals. Before their breakup, they were estimated to have made over $400 million for their role in takeover deals.[11] Their softer side was well appreciated by Yale University, which received substantial donations from them.

As the merger trend continued and junk bond financings increased, the Fed under Paul Volcker decided to take some action to restrict the use of junk. Often, takeovers were proposed by companies that had been created for the occasion and had no assets of their own, only what they were able to borrow in the form of junk bonds or junk bank loans. The Fed decided to apply its margin requirements to those shell companies.[12] The Fed ruled that only 50 percent of the purchase could be financed with junk bonds; the balance would have to be financed with cash. The ruling set off an uproar in the financial community. Investment bankers divided along traditional lines. The junk bond specialists predicted dire consequences for the economy, while the traditional investment bankers, who for the most part eschewed junk, applauded it. Felix Rohatyn of Lazard Frères applauded the Fed, saying, "I think it was a very sound, long overdue step to take." But the Fed deliberately left some loopholes in the ruling and acquisition-minded companies that were affected found alternative methods of raising cash.

The merger market was obscured somewhat by another notable trend on Wall Street at the same time. Divestitures, or spin-offs, were also extremely popular and required a great deal of investment bankers' time. They were part of the general synergy movement—the idea that some companies were worth more in pieces than as a whole. When their managements recognized this, they began to shed some unwanted parts, so that they could unlock the value hidden in their balance sheets. Many companies attempting to do so were the conglomerates, many of which had not fared particularly well since the early 1970s. ITT was first in the long list that began to divest. It had been doing so since the 1970s, when it was forced to liquidate some of its businesses because of its deal with the Justice Department. Many well-known names followed, including Westinghouse and Gulf + Western. The trend did not stop them from making new acquisitions, however, as many decided to reorient their businesses. Gulf + Western became Paramount Communications after liquidating most of the old Bluhdorn company, and then acquired Viacom and Simon & Schuster, a major book publisher. Westinghouse eventually sold its financial units and then acquired CBS in an attempt to become a communications company. Leaving its legacy and George Westinghouse in the past, it eventually took CBS's name and ceased to exist as a manufacturer.

GONE TO POT

Not content with merely changing the substance of antitrust activity, the Reagan administration began a drive to emasculate it completely in 1986. The secretary of commerce, Malcolm Baldrige, advocated abolishing the Sherman and Clayton Acts outright. In a package sent to Congress, the administration proposed that the president be allowed to give temporary exemptions from the antitrust laws to companies that claimed "injury" from foreign competition. It also proposed rolling back sections of the Clayton Act so that future Democratic administrations could not unravel the administration's measures. Most involved believed the proposed measures were too strong and predicted that Congress would rightfully refuse to acquiesce. Peter Rodino stated flatly that the proposals would not get through the House Judiciary Committee. One of those who did predict success, holding that the measures made perfectly good economic sense, was Douglas Ginsburg, then head of the Antitrust Division. Like his predecessors at the Justice Department, he believed that economic analysis rendered many of the antitrust laws obsolete.

Ginsburg studied law at the University of Chicago under two leading Chicago School advocates, George Stigler and Richard Posner. He then took a job at the budget office, which was already practicing economic analysis in the early 1970s. He then went into unfriendly territory to teach law at Harvard. "I got to test my ideas in a hostile environment," he later remarked. After being appointed to the Antitrust Division, he became the inside man to lead the Reagan attack on antitrust, espousing the Chicago approach while at the same time remaining a political favorite of the President and Attorney General Edwin Meese. As a result of his performance, Reagan nominated him to the Supreme Court when an opening occurred. But the resulting furor made administration officials wonder if they had gone too far in attempting to bring the "Reagan revolution" to antitrust.

Ginsburg was the second nominee put forward by Reagan to fill Justice Lewis Powell's vacant Supreme Court seat. The president had previously placed Robert Bork's name in nomination, but the ideological forces opposing Bork on antitrust as well as constitutional matters were ultimately successful in defeating his nomination. After remarks Bork made during his confirmation hearings portrayed him as somewhat ambivalent about the absolute right to privacy, the press made a fuss about polls that showed a majority of Americans were not in favor of his nomination. The confirmation process was especially virulent, with Bork being portrayed as one of the most dangerous ideologues in the country. After his defeat, many assumed that Ginsburg, nominated next, would be successful in his quest, because the anti-Bork forces would not dare to marshal their resources in such a fashion again. But they were wrong. Ginsburg was portrayed as being too young for the job, although his supporters noted that William O. Douglas had less experience than the 41-year-old judge when he was nominated to the Court by Franklin Roosevelt forty years before. Ginsburg's ultimate undoing was an admission that he had once used marijuana. Clearly, the nomination procedures were being overwhelmed with trivia in both instances, but the anti-Reagan forces won the day nevertheless. Two of the Chicago School's best-known proponents were denied a seat, not because of their qualifications but because of their ideology. The Senate Democrats opposing them, notably Edward Kennedy of Massachusetts and Joseph Biden of Delaware, both were members of the liberal camp in Congress, successors to what remained of the New Deal tradition. Antitrust alone did not defeat Bork but the strong views used to support his position on it did not enhance his chances with the opposing political camp.

The merger trend continued even after the severe stock market downturn following the 1987 collapse. In a classic sign of the times, a corporate raider teaching a course in mergers and acquisitions at Columbia University's business school offered his students a $100,000 finder's fee if they brought him a company for which he could make a tender offer. Needless to say, such courses became wildly popular at business schools around the country. Another business school professor, Mike Jensen at the University of Rochester, gained wide notoriety by being one of the few academics to defend corporate raids and takeovers. He also argued against a growing trend that decried executive compensation as being too high. He actually favored paying corporate executives more, not less. In his view, hostile takeovers were nothing more than businesses vying for position in a marketplace, a natural series of events. Views like that, plus the emphasis on competition and the salubrious effect it had on consumer prices, helped the takeover trend by giving it some theoretical ammunition and preaching the cause to another group of business school students who would shortly join the ranks of corporate financiers on Wall Street.

Looking back at the record in 1989, an American Bar Association (ABA) task force roundly criticized both Reagan administrations for being far too lax on antitrust enforcement. One of the ABA task force's members was Paul McGrath, since retired from the division and currently in private practice. During the previous eight years, the Antitrust Division's operating budget had been cut by over 50 percent. The task force report noted that some progress had been made in price-fixing prosecutions, but they were somewhat separate from antitrust. What the Justice Department needed was less "non-enforcement rhetoric" and more of a "positive enforcement agenda to reinvigorate . . . the division's resources and staff."[13] Even if the Justice Department had been more vigorous, it is doubtful that the judiciary would have been sympathetic. Reagan appointed about half of the federal judiciary during his two terms, and by the end of George Bush's administration almost two-thirds of federal judges had been appointed by Republicans. The overwhelming majority of the appointees were white, middle-class males who shared the administration's penchant for a competitive marketplace through deregulation. The true Reagan revolution was certainly found in antitrust theory and activity, although a shift to the right had been building even before he took the oath of office.

SECOND WIND

After the stock market collapse in 1987, the savings and loan crisis in 1989, and the recession that began in 1990, many pundits with short-term horizons thought that the merger and acquisition binge had finally ended. Between 1972 and 1988 the value of completed merger deals increased fifteen times, to a record $260 billion in that last year alone. Then, after the market collapse, deals and their values began a precipitous decline, falling to only $80 billion in 1992. Lower stock market values closed the window of opportunity for many companies to merge. Investment bankers and Wall Street in general felt the effects as well, suffering their own recession as fees declined. Goldman Sachs and Morgan Stanley remained the two premier merger-and-acquisition investment bankers during the 1980s and early 1990s. Both earned the majority of their fees advising target companies. First Boston found itself on the other side of the deals, advising many more acquirers than targets.

Prospects dimmed even further when Ivan Boesky and Michael Milken were found to have engaged in insider trading. Boesky was found to have conspired with an investment banker at Drexel Burnham to receive inside information on pending merger deals and then trade the stocks involved for his own gain. He was prosecuted by Rudolph Giuliani, the U.S. attorney for the Southern District of New York, and received a prison sentence and a $100 million fine. He provided evidence against Michael Milken, who was later indicted on one hundred counts of racketeering and fined almost $1 billion. He pleaded guilty to six charges and eventually spent three years in prison before being released. Drexel Burnham went out of business in 1990 after paying heavy fines and suffering serious losses in the junk bond market, which was undergoing a major correction because of the S&L crisis and the recession. But the market was kept alive by other Wall Street investment banks and by the mid-1990s was back to its previous form.

As the merger mania continued, it became more clear that investment bankers' compensation was playing a large role in the number of deals announced. Lured by fees that would have made Jay Gould envious, many investment bankers pressed deals upon aggressive corporate presidents, whom they knew were always looking for ways to expand. Even in relatively bad years by Wall Street standards, the compensation could be astronomical. In 1994, not a particularly good year in general, Thomas Lee of Boston was the highest paid executive in the financial community with compensation of around $170 million. Lee's fortune that year was derived from selling the Snapple beverage company, which he bought for 44 cents per share, to Quaker Oats for $14 a share, netting him over $150 million on the transaction. That earned him more than the legendary George Soros in the same year. Specializing in mergers and acquisitions accounted for about 30 percent of the richest Wall Street personalities that year alone.[14] Just as Morgan Stanley had broken the ice in 1974 by advising on a hostile takeover, the new breed of merger artists was setting new standards for compensation. And their advice seemed to be prompting many management buyouts, as it occurred to more than one corporate head that he and his management team could also realize profits by privatizing their own companies.

In 1986 one of the old names in the conglomerate-merger boom of the 1960s and 1970s fell on the hardest of times. LTV filed for Chapter 11 bankruptcy due to declining business and substantial pension fund liabilities. It would take the diversified steelmaker seven years to settle its liabilities and recapitalize itself into a new company, still bearing the LTV name. As if to add insult to injury, a Chicago securities firm was discovered to have sold a massive amount of LTV shares short, driving its price below $1 per share prior to its official reorganization. The company's demise officially marked the end of the conglomerate era. Those conglomerates that remained were much leaner operationally than they were in the late 1960s.

THE ENEMY IS DEAD

One of the subtle causes of the recent phase of the merger phenomenon was the dismemberment of the Soviet Union. As the old enemy crumbled, the face of industry quickly changed. Defense-related manufacturing industries faced an immediate crisis as military spending declined. Many new communications-related industries sprang up at the same time. Besides changing the industrial landscape, the collapse also added to the merger mania psychologically by showing the dominance of capital over politics and ideology. Ironically, the largest political merger in history—of disparate republics into the Soviet Union—failed for the lack of capital: It could not meet the West's spending on defense and technology, the only areas where it had historically claimed superiority. Once the myth collapsed, what Lenin once called "financial capital" emerged triumphant. After the victory, the idea of the evils of corporate bigness seemed more nonsensical than ever. The collapse of Ronald Reagan's "evil empire" demonstrated to free market advocates that no matter how big an entity, the threat it poses is still tempered by market mechanisms. Even if it is a gigantic organization, if it does not have the flexibility to respond to social needs, then it will eventually collapse under the weight of its own ineptitude.

Wall Street and the merger specialists in general became very sure of themselves in the new environment, where the market never appeared to retreat. That attitude did not go unnoticed by regulators, who were in the early stages of attempting to resurrect antitrust action from the doldrums. After Bill Clinton defeated George Bush for the presidency in 1992, antitrusters hoped that the pursuit of monopolies would again increase. But their hopes continued to be dashed by the conservative nature of the federal judiciary and an Antitrust Division that had become somewhat moribund over the past dozen years. The Clinton administration was presiding over a strong economy, and antitrust did not undergo a revival for fear of upsetting the applecart. Then a private antitrust case arose that had all the markings of cases from the past. In a dispute over the nature of competition in the market for cigarettes, Brooke Group, the parent of Liggett & Meyers, sued the Brown & Williamson Tobacco Corporation, claiming that Brown & Williamson was using predatory techniques to capture the market for generic cigarettes—those sold under unfamiliar brand names at a substantial discount from the nationally known brands. But the courts ruled that even though the top six firms controlled the cigarette industry, no harm resulted under the Robinson-Patman Act from Brown & Williamson's marketing techniques and that claims of predatory pricing had no bearing. The Supreme Court affirmed the decision, deflating antitrusters' hopes even more.[15] Predatory pricing, once the bête noire of alleged monopolists, had again been ruled ineffective as an argument. And Brooke Group's use of the Robinson-Patman Act as a part of their original suit appeared not to be in tune with the times.

After the 1992 recession, several minor business trends appeared that gave the general impression that the merger trend had abated. Corporate strategies such as downsizing—meaning that many companies were firing workers in a quest for reduced costs and higher profit margins—became household terms. But it soon became clear that mergers had only been on vacation, and after 1995 activity again increased dramatically. By the end of the decade, deals would be announced that, taken individually, outnumbered the total amounts announced in some individual years in the 1970s. And many of the deals were still using pool accounting as the accounting method of choice, especially mergers between banks and other financial institutions. The Financial Accounting Standards Board studied the method and the alternatives, but mergers using it looked very healthy in the strong stock market, raising the inevitable question of whether the 1960s were being replayed, this time with giant horizontal and vertical mergers rather than the conglomerates dominating the scene.

The last time the utility companies experienced merger mania was in the 1920s, during the days of Samuel Insull and Jack Morgan. After the Public Utility Holding Company Act of 1935 restricted their ability to expand, they remained within their home states, governed by public utility commissions. In the intervening years, they existed as tightly regulated companies, although they did enjoy government-granted monopolies in power production. But there were still vast differences in the price of electricity, as there were in the 1920s. The TVA produced power for as little as 4 cents a kilowatt-hour while in the Northeast it cost as much as 12 cents. As the 1990s began, pressure began to build to deregulate utilities, as so many other businesses had been deregulated during the Republican revolution of the 1980s. Congress obliged by passing the Energy Policy Act in 1992, which deregulated sales among the utilities themselves, opening the door for potentially cheaper wholesale power and lower rates for consumers. The individual states then quickly entered the arena by deregulating power sales and allowing freer competition, with California leading the way. As a result, some power companies sought to merge, arguing economies of scale and lower consumers rates if they were able to do so. This came at a time when the merger market began to increase its activity again, rebounding from the recession of 1990. The Clinton administration offered little resistance to the crumbling of the old monopolies, and the energy companies began seeking marriage partners. Several went as far afield as Britain, where they purchased utilities companies recently deregulated by the Conservative government in the 1980s.

Utilities were not the only recidivists on the merger scene in the 1990s. Railroads again began actively seeking merger partners in what had always been a delicate situation for regulators ever since the Interstate Commerce Commission was first established. After the Penn Central fiasco during the conglomerate era, truck transportation had increased its share of shipping at the expense of the rails, and in order to remain competitive, some of the larger railroads sought merger partners. As in the past, regulators tended to look favorably upon the deals. The industry had been consolidating since 1980, when Congress passed the Staggers Rail Act, and only ten large rail systems remained. But the railroads were generally considered to be more efficient and to have better access to capital than at any time since World War II.

Old names returned to capture headlines again. In an unpleasant battle for control of Burlington Northern, the Union Pacific lost a takeover battle with the Santa Fe. Both contenders had been actively seeking a merger partner in order to forge a nationwide railroad system. The Burlington–Santa Fe merger claimed to have saved over $500 million in costs in its first two years. The acquisitions-minded Union Pacific then found another potential partner in the Southern Pacific, a company whose finances had declined substantially. But the Southern Pacific was part of a glorious tradition, and in railroading, as in other businesses, name recognition is extremely valuable. In addition to the railroad business, Southern Pacific had also made a significant contribution to the communications business,

By Toles. © *Buffalo News.* Reprinted with permission of Universal Press Syndicate.

almost by default. Since the days of the first telephones and telegraph, Southern Pacific had been laying wires alongside its tracks so that its stations could communicate with each other. As time passed, the wires were upgraded and the system became extremely sophisticated. It became one of those companies whose private communications system rivaled AT&T in the 1970s. In 1983 the network was bought by a company named Sprint, which then began laying fiber-optic cables along the route. Southern Pacific made an invaluable contribution to the communications revolution simply because it originally needed to keep in touch with its stations. Had he been around in the 1980s, Jay Gould would have easily recognized the potential in communications, for that was originally one of his reasons for getting into the railroad business over a hundred years before.

Union Pacific aggressively made an offer for Southern Pacific. Clearly, the idea of a strong company taking over a weak one would play upon the sympathies of regulators, who would review the planned merger. "The Southern Pacific is a failing railroad," said Union Pacific chairman Drew Lewis, the architect of the merger. "Shippers have to be better off with the Union Pacific owning it." Lewis was secretary of transportation under Reagan and knew the merger business from the railroads' point of view. Like all railroad issues, the proposed merger had its advocates and detractors. Many of the arguments against a merger sounded like those of the prior century, when the robber barons pushed the railroads into the West for the first time and then began dictating rates to shippers. The chairman of a small cooperative that bought coal for utility companies in the West summarized the anxieties of smaller shippers, who feared that the newly expanded railroads would only raise their rates rather than lower them. "Those shippers who have the means of securing competitive bids among railroads are paying less and less while those of us who are captive shippers are paying more and more," he argued, echoing a lament that Andrew Carnegie knew well and used to his own advantage against the railroad barons a century earlier.[16] Ironically, the merger was proposed to the ICC as a formality and was one of the last proposals the agency heard before its dissolution.

The Interstate Commerce Commission was disbanded officially in late 1995, ending the agency's checkered history. A victim of the times and continued negative antitrust sentiment in Congress, the agency was portrayed as an anachronism in the latter part of the twentieth century, and some wondered why it had been allowed to exist as long as it did. No one expected railroad regulation to change substantially, but the tenor of the times was expressed by a Republican congressman sitting on the House Transportation Committee: "We'll be spending $35 million less per year and there will be a lot fewer regulations stifling surface transportation." The ICC's limited powers were absorbed by the Department of Transportation after President Clinton failed to give the agency a reprieve. The Surface Transportation Board (STB), within the Department of Transportation, assumed its functions; any transaction approved by it is exempt from the antitrust laws.

A second railroad merger battle developed when CSX agreed to merge with Conrail to form an enormous rail system. Within a short time, another railroad, Norfolk Southern, entered the fray with a counterbid almost 10 percent higher. The bidding war entered a second phase and was becoming somewhat unpleasant when the STB finally stepped in and exercised its new authority. As part of a negotiated deal between the warring parties, Conrail was split into two parts. CSX got the New York side, while Norfolk Southern purchased the Penn Central side. Twenty years after Vanderbilt and Scott's old railroads were merged into Conrail, they parted company and reverted to new owners, with the ICC's successor negotiating the regulatory side of the deal.

REVIVAL

While not particularly known for its antitrust policies, the Clinton administration nevertheless slowly began to mount some notable cases of its own. After almost two decades of neglect, the effort began with the appointment of new regulators in 1993, Robert Pitofsky at the FTC and Anne Bingaman at the Antitrust Division. What began somewhat slowly soon burgeoned into the greatest flurry of antitrust activity seen since the late 1960s. The bull market of the 1990s quickly awakened the antitrusters, who found themselves with an enormous workload. Politics reentered the game, too, as it became clear that a Democratic administration could not stand idly by and watch companies merge without regard for traditional antitrust concerns.

In the early 1990s, antitrust again became headline news, sometimes with a vaguely comical air. Two large food processors, Hormel and Conagra, were sued privately for conspiring to fix prices on processed catfish and eventually settled by paying over $20 million to settle a class action lawsuit against them. The states also awoke from the general antimonopoly slumber and began to pursue cases of their own, which often dovetailed with federal actions. And not all of the antitrust cases were brought against industrial companies. The agriculture company Archer Daniels Midland (ADM) was by far the biggest loser in a suit claiming that it conspired to fix the price of agricultural products. Before the incident was settled, all of the behind-the-scenes connivances of big business would come to the foreground.

ADM's problems began when one of its division presidents blew the whistle on its scheme to fix the price of one of the commodities it produced. The inquiry soon widened. Over seventy suits were eventually filed charging the company with antitrust violations and conspiracy to fix prices with other firms. On the board of the company was Ross Johnson, the former head of RJR/Nabisco in the 1980s before it was taken over by KKR. Speaking before a business school audience at Emory University, Johnson expressed some cynicism about the whistle-blower's motives. Next he went on to claim that the division president had been stealing from the company as well. "But then, you know, he tried to commit suicide. But he did it in a six car garage, which, I think, if you're going to do it, that's the place to do it. And his gardener just happened to come by [to save him]."[17] The employee became somewhat famous as the year's best-known whistle-blower. He was awarded a "Disgruntled Employee of the Year" award by a small Berkeley, California, magazine, which sent him a T-shirt and a commemorative certificate. It proved to be of little consolation. The whistle-blower and two other company executives were found guilty of conspiracy to fix prices. Separately, the company was fined $100 million, and it admitted responsibility for its errors.

The consolidation movement extended to banking as well as utilities and railroads. One of the last vestiges of outdated regulation finally disappeared when Congress passed the Interstate Banking Act in 1994, allowing banking companies to merge across state lines. Since 1927, when Congress passed the McFadden Act, banks had not been allowed to open new branches across state lines. Equally, the Bank Holding Company Act prohibited them from owning more than one banking company. Now, after decades of lobbying and exceptions to the rule, interstate banking became a reality as the old prohibitions against merger vanished. Banking mergers began almost immediately, and the top ten banks in the country changed their complexion very quickly. The new Chase, the result of a merger between Chase Manhattan and Chemical Bank, became the country's largest commercial bank. In banking circles, it was known as a "merger among equals," an idea that would have been unthinkable before the Antitrust Division changed tack. As a result of directives from the Federal Reserve beginning in 1989, the banks also moved into investment banking. With the merger between Citicorp and Traveler's in 1998, the banking industry was again united with most of the businesses it had been divorced from in previous decades, although the Glass-Steagall Act remained on the books and its proposed successor legislation still had not been passed by Congress. Under Alan Greenspan, an advocate of allowing the banks to engage in the securities business, the Fed began loosening its grip on the banks' activities under Section 20 of the Glass-Steagall Act and began allowing them to derive more and more of their revenue from securities-related activities. That action also sparked a number of commercial banks to buy medium-sized investment banks that fit the Fed's guidelines. After sixty years of Glass-Steagall prohibitions, the wall of separation that had been constructed between the two sides of banking began to fall. Pundits would note that it was the second type of wall to fall within the decade. What Congress had been unable to accomplish in decades was done by the Fed over a ten-year period. Fears of the old money trust had long since receded and been replaced by an urge to merge commercial banks and investment banks into larger, full-service financial institutions able to complete on a global scale. The abolition of the New Deal restrictions in banking was the deregulators' greatest victory in the new environment. Business in general was becoming extremely capital-intensive because of globalization. As a result, the pocketbooks of many companies that wanted to expand were severely stretched, and banking was no exception. Now, with global competition, banks needed more capital and facilities. Expansion through merger was the only viable method of achieving it, and the merger environment on Wall Street proved ideal for putting together large deals that would have been unheard of ten years before.

Like many other industries in the 1990s, the telecommunications industry once again underwent a major deregulatory phase when Congress passed the Telecommunications Act of 1996. This law allowed the traditional line of demarcation between local and long-distance telephone companies to fall, enabling each to offer services in the other's traditional marketplace, which had been established fifteen years before with the breakup of AT&T. Now, in the name of greater competition, the Baby Bells were allowed back into the old parent company's market and vice versa. Detractors asked what the point was of breaking up AT&T to begin with. The short answer was increased competition and lower prices. Like utilities and banking, the telecommunications industry was set for more competition than it had seen since the early days of the twentieth century, before the Bell system was assembled by bankers intent on dominating the industry.

Greenmail debates continued well into the 1990s. One of the largest concerned a proposed takeover of the Chrysler Corporation, valued at $22 billion, by investor Kirk Kerkorian and former Chrysler president Lee Iacocca. Like Iacocca, Kerkorian was the son of immigrants; he had dropped out of high school and trained pilots for the Royal Air Force during World War II. Most of his estimated net worth of $2.5 billion had been made buying and selling entertainment companies, so Chrysler was something of a departure for him. In 1995 Kerkorian made $55-a-share offer for the 90 percent of the auto manufacturer he did not already own. Iacocca joined the offer, putting up $50 million of his own money in the process. Kerkorian had been at odds with Chrysler's board for some time over the market price of the stock, which had been languishing. Both men thought the share price should be higher, and their offer reflected their optimism in the future of the company. But the fly in the ointment was that prior financing had not been arranged, so most Chrysler executives believed that the offer was really greenmail in disguise. Kerkorian claimed that the offer would "provide Chrysler's shareholders with a substantial premium for their shares." Chrysler saw it differently. The company had over $7 billion in cash, which made it an enviable target in itself. Its chairman said flatly that the company was not for sale. But one of its senior managers advised his employees to begin reading the account of the RJR/Nabisco merger, *Barbarians at the Gate*, just in case.[18]

Chrysler had poison pill defenses set up against any unwanted takeovers. In this case they could have proved useful since one of Kerkorian's best-known deals was a hostile takeover of MGM in 1969. He also bought a major stake in United Artists a decade later. He subsequently sold both to Ted Turner. Skeptics who thought that the entire affair was nothing more than greenmail were disappointed when Kerkorian and Chrysler negotiated a truce in 1996. In a complicated deal, Kerkorian gave up the takeover battle in exchange for representation on Chrysler's board. Iacocca was paid over $20 million by the company to have nothing more to do with it after he committed what it considered an act of extreme disloyalty by allying with Kerkorian in the first place. As the stock market continued to rise in the mid-1990s, the substantial stake Kerkorian held in the company continued to gain value until the company eventually merged with Daimler Benz of Germany. His stake was then reputed to be worth over \$1 billion more when the merger was completed, putting his total assets at more than \$5 billion.

The latest consolidation phase of the 1990s evoked many familiar arguments, heard in the past, about the future of business in the face of what appeared to be relentless merging and cost cutting. The large chain stores again became an issue, as they originally had in the 1920s. Retailing and bookselling, to name but two businesses, began to lose many smaller stores as the larger began to dominate their respective businesses. Sam Walton, of Arkansas, began a career in retailing as a trainee at a JC Penney store after college. He opened his first five-and-dime store in Arkansas in 1945 and had a chain of thirty stores by 1970. After going public to raise cash, he began to vigorously expand, and within twenty-five years his Wal-Mart Stores had become the world's largest retailer, with over \$75 billion a year in sales. When he opened a store in a rural or semirural area, many small retailers went out of business within a short period of time, not being able to compete on price or variety. When combined with the sales of the other retailing giants, Wal-Mart rapidly changed the shopping habits of many and altered the economics of the entire industry.

The publishing industry underwent a similar transformation as giant booksellers such as Barnes & Noble began to force smaller booksellers to the brink. Able to achieve economies of sale and distribution arrangements with publishers that smaller retailers could not match, the chains could offer discounts off list prices that their smaller competition could not. Noting the mergers taking place among the publishers themselves, critics claimed that the small bookseller was quickly becoming extinct. The American Booksellers Association filed an antitrust suit against the two largest book chains in federal court in 1998, claiming that the large chains were receiving extra discounts and incentives from publishers that were unavailable to smaller stores. They sued under the Robinson-Patman Act and similar California antitrust statutes.

In response to the radical changes in the defense industry after the demise of the Soviet Union, the Lockheed Martin Corporation proposed a union with Northrop Grumman Corporation in a planned \$8 billion merger between the two defense contractors. The Justice Department objected that the merger would create too much vertical integration within the industry, which would in turn harm competitive bidding (a government requirement) among other companies doing business with the Defense Department. In the face of the opposition, Lockheed finally dropped its merger plans. The head of the Antitrust Division, Joel Klein, praised the decision, saying, "This means that the United States Government and the American people will continue to receive the highest possible quality of military products and services." The emphasis on competition and its link to price and quality was not completely dead.

A similar merger between the Boeing Corporation and the McDonnell Douglas Corporation was successful despite some intense scrutiny. The two aircraft manufacturers proposed a merger valued at $14 billion, large but certainly not gigantic by 1990s standards. The case was investigated by the FTC, which was often in open competition with the Antitrust Division for noteworthy cases. The FTC assembled an army of investigators to examine the potential merger, and it quickly became its most intensive investigation in history. The two companies also faced enormous paperwork problems and costs associated with the merger. They estimated that they had over six hundred lawyers and paralegals on their staffs in order to deal with the FTC's myriad requests. While the decade itself was one of large mergers, one military analyst said bluntly, "This is what President Eisenhower warned us about back in 1961—a massive military-industrial complex—this concentration of power."[19] Eventually the FTC disagreed and allowed the merger to proceed, claiming that the merger would not lessen competition in the manufacturing of either military or civilian aircraft, especially in light of the fact that McDonnell Douglas was no longer a factor on the market for civilian aircraft. The European Union initially demurred and challenged the merger, but it too eventually quieted its misgivings, and the two companies formally merged in the summer of 1997.

The computer industry again began to attract the attention of antitrusters in the 1990s. Both the Microsoft Corporation, headed by Bill Gates, and the Intel Corporation drew fire from antitrusters investigating the virtual monopolies that both companies had developed in their respective corners of the market. Probably the most successful American company of the postwar period, Microsoft emerged from obscurity to become one of the country's largest in a short period of twenty years. During that time, its major product had become the standard for operat-

By Oliphant. © Universal Press Syndicate. Reprinted with permission.

ing systems on personal computers worldwide. Gates himself reportedly became the world's richest man, with his holdings valued at slightly under $70 billion. That put him roughly on par with William Vanderbilt and ahead of Jay Gould but still far behind John D. Rockefeller.[20] Much of that amount was due to the escalating stock market. Less than four years before, his stake in Microsoft had been valued at less than $10 billion. Using the old adage that where there is that much smoke there must be fire, the Antitrust Division began investigating Microsoft to see whether a monopoly existed. It filed suit against the company in 1998, charging it with antitrust violations against its competition in the Internet browser business. A month later, the FTC filed suit against the Intel Corporation, the largest maker of computer chips, which held over 90 percent of its respective market. But the chipmaker chose a different, less combative road than Microsoft and settled its suit amicably with regulators rather than face a long court battle.

The Microsoft suit was not totally surprising but still was not as clear-cut as it might have appeared on the surface. A suit against the company had originally been filed in 1993 by Anne Bingaman, the first head of the Antitrust Division in the Clinton administration. But that suit was settled in 1995, leaving the door open for another. Her successor, Joel Klein, filed the second, more notable suit. It was eventually joined by a number of state suits as well. There was no doubt that Microsoft held a virtual monopoly over computer operating systems; its Windows was used on over 90 percent of personal computers across the globe. In terms of efficiency and consumer preferences, it was clear that the monopoly had been earned and no one, including the Antitrust Division, claimed that Microsoft had achieved its dominant market share by anything but ingenuity and clever marketing. But competitors claimed that by bundling its Internet browser with the operating system, Microsoft prevented them from selling their own products to customers. In other words, Microsoft was providing barriers to entry to its competition. If a customer used Windows, then he or she was forced to use the Microsoft's browser as well.

The United States charged Microsoft with tactics designed to stifle competition in the market for Internet browsers. It quoted a Microsoft official telling industry executives that, as far as the competition for alternative browsers were concerned, "We are going to cut off their air supply. Everything they are selling, we're going to give away for free." As a result, the government sought to restrain the company from such tactics, citing it as being in violation of the Sherman Act. Unlike previous notable cases, however, the government originally did not seek the breakup of Microsoft, only to "enter such other preliminary and permanent relief as is necessary and appropriate to restore competitive conditions in the markets affected by Microsoft's unlawful conduct."[21]

The widely publicized case also brought some familiar faces to the bar. Robert Bork announced that he would advise Netscape, one of Microsoft's main competitors in the browser market, on legal strategies in the case. "This is a challenge not to Microsoft's size but to predatory practices," he stated when announcing that he would assist Netscape. He was joined in the effort by the former presidential candidate Robert Dole. Dole was enlisted to press the case against the company in political circles. Dole claimed that the company wanted to erect "a toll booth to charge admission to the Internet . . . Microsoft may have earned that monopoly through legal, aggressive competition but it cannot be allowed to violate antitrust laws." Bork stated that the restrictions Microsoft placed upon computermakers that used its operating systems were designed to ensure that no competitor could enter the market effectively. "Microsoft's insistence upon integrating its own browser with its operating system is a tactic deliberately chosen to bury Netscape," he explained, seeking to explain why the Microsoft case was misunderstood among the press and some lawyers as well.[22]

Bork's remarks on behalf of Netscape surprised some who remembered him as one favoring little or no antitrust action unless an economic case could be made against an alleged monopolist, since the Microsoft case did not quite qualify. But the charge of predatory tactics was not one that necessarily needed to be supported by extensive economic analysis. Since a new technology was involved, with potentially enormous economic consequences, the Microsoft case involved barriers to entry to a new, revolutionary form of information gathering and commerce rather than to a long-established industry. Rather than allow Microsoft to reach the mature stage that Standard Oil had earlier in the century, dominating its industry almost totally, the suit was as much a warning shot across the company's bow as it was a challenge to its alleged bullying tactics with its browser. Being a monopolist *and* a bully would not be tolerated despite Microsoft's admitted success in leading the world's software industry.

While the 1980s and 1990s were certainly two decades of relative affluence and growth, there was also an element of deflation evident in the economy that influenced mergers. As in the period of trust formation in the 1880s and 1890s, stable prices forced many companies to search for merger partners so that they could cut costs and achieve greater economies of scale. Since monopolies and antitrust have a relatively short history, it is difficult to say whether mergers rise to the surface in times of deflation or potential deflation. But it is clearly evident that they cannot proceed at the frenetic pace of the 1920s, 1960s, or 1980s and 1990s without friendly federal governments willing to give business the benefit of the doubt in the constant tug-of-war over what is in the public's best interests. But even this short history leaves one indelible impression: Monopoly is the logical outcome of free market economic organization. Antitrust claims to be the antidote if that power overextends itself and ceases to provide benefits. But the medicine has always been political, with doses of economics applied only within the last twenty-odd years. The history of monopoly in the United States since the early nineteenth century still relies upon a watchful government to keep big business in check. The American civil religion, with its inherent distaste of arbitrary bigness, still drives antitrust policy, despite all of the applications of antitrust law and economics. Despite its successes and failures, applications of the antitrust laws are still very susceptible to prevailing political trends. The ghosts of Hamilton and Jefferson still hover over antitrust debate today, much as they did in the past.

NOTES

CHAPTER I

1. J. C. Black, *The Reign of Elizabeth*, 2nd ed. (Oxford: Clarendon Press, 1959), p. 232.

2. John Moody, *The Trust About the Trusts* (New York: Moody Publishing Co., 1904), p. xv.

3. Charles Adams, "The Railroad System" in Charles Adams and Henry Adams, *Chapters of Erie and Other Essays* (Boston: James R. Osgood, 1871), p. 383. Henry Adams was also well known for making similar arguments against those he disagreed with. Better acquainted with finance than Charles, Henry Adams wrote several essays on British and American finances in the late 1860s. In one, he attacked the Legal Tender Act passed during the Civil War and the congressmen who voted for it as bad legislation passed by mediocre men with no expertise in finance.

4. Alastair Burnet, *America 1843–1993: One Hundred Fifty Years of Reporting the American Connection* (London: The Economist Books, 1993), p. 55.

5. *India Bagging Association v. B. Kock and Company*, a case before a Louisiana court.

6. Gustavus Myers, *History of the Great American Fortunes* (New York: Modern Library, 1936), p. 287.

7. Thomas K. McGraw, *Prophets of Regulation* (Cambridge, MA: Harvard University Press, 1984), p. 59.

8. Myers, *Great American Fortunes*, p. 310.

9. Edmund Morris, *The Rise of Theodore Roosevelt* (New York: Ballantine Books, 1979), p. 173.

10. Maury Klein, *The Life and Legend of Jay Gould* (Baltimore: Johns Hopkins University Press), p. 474.

11. Adams, "The Railroad System," p. 403.

12. Quoted in Richard Hofstadter, *Anti-intellectualism in American Life* (New York: Alfred A. Knopf, 1970), p. 258.

13. 9 Wheat. 1, 6 L.Ed. 23 (1824).

14. *Poor's Manual of the Railroads of the United States* (New York: H. V. & H. W. Poor, 1884), p. iii.

15. 94 U.S. 113, 24 L.Ed. 77 (1877).

16. Adams, "The Railroad System," p. 417.

17. 118 U.S. 557 (1886).

18. Quoted in Lawrence Friedman, *A History of American Law* (New York: Simon & Schuster, 1973), p. 395.

19. Matthew Josephson, *The Robber Barons* (New York: Harcourt Brace, 1934), p. 186.

20. Andrew Carnegie, "My Experience with Railway Rates and Rebates," in Joseph Frazier Wall, ed., *The Andrew Carnegie Reader* (Pittsburgh: University of Pittsburgh Press, 1992), p. 86.

21. Klein, *Jay Gould*, p. 436 ff.

22. Ibid., p. 310.

23. Charles Francis Adams, *An Autobiography* (Boston: Houghton Mifflin Co., 1916), p. 195.

24. Ibid., p. 136.

25. *New York Times*, April 6, 1890.

26. Ida M. Tarbell, *The History of the Standard Oil Company* (Gloucester, MA: Peter Smith, (1964), pp. 133–34.

27. Ibid., p. 142.

28. Quoted in Allan Nevins, *John D. Rockefeller* (New York: Charles Scribner's Sons, 1959), p. 208.

29. Nevins, *Rockefeller*, p. 208.

30. Antitrust laws, as opposed to the antimonopoly laws of the previous century passed in some of the original states.

31. Quoted in Jeremiah Whipple Jenks and Walter E. Clark, *The Trust Problem* (Garden City, N.Y.: Doubleday, Doran & Co., 1929), p. 224.

32. Theodore E. Burton. *John Sherman* (Boston: Houghton Mifflin Co., 1906), p. 356.

33. Klein, *Jay Gould*, p. 453.

34. Adams, *Autobiography*, p. 198.

35. Henry Adams, *The Education of Henry Adams* (Boston: Houghton Mifflin, 1966), p. 266.

CHAPTER 2

1. Matthew Josephson, *The Politicos* (New York: Harcourt Brace, 1966), p. 663.

2. Burnet, *One Hundred Fifty Years*, p. 70.

3 V I Lenin, "Imperialism, the Highest Stage of Capitalism," in *Selected Works* (Moscow: Progress Publishers, 1970), p. 709.

4. 156 U.S. 1.

5. November 11, 1909.

6. William Howard Taft, *The Antitrust Act and the Supreme Court* (New York: Harper & Brothers, 1914), p. 60.

7. 166 U.S. 313.

8. Theodore Roosevelt, *The Works of Theodore Roosevelt* (New York: Charles Scribner's Sons, 1926), vol. 15, p. 92.

9. Theodore Roosevelt, *An Autobiography* (New York: Charles Scribner's Sons, 1921), p. 428.

10. 193 U.S. 327.

11. Tarbell, *Standard Oil*, vol. 2, p. 284.

12. *Standard Oil Company of New Jersey v. United States*, 221 U.S. 1 (1911).

13. Ron Chernow, *Titan: The Life of John D. Rockefeller* (New York: Random House, 1998), pp. 556–57.

14. 221 U.S. 60.

15. Roosevelt, *Autobiography*, p. 431.

16. *Interstate Commerce Commission v. Cincinnati, New Orleans and Texas Pacific Railroad Company*, 167 U.S. 479, 494.

17. Roosevelt, *Works*, vol. 15, p. 276.

18. Quoted in John Wilber Jenkins, *James B. Duke, Master Builder* (New York: George H. Doran Co., 1927), p. 151.

19. *United States v. American Tobacco Co.*, 221 U.S. 106 (1911).

20. Quoted in Ron Chernow, *The House of Morgan: An American Banking Dynasty and the Rise of Modern Finance* (New York: Simon & Schuster, 1990), p. 109.

21. See Eliot Jones, *The Trust Problem in the United States* (New York: Macmillan, 1921), p. 495 ff.

22. J. A. Hobson, *Imperialism* (Ann Arbor: University of Michigan Press, 1965), p. 77.

23. Ibid.

24. Chernow, *The House of Morgan*, pp. 190–91.

25. Quoted in Robert A. Hart, *The Great White Fleet: Its Voyage Around the World 1907–1909* (Boston: Little, Brown, 1965), p. 14.

26. *New York Times,* May 12, 1915.

27. Harold Brayman, *The President Speaks Off the Record* (Princeton: Dow Jones Books, 1976) p. 74.

28. A more detailed discussion of the money trust can be found in my *Wall Street: A History* (New York: Oxford University Press, 1997), chapter 5.

29. Robert M. La Follette, *A Personal Narrative of Political Experiences* (Madison, WI: Robert M. La Follette Company, 1913), p. 762.

30. Myers, *Great American Fortunes,* p. 636.

31. Louis D. Brandeis, *Other People's Money and How the Bankers Use It* (New York: Frederick A. Stokes Co., 1913), p. 4.

32. Roosevelt, *Works,* vol. 15, p. 147.

33. Myers, *Great American Fortunes,* p. 366.

34. Quoted in Bernard A. Weisberger, *The Dream Maker: William C. Durant, Founder of General Motors* (Boston: Little, Brown & Co., 1979), p. 120.

35. Clarence Barron, *They Told Barron* (New York: Harper & Brothers, 1930), p. 103.

36. Heinrich Kronstein, John T. Miller and Ivo Schwartz, *Modern American Antitrust Law* (New York: Oceana Publications, 1968), p. 60.

37. Section 7. Italics added.

38. *New York Times,* August 7, 1914.

39. The FTC absorbed the functions of the Bureau of Corporations, which was established in 1903.

40. *New York Times,* August 11, 1914.

41. Roosevelt, *Autobiography,* p. 439.

42. Brayman, *The President Speaks,* p. 51.

43. See Geisst, *Wall Street,* pp. 119–20.

44. Arundel Cotter, *United States Steel* (Garden City, NY: Doubleday, Page & Co., 1921), p. 205.

45. Quoted in Alpheus T. Mason, *Brandeis: A Free Man's Life* (New York: Viking Press, 1946), p. 355.

46. Ibid, p. 546.

CHAPTER 3

1. Brayman, *The President Speaks Off-the-Record,* p. 190.

2. Thurman Arnold, *The Folklore of Capitalism* (New Haven: Yale University Press, 1937), p. 220.

3. 262 U.S. 522.

4. Richard Hofstadter, *The Age of Reform* (New York: Alfred A. Knopf, 1955), p. 286.

5. Clarence Barron, *They Told Barron* (New York: Harper & Brothers, 1930), p. 226. Whelan went on to claim that the real estate ventures were not actually for speculation but simply for the location of his retail stores.

6. The original authority of the Federal Radio Commission, created by the act, lasted for only one year, after which authority was reassigned to the Department of Commerce.

7. July 20, 1928.

8. Alfred E. Smith, *Campaign Addresses of Governor Alfred E. Smith* (Washington, D.C.: Democratic National Committee, 1929), pp. 14, 22.

9. Quoted in Arthur M. Schlesinger Jr., *The Coming of the New Deal* (Boston: Houghton Mifflin Co., 1959), p. 322.

10. Barron, *They Told Barron*, p. 51.

11. Quoted in John Wilber Jenkins, *James B. Duke, Master Builder* (New York: George H. Doran Co., 1927), p. 176.

12. Ibid., p. 266.

13. *New York Times*, January 15, 1928.

14. Bernard Bellush, *Franklin D. Roosevelt as Governor of New York* (New York: Columbia University Press, 1955), p. 217.

15. Forrest McDonald, *Insull* (Chicago: University of Chicago Press), p. 272.

16. Quoted in M. L. Ramsay, *Pyramids of Power: The Story of Roosevelt, Insull and the Utility Wars* (Indianapolis: Bobbs-Merrill Co., 1937), p. 52.

17. George W. Norris, *Fighting Liberal: The Autobiography of George W. Norris* (New York: Macmillan, 1946), p. 160.

18. As Forrest McDonald noted, Pinchot's charges claimed that the power industry was dominated by General Electric, the Mellon group, the Morgan group, and Samuel Insull, among others. The problem was that General Electric had sold out its share of power production earlier, as did the Mellon group. Morgan only joined the industry several weeks before the charges were leveled, when the United Corporation was formed. However, the general basis of Pinchot's charges was true, leaving the narrow chronological interpretation aside. While the United Corporation was just being formed, Morgan's interest in utilities preceded it by some years, so the creation of the giant corporation was the culmination of his interests, not the beginning. See McDonald, *Insull*, p. 269. Ramsay claimed that Hearst had no particular axe to grind with Insull other than his long-standing distrust of giant utilities in general. Ramsay went on to write *Pyramids of Power*, one of the few books written about Insull and the utilities problem of the period.

19. Cited in Bernard A. Wesiberger, *The Dream Maker: William C. Durant, Founder of General Motors* (Boston: Little, Brown & Co., 1979), p. 324.

20. E. G. Nourse et al., *America's Capacity to Produce* (Washington, D.C.: Brookings Institution, 1934), p. 132 ff.

21. Ramsay, *Pyramids of Power*, p. 221.

22. Quoted in McDonald, *Insull*, p. 247. This material follows his account of Insull's financing of the Eaton buyout.

23. A detailed account of the bear raid can be found in my *Wall Street: A History*, Chapter 7. I am indebted to McDonald's account of the Insull financing against Eaton for this point. See McDonald, *Insull*, p. 290 ff.

24. See also *Wall Street: A History*, pp. 231–32, for more on the FDR-Brandeis connection.

25. Adolph A. Berle and Gardiner C. Means, *The Modern Corporation and Private Property* (New York: Harcourt Brace & World, 1932), p. 18. I am using the revised edition here, published in 1967.

26. Ibid., p. 27.

27. Ibid., Chapter 3.

CHAPTER 4

1. Quoted in Eugene Lyons, *David Sarnoff: A Biography* (New York: Harper & Row, 1966), p. 173.

2. Quoted in Gustavus Myers, *The Ending of Hereditary American Fortunes* (New York: Julian Messner, Inc., 1939), p. 345.

3. Edward M. Lamont, *The Ambassador from Wall Street* (Lanham, MD: Madison Books, 1994), p. 405.

4. The Economist, *The New Deal: An Analysis and Appraisal* (New York: Alfred A. Knopf, 1936), p. 149.

5. Hugh S. Johnson, *The Blue Eagle from Egg to Earth* (Garden City, NY: Doubleday, Doran & Co.), p. 176.

6. Quoted in Arthur Schlesinger Jr., *The Politics of Upheaval* (Boston: Houghton Mifflin Co., 1960), p. 280.

7. Brayman, *The President Speaks*, p. 331.

8. Cited in Philip La Follette, *Adventure in Politics: The Memoirs of Philip La Follette* (New York: Holt, Rinehart & Winston, 1970), p. 170.

9. The Economist, *The New Deal*, pp. 136–37.

10. Quoted in Carl D. Thompson, *Confessions of the Power Trust* (New York: E. P. Dutton & Co., 1932), p. 270.

11. Ibid., p. 307.

12. Ibid, p. 367.

13. *New York Times*, February 21, 1938.

14. Rexford G. Tugwell, *The Brains Trust* (New York: Viking Press, 1968), p. 74.

15. See Geisst, *Wall Street*, p. 216.

16. Quoted in Jordan Schwarz, *The New Dealers: Power Politics in the Age of Roosevelt* (New York: Alfred A. Knopf, 1993), p. 289.

17. Wright Patman, *Complete Guide to the Robinson–Patman Act* (Englewood Cliffs, NJ: Prentice Hall, 1938), p. 3.

18. *New York Times*, June 22, 1936.

19. A subsequent analysis of the Robinson-Patman Act showed that in the twenty years after its passage, only eight cases had been instituted by the Department of Justice under its provisions. Overall, in the twenty years, 311 violations were filed under the law either by the FTC or before the courts, of which

119 were dismissed. See Corwin D. Edwards, *The Price Discrimination Law: A Review of Experience* (Washington, DC: The Brookings Institution, 1959), p. 661 ff.

20. Arthur Schlesinger Jr., *The Politics of Upheaval* (Boston: Houghton Mifflin Co., 1960), p. 510.

21. Gallup polls of October 1937 and April 1938. See George H. Gallup, *The Gallup Poll: Public Opinion 1935–71* (New York: Random House, 1972), pp. 75, 99.

22. Thurman Arnold, *The Symbols of Government* (New Haven: Yale University Press, 1935), p. 185.

23. Quoted in Ellis W. Hawley, *The New Deal and the Problem of Monopoly* (Princeton: Princeton University Press, 1966), p. 423.

24. Thurman W. Arnold, *The Bottlenecks of Business* (New York: Reynal & Hitchcock, 1940), p. 4.

25. *New York Times*, December 31, 1937.

26. Ickes, *The Inside Struggle*, pp. 284–85.

27. Brayman, *The President Speaks*, p. 329.

28. David Lynch, *The Concentration of Economic Power* (New York: Columbia University Press, 1946), p. 185.

29. Ibid., p. 323.

CHAPTER 5

1. George H. Gallup, *The Gallup Poll: Public Opinion 1935–1971* (New York: Random House, 1972), p. 298.

2. Quoted in Eliot Janeway, *The Struggle for Survival* (New Haven: Yale University Press, 1951), p. 65.

3. John Morton Blum, *Years of Urgency, 1938–1941* (Boston: Houghton Mifflin Co., 1965), p. 98.

4. Quoted in Jordan Schwarz, *The New Dealers: Power Politics in the Age of Roosevelt* (New York: Alfred A. Knopf, 1993), p. 65.

5. Jesse Jones with Edward Angly, *Fifty Billion Dollars: My Thirteen Years with the RFC* (New York: Macmillan, 1951), p. 397.

6. *New York Times*, September 11, 1940.

7. Blum, *Years of Urgency*, p. 209.

8. Edward R. Stettinius Jr., *Lend-Lease: Weapon for Victory* (New York: Macmillan, 1944), p. 323.

9. Burnet, *America*, p. 139.

10. Ibid., p. 298.

11. Bernard Baruch, *My Own Story* (New York: Holt, Rinehart & Winston, 1957), p. 265.

12. Jones, *Fifty Billion Dollars*, p. 325 ff.

13. *New York Times*, June 9, 1944.

14. Quoted in Robert Lacey, *Ford: The Men and the Machine* (Boston: Little, Brown & Co., 1986), p. 393.

15. Burnet, *America*, p. 137.

16. *New York Times*, October 29, 1944.

17. John B. Rae, *The American Automobile: A Brief History* (Chicago: University of Chicago Press, 1965), p. 165.

18. See George David Smith, *From Monopoly to Competition: The Transformations of Alcoa, 1888–1986* (New York: Cambridge University Press, 1988), Chapter 5.

19. *United States v. Aluminum Company of America et al.*, 148F 2nd, 416, 446.

20. In *United States v. Carroll Towing,* Hand ruled using a formula based upon economic analysis to determine liability for negligent behavior. In the formula, he attempted to show that the liability should be based upon the loss incurred multiplied by the probability of the accident occurring to determine the actual dollar liability owed to the injured party.

21. *New York Times*, February 8, 1948.

22. *Life*, August 13, 1951.

23. *New York Times*, June 6, 1944.

24. *Corrected Opinion of Harold R. Medina United States Circuit Judge*, in *United States of America v. Henry S. Morgan et al.*, February 4, 1954, p. 2. For a more detailed description of the Morgan case, see *Wall Street: A History*, Chapter 7.

25. Ibid., p. 416.

CHAPTER 6

1. Estes Kefauver, *In a Few Hands: Monopoly Power in America* (New York: Pantheon Books, 1965), p. 189.

2. William Proxmire, *Report from Wasteland: America's Military-Industrial Complex* (New York: Praeger, 1970), p. 14.

3. 353 U.S. 586 (1957). The ruling did not include the Celler-Kefauver amendment because the case originally was brought before the amendment was passed.

4. *United States v. Arnold, Schwinn & Co.*, 388 U.S. 365 (1967).

5. Quoted in Joseph Bruce Gorman, *Kefauver: A Political Biography* (New York: Oxford University Press, 1971), p. 298.

6. Ibid., p. 310.

7. Walter Adams, "The Antitrust Alternative," in Ralph Nader and Mark J. Green, editors, *Corporate Power in America* (New York: Grossman Publishers, 1973), p. 131.

8. Ibid., p. 104.

9. Ibid., p. 83.

10. John Kenneth Galbraith, *The New Industrial State* (Boston: Houghton Mifflin, 1967), p. 186.

11. Kefauver, *In a Few Hands*, pp. 92–93.

12. Ibid., p. 135.

13. *Wall Street Journal*, April 17, 1970.

14. Quoted in John F. Winslow, *Conglomerates Unlimited: The Failure of Regulation* (Bloomington: Indiana University Press, 1973), p. 144.

15. Joel Seligman, *The Transformation of Wall Street: A History of the Securities and Exchange Commission and Modern Corporate Finance* (Boston: Houghton Mifflin Co., 1982), p. 419.

16. Harold Geneen, *The Synergy Myth* (New York: St. Martin's Press, 1997), p. 19.

17. Quoted in John Brooks, *The Go-Go Years* (New York: Weybright & Talley, 1973), p. 178.

18. *Investigation of Conglomerate Mergers*, House of Representatives, 92nd Congress, 1st sess., 414 (June 1, 1971).

19. Prohibitions against reciprocity could be found in the Sherman Act and the Clayton Act, although it was not specifically mentioned by name.

20. *Wall Street Journal*, April 10, 1969.

21. *New York Times*, July 20, 1974.

22. Brayman, *The President Speaks*, p. 808.

23. Winslow, *Conglomerates Unlimited*, Chapter 9.

24. Ibid.

25. Seligman, *Transformation*, p. 419.

26. Winslow, *Conglomerates Unlimited*, p. 188 ff.

27. Edward F. Cox, Robert Fellmeth, and John Schulz, *"The Nader Report" on the Federal Trade Commission* (New York: Richard W. Baron, 1969), p. vii.

28. *Wall Street Journal*, May 23, 1969.

29. April 30, 1970.

30. In 1955 FDR appointees Hugo Black, Stanley Reed, Felix Frankfurter, and William O. Douglas were still on the Court. They were joined by Truman appointees Sherman Minton, Harold Burton, and Tom Clark. By 1965 only Black, Douglas, and Clark remained.

31. John S. McGee, "Predatory Price Cutting: The Standard Oil (N.J.) Case," *Journal of Law and Economics* 137 (1958).

32. Arthur F. Burns, *Reflections of an Economic Policymaker* (Washington, DC: American Enterprise Institute, 1978), p. 204.

CHAPTER 7

1. *New York Times*, August 16, 1971.

2. *Wall Street Journal*, January 24, 1974

3. Ibid, July 5, 1974

4. Geneen, *The Synergy Myth*, p. 194.

5. Robert H. Bork, *The Antitrust Paradox: A Policy at War with Itself* (New York: Basic Books, 1978), p. 6.

6. Kenneth W. Dam, "Kennedy's 'Big Is Bad' Bill," *Wall Street Journal*, May 22, 1979. A reprint of the testimony.

7. Federal Communications Commission, *Telephone Investigation: Proposed Report* (Washington, DC: Government Printing Office, 1938).

8. Quoted in Alan Stone, *Wrong Number: The Breakup of AT&T* (New York: Basic Books, 1989), p. 61.

9. Ibid., p. 71 ff.

10. See *Wall Street: A History*, Chapter 7.

11. Ralph Nader and William Taylor, *The Big Boys: Power and Position in American Business* (New York: Pantheon Books, 1986), p. 400.

12. See Peter Temin, *The Fall of the Bell System: A Study in Prices and Politics* (Cambridge: Cambridge University Press, 1987), p. 33 ff.

13. Ibid., p. 41.

14. Cited in Nader, *The Big Boys*, pp. 401–2.

15. Steve Coll, *The Deal of the Century: The Breakup of AT&T* (New York: Atheneum, 1986), Chapter 4.

16. *New York Times*, July 31, 1974.

17. Temin, *Fall of the Bell System*, p. 108.

18. Vertical integration meant that the phone company's divisions did not replicate services but all individually provided different services that when combined formed the Bell system.

19. *Wall Street Journal*, November 22, 1974.

20. Stone, *Wrong Number*, p. 294.

21. Ibid., p. 311.

22. Since 1927, banks were not allowed to open *de novo* (new) branches across state lines by the McFadden Act, and the Glass-Steagall Act prohibited them from engaging in securities activities if those market activities contributed more than 10 percent of their revenues. As a result, no commercial banks entered the securities business.

23. Mark J. Green, Beverly C. Moore, and Bruce Wasserstein, *The Closed Enterprise System* (New York: Grossman Publishers, 1972), p. 4.

24. *Wall Street Journal*, May 7, 1975.

CHAPTER 8

1. Edwin Meese III, *With Reagan: The Inside Story* (Washington, DC: Regnery Gateway, 1992), p. 156.

2. *Wall Street Journal*, January 5, 1984.

3. The HHI was determined by taking the market share of the dominant firms in an industry, squaring them, and adding them up. Then the market shares of the

merging parties, multiplied times each other and multiplied by 2, were compared with the index to determine if a new concentration emerged that might compromise competition. A score of 10,000 on the test suggested that a monopoly was imminent.

4. *Continental TV, Inc. v. GTE Sylvania, Inc.*, 433 U.S. 36 (1977).

5. Barrie Wigmore, *Securities Markets in the 1980s: The New Regime 1979–1984* (New York: Oxford University Press, 1997), p. 302.

6. Ivan Boesky, *Merger Mania: Arbitrage, Wall Street's Best-kept Money-making Secret* (New York: Holt, Rinehart & Winston, 1985), p. 160.

7. Investment grade means a Standard & Poor's rating of BBB or higher. Junk is BB or lower.

8. *Wall Street Journal*, June 28, 1985.

9. Many states subsequently passed antigreenmail laws that prohibited a company from buying back stock that was not held for a specified amount of time.

10. *Detroit News*, January 25, 1987.

11. Wigmore, *Securities Markets*, pp. 353–54.

12. Margin is the amount of cash that an investor in securities must deposit in cash in order to make a purchase or sale. At the time of the proposal, the margin requirement was 50 percent.

13. *Wall Street Journal*, July 19, 1989.

14. *Financial World*, July 4, 1995.

15. *Brooke Group Ltd. v. Brown & Williamson Tobacco Corp.*, 509 U.S. 209 (1993).

16. *Forbes*, December 18, 1995.

17. *Fortune*, October 30, 1995.

18. *Wall Street Journal*, April 13, 1995.

19. *St. Louis Post-Dispatch*, July 27, 1997.

20. Comparing the fortunes of Vanderbilt and Gould at their deaths, some $200 million and $100 million respectively, would put Gates ahead of both in the strong market of the late 1990s. Calculating their fortunes in present terms, Vanderbilt's would be worth around $54 billion while Gould's would be around $27 billion, compounded at 5 percent over 115 years. A higher rate would put Vanderbilt ahead.

21. *New York Times*, May 19, 1998.

22. Ibid, May 22, 1998.

BIBLIOGRAPHY

PRIMARY SOURCES

Adams, Charles Francis. *An Autobiography*. Boston: Houghton Mifflin Co., 1916.

Adams, Charles F. and Henry Adams. *Chapters of Erie and Other Essays*. Boston: James R. Osgood & Co., 1871.

Adams, Henry. *The Degradation of the Democratic Dogma*. New York: Peter Smith, 1949.

———. *The Education of Henry Adams*. Boston: Houghton Mifflin Co., 1961.

Arnold, Thurman. *The Bottlenecks of Business*. New York: Reynal & Hitchcock, 1940.

———. *The Folklore of Capitalism*. New Haven: Yale University Press, 1937.

———. *The Symbols of Government*. New Haven: Yale University Press, 1935.

Blackstone, William. *Commentaries on the Laws of England*. Boston: Beacon Press, 1962.

Brandeis, Louis D. *Other People's Money and How the Bankers Use It*. New York: Frederick A. Stokes Co., 1913.

Burns, Arthur F. *Reflections of an Economic Policy Maker*. Washington, D.C.: American Enterprise Institute, 1978.

Coolidge, Calvin. *The Autobiography of Calvin Coolidge*. New York: Cosmopolitan Book Corp., 1929.

Gallup, George H. *The Gallup Poll: Public Opinion 1935–1971*. New York: Random House, 1972.

Hobson, J. A. *Imperialism*. Ann Arbor: University of Michigan Press, 1965.

Holmes, Oliver Wendell Jr. *The Common Law*. New York: Dover Books, 1991.

Ickes, Harold L. *The Secret Diary of Harold L. Ickes: The First Thousand Days*. New York: Simon & Schuster, 1953.

———. *The Inside Struggle 1936–1939*. New York: Simon & Schuster, 1954.

Johnson, Hugh S. *The Blue Eagle from Egg to Earth*. Garden City, NY: Doubleday, Doran & Co., 1935.

Jones, Jesse, with Edward Angly. *Fifty Billion Dollars: My Thirteen Years with the RFC*. New York: Macmillan, 1951.

Kefauver, Estes. *In a Few Hands: Monopoly Power in America*. New York: Pantheon, 1965.

La Follette, Philip. *Adventure in Politics: The Memoirs of Philip La Follette*. Ed. Donald Young. New York: Holt, Rinehart & Winston, 1970.

La Follette, Robert M. *A Personal History of Political Experiences*. Madison, WI: Robert M. La Follette Co., 1913.

Lloyd, Henry Demarest. *Wealth Against Commonwealth*. Englewood Cliffs, NJ: Prentice Hall, 1963.

Meese, Edwin III. *With Reagan: The Inside Story*. Washington, DC: Regnery Gateway, 1992.

Morgenthau, Henry. *Years of War, 1941–1945*. Ed. John Morton Blum. Boston: Houghton Mifflin, 1967.

———. *Years of Urgency, 1938–1941*. Ed. John Morton Blum. Boston: Houghton Mifflin, 1965.

———. *Years of Crisis, 1928–1938*. Ed. John Morton Blum. Boston: Houghton Mifflin, 1959.

Nader, Ralph. *Unsafe at Any Speed: The Designed-In Dangers of the American Automobile*. New York: Grossman Publishers, 1965.

Norris, George W. *Fighting Liberal: The Autobiography of George W. Norris*. New York: Macmillan, 1946.

Patman, Wright. *Complete Guide to the Robinson-Patman Act*. Englewood Cliffs, NJ: Prentice Hall, 1938.

Poor's Manual of the Railroads of the United States. New York: H. V. & H. W. Poor, 1869–1893.

Roosevelt, Franklin D. *The Public Papers and Addresses of Franklin D. Roosevelt*. New York: Random House, 1938.

Roosevelt, Theodore. *An Autobiography*. New York: Charles Scribner's Sons, 1921.

———. *The Works of Theodore Roosevelt*. New York: Charles Scribner's Sons, 1926.

Smith, Alfred E. *Campaign Addresses of Governor Alfred E. Smith*. Washington, D.C.: Democratic National Committee, 1929.

Stettinius, Edward R. Jr. *Lend-Lease: Weapon for Victory*. New York: Macmillan, 1944.

———. *The Diaries of Edward R. Stettinius, Jr. 1943–1946*. Ed. Thomas Campbell and George Herring. New York: New Viewpoints, 1975.

Taft, William Howard. *The Anti-Trust Act and the Supreme Court*. New York: Harper & Brothers, 1914.

Tugwell, Rexford G. *The Brains Trust*. New York: Viking Press, 1968.

Wall, Joseph Frazier, ed. *The Andrew Carnegie Reader*. Pittsburgh: University of Pittsburgh Press, 1992.

SECONDARY SOURCES

Adams, Walter, and James Brock. *Dangerous Pursuits: Mergers and Acquisitions in the Age of Wall Street*. New York: Pantheon Books, 1989.

——— and Horace M. Gray. *Monopoly in America*. New York: Macmillan, 1955.

Bain, J. S. *Barriers to New Competition*. Cambridge, MA: Harvard University Press, 1956.

Bellush, Bernard. *Franklin D. Roosevelt as Governor of New York*. New York: Columbia University Press, 1955.

Berglund, Abraham. *The United States Steel Corporation*. New York: Columbia University Press, 1907.

Berle, Adolph A., and Gardiner C. Means. *The Modern Corporation and Private Property*. Revised edition. New York: Harcourt Brace & World, 1968.

Bork, Robert H. *The Antitrust Paradox: A Policy at War with Itself*. New York: Basic Books, 1978.

Brayman, Harold *The President Speaks Off-the-Record*. Princeton: Dow Jones Books, 1976.

Brooks, John *The Go Go Years* New York: Weybright & Talley, 1973.

Brown, Stanley H. *Ling: The Rise, Fall, and Return of a Texas Titan*. New York: Atheneum, 1972.

Buckhorn, Robert F. *Nader: The People's Lawyer*. Englewood Cliffs, NJ: Prentice-Hall, 1972.

Burnet, Alastair. *America 1843–1993: One Hundred Fifty Years of Reporting the American Connection*. London: The Economist Books, 1993.

Burns, Arthur R. *The Decline of Competition: A Study of the Evolution of American Industry*. New York: McGraw-Hill, 1936.

Burrough, Brian, and John Helyar. *Barbarians at the Gate: The Fall of RJR Nabisco*. New York: Harper, 1991.

Burton, Theodore E. *John Sherman*. Boston: Houghton Mifflin Co., 1906.

Carr, Charles C. *Alcoa: An American Enterprise*. New York: Rinehart & Co., 1952.

Chamberlain, Edward. *The Theory of Monopolistic Competition*. Cambridge, MA: Harvard University Press, 1938.

Chandler, Lester V. *Inflation in the United States, 1940–1948*. New York: Harper & Brothers, 1951.

Chernow, Ron. *Titan: The Life of John D. Rockefeller, Sr.* New York: Random House, 1998.

———. *The House of Morgan: An American Banking Dynasty and the Rise of Modern Finance*. New York: Simon & Schuster, 1990.

Coll, Steve. *The Deal of the Century: The Breakup of AT&T*. New York: Atheneum, 1986.

Cotter, Arundel. *United States Steel*. Garden City, NY: Doubleday, Page & Co., 1921.

Cox, Edward F., Robert Fellmeth, and John Schulz. *The Nader Report on the Federal Trade Commission*. New York: Richard W. Baron, 1969.

Davis, Kenneth S. *FDR: The New York Years 1928–1933*. New York: Random House, 1979.

The Economist. *The New Deal: An Analysis and Appraisal*. New York: Alfred A. Knopf, 1937.

Edwards, Corwin D. *The Price Discrimination Law: A Review of Experience*. Washington, D.C.: The Brookings Institution, 1959.

Friedman, Lawrence M. *A History of American Law*. New York: Simon & Schuster, 1973.

Galbraith, John Kenneth. *The New Industrial State*. Boston: Houghton Mifflin Co., 1967.

Geisst, Charles R. *Wall Street: A History*. New York: Oxford University Press, 1997.

Geneen, Harold, with Brent Bowers. *The Synergy Myth*. New York: St. Martin's Press, 1997.

Gorman, Joseph Bruce. *Kefauver: A Political Biography*. New York: Oxford University Press, 1971.

Green, Mark, ed. *The Monopoly Makers: Ralph Nader's Study Group Report on Regulation and Competition*. New York: Grossman Publishers, 1973.

Green, Mark, Beverly C. Moore, and Bruce Wasserstein. *The Closed Enterprise System*. New York: Grossman Publishers, 1972.

Gunther, Gerald. *Learned Hand: The Man and the Judge*. New York: Alfred A. Knopf, 1994.

Halberstam, David. *The Best and the Brightest*. New York: Random House, 1972.

Hart, Robert A. *The Great White Fleet: Its Voyage Around the World 1907–1909*. Boston: Little, Brown & Co., 1965.

Hawley, Ellis W. *The New Deal and the Problem of Monopoly*. Princeton: Princeton University Press, 1966.

Hofstadter, Richard. *Anti-intellectualism in American Life*. New York: Alfred A. Knopf, 1970.

———. *The Age of Reform: From Bryan to F.D.R.* New York: Alfred A. Knopf, 1955.

Hovenkamp, Herbert. *Enterprise and American Law.* Cambridge, MA: Harvard University Press, 1991.

Hoyt, Edwin P. *The Goulds: A Social History.* New York: Weybright & Talley, 1969.

———. *The Vanderbilts and Their Fortunes.* Garden City, NY: Doubleday & Co., 1962.

Jenkins, John Wilber. *James B. Duke, Master Builder.* New York: George H. Doran Co., 1927.

Janeway, Eliot. *The Struggle for Survival.* New Haven: Yale University Press, 1951.

Jenks, Jeriamiah Whipple, and Walter E. Clark. *The Trust Problem.* Garden City, NY: Doubleday, Doran & Co., 1917.

Jones, Eliot. *The Trust Problem in the United States.* New York: Macmillan, 1921.

Josephson, Matthew. *The Politicos.* New York: Harcourt Brace, 1966.

———. *The Robber Barons.* New York: Harcourt Brace, 1962.

Kaysen, Carl, and Donald Turner. *Antitrust Policy: An Economic and Legal Analysis.* Cambridge, MA: Harvard University Press, 1959.

Klein, Maury. *The Life and Legend of Jay Gould.* Baltimore: The Johns Hopkins University Press, 1986.

Koontz, Harold D. *Government Control of Business.* Boston: Houghton Mifflin Co., 1941.

Kostinen, Paul. *The Military-Industrial Complex: A Historical Perspective.* New York: Praeger, 1980.

Lacey, Robert. *Ford: The Men and the Machine.* Boston: Little, Brown & Co., 1986.

Lamont, Edward M. *The Ambassador from Wall Street.* Lanham, MD: Madison Books, 1994.

Link, Arthur S. *Woodrow Wilson and the Progressive Era.* New York: Harper & Brothers, 1954.

Lippmann, Walter. *Interpretations.* Ed. Allan Nevins. New York: Macmillan, 1932.

Lynch, David. *The Concentration of Economic Power.* New York: Columbia University Press, 1946.

McCarry, Charles. *Citizen Nader.* New York: Saturday Review Press, 1972.

McCraw, Thomas K. *Prophets of Regulation.* Cambridge, MA: Harvard University Press, 1984.

McDonald, Forrest. *Insull.* Chicago: University of Chicago Press, 1962.

Mason, Alpheus T. *Brandeis: A Free Man's Life.* New York: Viking Press, 1946.

Means, Gardiner. *The Corporate Revolution in America.* New York: Crowell-Collier Press, 1962.

Montague, Gilbert Holland. *Trusts of Today.* New York: Greenwood Press, 1968.

Moody, John. *The Truth About the Trusts.* New York: Moody Publishing Co., 1904.

Morris, Edmund. *The Rise of Theodore Roosevelt*. New York: Ballantine Books, 1979.

Myers, Gustavus. *The Ending of Hereditary American Fortunes*. New York: Julian Messner, Inc., 1939.

———. *History of the Great American Fortunes*. New York: Modern Library, 1936.

Nader, Ralph, and William Taylor. *The Big Boys: Power and Position in American Business*. New York: Pantheon Books, 1986.

Nader, Ralph, and Mark Green. *Corporate Power in America*. New York: Grossman Publishers, 1973.

Nevins, Allan. *John D. Rockefeller*. New York: Charles Scribner's Sons, 1959.

Nevins, Allan, and Frank Ernest Hill. *Ford*. 3 vols. New York: Arno Press, 1976.

Nourse, E. G., et al. *America's Capacity to Produce*. Washington, DC: Brookings Institution, 1934.

Nutter, G. Warren, and Henry Adler Einhorn. *Enterprise Monopoly in the United States: 1899–1958*. New York: Columbia University Press, 1969.

Rae, John B. *The American Automobile: A Brief History*. Chicago: University of Chicago Press, 1965.

Ramsay, M. L. *Pyramids of Power: The Story of Roosevelt, Insull and the Utility Wars*. Indianapolis: Bobbs-Merrill Co., 1937.

Ritter, Gretchen. *Goldbugs and Greenbacks: The Antimonopoly Tradition and the Politics of Finance in America, 1865–1896*. New York: Cambridge University Press, 1997.

Robinson, Joan. *The Economics of Imperfect Competition*. London: Macmillan, 1933.

Sampson, Anthony. *The Sovereign State of ITT*. New York: Stein & Day, 1973.

Schlesinger, Arthur M. Jr. *The Politics of Upheaval*. Boston: Houghton Mifflin Co., 1960.

———. *The Coming of the New Deal*. Boston: Houghton Mifflin Co., 1959

———. *The Crisis of the Old Order*. Boston: Houghton Mifflin Co., 1957

Schwartz, Jordan A. *The New Dealers: Power Politics in the Age of Roosevelt*. New York: Alfred A. Knopf, 1993.

Seligman, Joel. *The Transformation of Wall Street: A History of the Securities and Exchange Commission and Modern Corporate Finance*. Boston: Houghton Mifflin Co., 1982.

Smith, Gene. *The Shattered Dream: Herbert Hoover and the Great Depression*. New York: William Morrow, 1970.

Smith, George David. *From Monopoly to Competition: The Transformation of Alcoa, 1888–1986*. New York: Cambridge University Press, 1988.

Sobel, Robert. *The Rise and Fall of the Conglomerate Kings*. New York: Stein & Day, 1984.

Stone, Alan. *Wrong Number: The Breakup of AT&T*. New York: Basic Books, 1989.

Tarbell, Ida M. *The History of the Standard Oil Company.* Gloucester, MA: Peter Smith, 1963.

———. *The Nationalizing of Business, 1878–1898.* New York: Macmillan, 1927.

Temin, Peter. *The Fall of the Bell System: A Study in Prices and Politics.* Cambridge: Cambridge University Press, 1987.

Thompson, Carl D. *Confessions of the Power Trust.* New York: E. P. Dutton & Co., 1932.

Timmons, Bascom N. *Jesse H. Jones: The Man and the Statesman.* New York: Henry Holt & Co., 1956.

Traxel, David. *1898: The Birth of the American Century.* New York: Alfred A. Knopf, 1998.

Warren, Kenneth. *Triumphant Capitalism: Henry Clay Frick and the Industrial Transformation of America.* Pittsburgh: University of Pittsburgh Press, 1996.

Wasserstein, Bruce. *Big Deal: The Battle for Control of America's Leading Corporations.* New York: Warner Books, 1998.

Weisberger, Bernard. *The Dream Maker: William C. Durant, Founder of General Motors.* Boston: Little, Brown & Co., 1979.

Wendt, Lloyd. *Chicago Tribune: The Rise of a Great American Newspaper.* Chicago: Rand McNally & Co., 1979.

White, J. B. *The Age of Elizabeth.* 2nd ed. Oxford: Clarendon Press, 1959.

Whitney, Simon N. *Antitrust Policies: American Experience in Twenty Industries.* New York: Twentieth Century Fund, 1958.

Wigmore, Barrie. *Securities Markets in the 1980s: The New Regime 1979–1984.* New York: Oxford University Press, 1997.

Wilner, Frank. *Railroad Mergers: History, Insight, Analysis.* Omaha, NE: Simmons, Boardman, 1997.

Winslow, John F. *Conglomerates Unlimited: The Failure of Regulation.* Bloomington: Indiana University Press, 1973.

Wood, Gordon. *The Radicalism of the American Revolution.* New York: Alfred A. Knopf, 1992.

Yergin, Daniel. *The Prize: The Epic Quest for Oil, Money & Power.* New York: Simon & Schuster, 1991.

INDEX